ACROSS the LAND

...a Canadian journey of discovery

Printed in Victoria, Canada

National Library of Canada Cataloguing in Publication Data

A cataloguing record for this book that includes the U.S. Library of Congress Classification number, the Library of Congress Call number and the Dewey Decimal cataloguing code is available from the National Library of Canada. The complete cataloguing record can be obtained from the National Library's online database at: www.nlc-bnc.ca/amicus/index-e.html

ISBN 1-4120-2276-2

TRAFFORD

This book was published on-demand in cooperation with Trafford Publishing. On-demand publishing is a unique process and service of making a book available for retail sale to the public taking advantage of on-demand manufacturing and Internet marketing. On-demand publishing includes promotions, retail sales, manufacturing, order fulfilment, accounting and collecting royalties on behalf of the author.

Suite 6E, 2333 Government St., Victoria, B.C. V8T 4P4, CANADA
Phone   250-383-6864   Toll-free   1-888-232-4444 (Canada & US)
Fax   250-383-6804   E-mail   sales@trafford.com
Web site   www.trafford.com   TRAFFORD PUBLISHING IS A DIVISION OF TRAFFORD HOLDINGS LTD.
Trafford Catalogue #04-0104   www.trafford.com/robots/04-0104.html

20 19 18 17 16 15 14 13 12 11 10 9

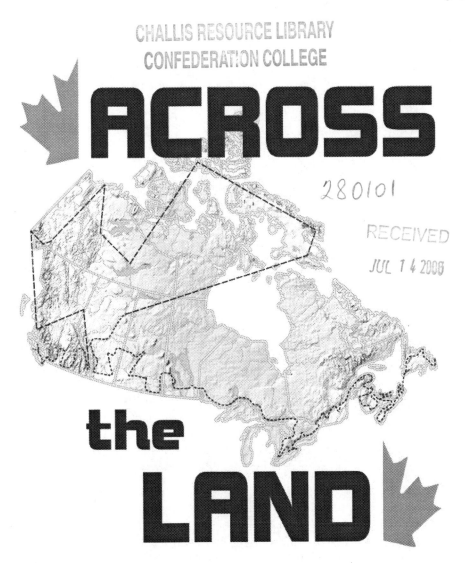

ACROSS

the

LAND

...a Canadian journey of discovery

Barry D. Stewart

This book is dedicated to my grandchildren, Jonathan, Alexander, Marina, Ethney, Marshall and any others that may arrive, along with everyone of their generation. I hope all of you develop a love for Canada's history and traditions and that you travel the country far and wide.

I appreciate the help of everyone who contributed to this endeavour, particularly my wife Pat, who encouraged me to undertake the project and spent many hours reading and editing various drafts. Her suggestions have created a much more focused and readable tale of the journey.

Thanks to the family members and friends, especially my sons Deane and Deron and friend Rae, who provided comments and suggestions; they greatly improved the book. Any errors of fact or structure, however, are all mine – I made the final decisions.

The cover and maps were enhanced by the skills of Rob Edge and his team at Western Sky Creative Inc. in Calgary.

The folks at Trafford Publishing have been exceptionally helpful, especially Annette Humphries and Jennifer Jenkins.

Table of Contents

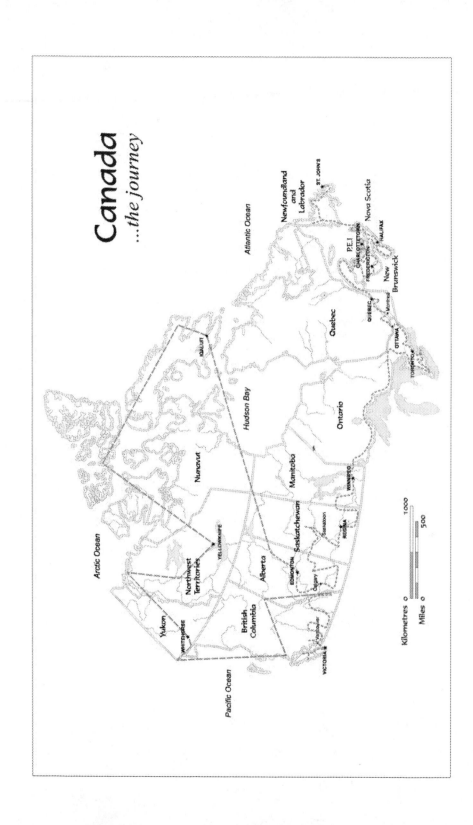

Canada
...the journey

Foreword

We are about to take a fascinating journey together – across all of Canada, visiting essentially every corner of the land as we take in its beauty, happenings, history and traditions. We'll also observe some of the idiosyncrasies of our country, having a lot of fun along the way.

Before you get in the car and join me for the trip, you probably want to know who I am and why I want you to come along.

I have a love for Canada. Having been born here and lived here for most of my 60-plus years, I have come to see it and appreciate it for all of its virtues and anomalies. This is my personal perspective of our country. If it is targeted at anyone in particular, it is Canadians who have not experienced many parts of the country. I often find that people can develop some erroneous, even strange, perspectives about other regions when they have not visited them first-hand.

I have lived in five provinces. I was born and raised in Winnipeg, Manitoba. I completed high school and university in Ontario. During my career I lived in Alberta, Saskatchewan, British Columbia and Ontario. I have conducted business in and traveled around all of the ten provinces and the three territories. In talking with others, I realize that not many Canadians can say that. That's a shame, as our country has so much to show in its geographic and community diversity, all within a common identity.

I have also lived outside of Canada, in the United States and South America, and have traveled for business and pleasure in Europe, the Middle East, Southeast Asia and Australia. These experiences have allowed me to see Canada from an external perspective and through the eyes of others.

My approach to writing this book is to have a dialogue with you, the reader, about a trip from coast to coast that we are taking together. It is an imaginary journey in the sense that it is a composite of a number of trips that I have taken, and some of the experiences that I will relate have been gathered over a lifetime. Be assured that I have been to every place that I describe. I have also driven over 25,000 kilometers around the country during the creation of this book to update my information.

Our route will be a bit tortuous at times, since we are covering the country in a one-way journey. Maps are provided for each chapter to help keep track of where we are at any time.

Our dialogue will touch on three dimensions: a cross-Canada tour, Canada's history, and some of the country's issues and dynamics.

The structure will read like a travelogue, but it is not full of all the detailed descriptions that can be found in major tour guides or weekend newspaper articles. It is an overview, augmented by specific fascinating or unusual sights.

We will uncover some of our history; there are descriptions of historical events and many local stories. I am a reader of history and a collector of antique maps and books which will show through. Our historical discussions will focus on the area we are visiting at any point in time; thus they will not be chronological. I believe you may be surprised how colourful and interesting our history can be.

I will not provide any extensive discussion of social or political issues, but it is impossible to travel across this country and observe its people and events without commenting on some of the things we see and hear. I think of myself as a typical middle-of-the-road Canadian, with a quiet passion for the country, a conservative fiscal attitude, a somewhat liberal social attitude and a centralist voting habit.

My commentary will be mostly positive since that is how I feel about the country. However, I will also describe the oddities, the irregularities, and the various foibles and follies that we encounter along the way. I believe that a few of these observations will amuse you. As commentators and comedians like to say, "You couldn't make this stuff up, even if you tried." I'll express that thought more than once.

This is a personal narrative, full of experiences, observations and general commentary. It is by necessity selective and anecdotal — Canada is so large and diverse in its cultural heritage, geography and history. I have spoken to many people during my travels, but the thoughts that I express are my own.

I hope you enjoy our trip together. More importantly, I hope it motivates you to go and actually see some new part of our country.

With that, let's get started. Canada, here we come!

Atlantic Canada

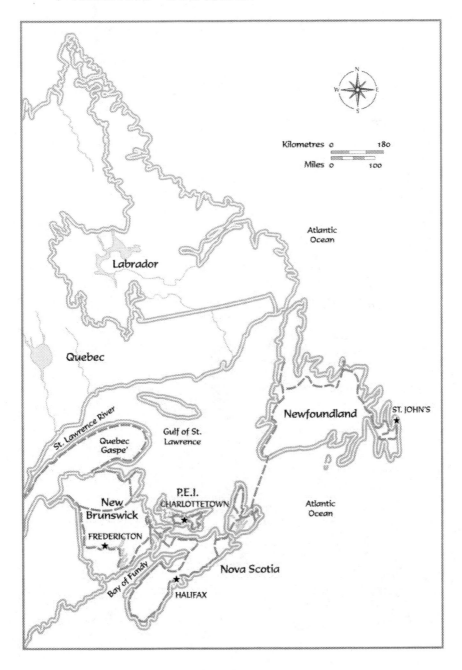

Labrador

Atlantic
Ocean

Quebec

St. Lawrence River

Quebec
Gaspe'

Gulf of St.
Lawrence

Newfoundland

ST. JOHN'S
★

New
Brunswick

P.E.I.
CHARLOTTETOWN
★

FREDERICTON
★

Atlantic
Ocean

Bay of Fundy

Nova Scotia

HALIFAX
★

Kilometres 0   180

Miles 0   100

Newfoundland and Labrador

LABRADOR

Churchill Falls

Goose Bay

Kilometres 0   180

Miles 0   100

NEWFOUNDLAND

L'Anse-aux-Meadows

St. Anthony

Gulf of St. Lawrence

White Bay

Cow Head

Rocky Harbour

Gros Morne

Deer Lake

Notre Dame Bay

Atlantic Ocean

Twillingate

Gander

Bonavista Bay

Grand Falls-Windsor

Gambo

Cornerbrook

Port Blandford

Terra Nova

Trinity Bay

Conception Bay

Stephenville

Bay Robert

Dildo

Bull Arm

Briaus

ST. JOHN'S

Come-by-Chance

Cape Spear

Argentia

Placentia Bay

Witless Bay

Port-aux-Basques

St. Pierre-Miquelon

Ferry to N.S.

Ferry to N.S.

Gulf of St. Lawrence

Avalon Peninsula

1. Newfoundland and Labrador

What better place to start our journey than standing on the bluffs of eastern Newfoundland and looking out to the North Atlantic? I have stood on Signal Hill, above St. John's, a number of times; always it seems when the skies are grey, the wind is blowing and a fog is hanging over the land and the sea.

But then, this should not be a surprise since Environment Canada has declared St. John's to be the foggiest and windiest city in Canada, averaging 199 days a year with fog and 23 km/h winds year round. I guess I could have started with the famous line, "It was a dark and stormy night ..." but I'll leave that for Snoopy.

From up here on Signal Hill we can visualize the time over 500 years ago, shortly after the discoveries of Columbus in Central America, when John Cabot sailed to these northern waters and discovered the Grand Banks. That area of relatively shallow water was teeming with cod such that they could gather them in buckets over the sides of the ship. Off on the horizon could be seen the grey and rocky shores of this new found land. Although we now know that Viking travelers had been this way before, those memories had been lost and this was the start of the European travel, migration and colonization of northern America that would lead to the creation of what is now Canada.

Cod was king in those early days and the early fishing fleets preferred not to seek out land at all. It was for a very pragmatic reason that the early English fishermen set up in the sheltered harbour of St. John's – the price of salt. Due to their warmer climates for evaporating seawater and natural salt beds, the fleets from Portugal and other parts of southern Europe had access to plentiful supplies of cheap salt to preserve their huge catches of fish for the journey back home; the English did not. They resorted to drying their fish on racks in the sun, which required much less salt for preservation, but required that they set up seasonal colonies on the shore of Newfoundland. In doing so they became the first European residents of "Canada." The fishing logistics dominated the settlements, the government and the social structure of the area for centuries. These early activities result in St. John's claim to be the oldest city in North America, although, because of its seasonal use in the early periods, St. Augustine, Florida and Quebec City lay claim to being older permanent settlements.

We can best understand this heritage through the displays and presentations at the national park's visitor's centre near the brow of Signal Hill, a stop well worth making to get our bearings on the origins of the area. The huge three-dimensional map at the entrance gives us a good overview of the area, showing the relief both onshore and under the offshore ocean. It makes us realize the immense scale of the Grand Banks and gives us a sense of the tortuous paths of the majestic icebergs that march down the northern and eastern shores of the province.

The North Atlantic can be a treacherous place. It has claimed the lives of many sailors, fishermen and travelers. Its fury can be immense.

My first trips to Newfoundland were in the mid-1980s when I was involved with the offshore oil industry. We were developing concepts to produce oil from the Grand Banks area discoveries such as the large Hibernia oil field. Designs to withstand the wild North Atlantic storms and the impact of icebergs demanded new engineering and construction methods. It was always a reminder of the reality of the threats when we checked the maps and realized the facility was going to be farther north and farther offshore than the site of the sinking of the *Titanic*.

The harsh reality was also ever-present in the memory of the overturning of the world's largest offshore drilling rig *Ocean Ranger* that was exploring for oil on the Grand Banks in 1982. The flotation chambers were flooded with seawater in a big storm; all 84 crew members on board were lost.

By the way, Signal Hill gets its name from being the site of the first trans-Atlantic wireless communication, conducted by Marconi in 1901. This proved that radio communications could reflect off the atmosphere and carry around the curvature of the Earth.

During the summer months, students dressed in the colourful British grenadier costumes from colonial times set up a tent village and perform marches and military exercises to entertain the tourists. The sounds of the drums and musket fire in response to the barked-out orders of the officers add to the spectacle.

Looking back down the hill, landward, we can see a complete panorama of St. John's harbour. A narrow entrance between steep shores leads to the long harbour tucked in at a right angle from the entrance, well protected by the surrounding hills. It is smaller than one might expect, given its historical reputation. It is only two kilometers long and less than one kilometer wide, but what a welcome shelter from the wild North Atlantic it has been over the centuries. As we gaze over the sight, we can sense history, whether it is of the early fishing fleets or the later marshalling of naval forces heading out to the world wars of the twentieth century.

Going down into the city itself, we can see that the main business streets run parallel to the tidy harbour front, rising in tiers up the hillside. The cross streets are narrow and steep, seemingly all called *lanes* or *hills* or *coves* or *alleys*, which seems much more colourful than just the *streets* and *avenues* of other places.

The harbour appears very orderly and businesslike, with the powerful offshore work boats, the large container cargo ships, the multi-boomed fishing trawlers and the bold red-and-white Canadian Coast Guard vessels all in their places.

The first thing we notice is the architecture, or, more specifically, the many houses and buildings with brightly-coloured wood-siding finishes. The houses are red and yellow and green and orange and turquoise and purple. It is a cheerful relief from the weather that is often grey and dull, especially in the winter. As we travel around, we will find that this is a province-wide phenomenon. What a delight it is to see!

The spoken language of the Newfoundlanders is truly a unique creation of accent and new words, or, at least, words with new meanings. The cadence is similar to the Irish — no surprise, I guess, with the strong historical links to Ireland.

Their words and meanings are a puzzle to newcomers, or "mainlanders." "Where you to, b'y?" is simply an inquiry as to where you live or where you have come from, not where you are going. I certainly confused people in my early encounters here when I replied by describing the planned next stages of my trip.

Traditions and heritage are strong here. It is said that you are considered "CFA," which means come-from-away, for generations.

Believe it or not, there is a 700-page dictionary of the Newfoundland language. This is a serious piece of work, not a tourist gimmick, which involved years of research, especially in the more remote towns and villages. It is a treat to browse through it. For the tourist trade there is a thriving business in tee shirts with local words explained. How else would we know that to *twack* means to window shop? It's a refreshing change from the same old tee shirts you see everywhere else.

However, the most popular tee shirt has a map of the 36 pubs of the George Street area. They are stacked side-by-side; this must be the most concentrated collection of drinking establishments in the country. Signs declare that outside street-drinking must stop by 2:00 a.m.

Another unique thing about Newfoundland is its music. The high-energy jigs and the local dialect make for great listening. When you hear the *Ode to Newfoundland* or *I'se the B'y*, you can't help but get caught up in the mood. And they seem to have so much fun in playing it.

Every two years they hold a Sound Symposium here in St.John's. It features a wide range of music performances and workshops. Perhaps the most unusual feature is the Harbour Symphony each mid-day during the festival. A melody of "tunes " is played by the horns of the ships in harbour; the long low tones of large ships blend with the lighter tones and whistles of the smaller ones. This is quite a feat of creation and coordination, especially considering that a different array of ships is in harbour each day.

Then there is the time dimension. Here we are on Newfoundland time, which is a half-hour displaced from the cycle in the rest of Canada. That is, it is one-half hour earlier than Halifax, one-and-a-half hours earlier than Toronto and four-and-a-half hours earlier than Vancouver. It does take some careful attention when you are going to phone someone elsewhere, or even to just figure out when something familiar is going to be on television. Of course, most Canadians know about this phenomenon, as it has been a running commentary on the CBC or by comedians for decades as they say, "News highlights at nine o'clock, seven thirty in Newfoundland," or "The world ends at midnight, 12:30 in Newfoundland."

This contrasts with my experience in Australia. There, the state of South Australia also has a half-hour time zone adjustment. Once, I was traveling to Adelaide, South Australia, from Brisbane, in the state of Queensland. When I asked some acquaintances, senior executives from Australia, they did not know what time it would be in Adelaide. When I returned, they were surprised to hear about a similar half-hour situation there — they didn't know it existed! In Canada we know about Newfoundland time; it's a national icon.

In St. John's there are many and varied restaurants to choose, and an amazing number of pubs. Hotels and restaurants that sit on the hillside and look over the harbour are my favourite. Seafood, of course, is readily available, with cod being the centrepiece on many menus. Pan-fried is the traditional way and always recommended. I am always surprised to see cod cheeks and cod tongues on the menus. Always ready to try anything, I have tried them and they are delicious. And they are popular – on one visit I was told in a restaurant that they were out of cod cheeks that evening since there had been a big run on them that day; and they were serious!

Other new items you see on the menus are bakeapple berry pies or partridgeberry jams for breakfast toast, both variations on raspberries found in the marshy bogs, the former being yellow-orange and the latter dark red. Also, they always have vinegar on the table for french fries, a forgotten habit in so many places.

Another tradition for a newcomer is to be "screeched in," which makes you an honourary Newfoundlander. It involves taking an oath, throwing back a shot of Screech (strong rum) and kissing a cod fish.

Not for the squeamish, but since it usually happens in a bar with lots of loud cheering and encouragement from the locals, after a drink or two in preparation, it seems like fun at the time.

At the end of Water Street in St. John's is the Newman wine store, a rustic stone building with the inside constructed as arched stone rooms or vaults. We are in a simple building downtown, but feel like we are in some remote cave system. There are displays about wine and port making, various pieces of old tools and equipment, and many wine racks. The specialty is their port, imported from Portugal in kegs and bottled locally. This is all positioned with a story of a wayward ship hauling port from Portugal to England in 1679 that ventured via Newfoundland. The extra-long journey, with the port sloshing about in the rough wooden casks, seemed to add to its flavour and, thus, a tradition was born.

On the hills a kilometer or so above the harbour sits the provincial House of Assembly, a stepped-structure of yellow-beige brick that goes from two stories at the edge to a ten-story tower in the centre. It commands a view in all directions.

Nearby is Memorial University, a spread-out campus with modern brick buildings, many connected by raised, covered walkways and all centred on a tall distinctive concrete clock tower.

One thing I will comment on as we travel across the country is traffic and how it works or doesn't work in various places. I think I have a pretty good sense of direction and awareness of maps and traffic patterns. Having said that, there is no place in Canada where I make more wrong turns, or cannot find my way, than in the St. John's area. Streets angle off in random directions, street names change arbitrarily on a route, one-way streets and non-intersecting crossovers are not shown on local maps. Some might say this is just a weakness in a guy who lives in Calgary, where the streets are nicely laid out on a regular grid and most of them are sequentially numbered. I don't think so, since there are many other cities with St. John's attributes. It's the lack of signs — a province-wide issue. There may be a sign warning you about a turn in a few kilometers or a number of exits down the road, but, too often, nothing when you reach the spot. I have the same problems in Gander and Cornerbrook, cities of only ten or twenty thousand people! If you live here, I guess you just watch your odometer closely and diligently count exits until the route becomes familiar.

Of course, we see another St. John's as we drive around. Modern subdivisions, shopping malls and movie complexes are also here, with all of the familiar names from A&W to Zellers. They are everywhere we go these days. But let's put that out of our mind and get back to the real tour.

Going south through the city and up over rolling hills and past small villages, we come to the cliff lookout of Cape Spear, the easternmost point of land in North America. Standing on the cliff and looking out to sea, we can see the breaking waves of the North Atlantic. High above us is the dominant, colourful lighthouse that commands the whole area from its perch. Down near the shoreline, we can spot the blows and swells of the seemingly-playful whales as they work their feeding grounds. There are large humpbacks and the smaller minkes. It's a patient game of observation, guesswork and timing to catch a photo of one of the whales as they surface for air. After a while, you learn to see the fluorescent green baleen of a whale in the water as it nears the surface, and to be prepared for a quick shutter release when it breaches and spouts water high into the air before it dives again, sometimes with a great flourish of its tail. It's a fun game of anticipation and reflex.

Driving south along the Atlantic shore, the area continues to be rugged with high, tree-covered hills and steep cliffs at the sea's edge. There are many bays that carve the shoreline, most of which have a town or village at the upper end. I know I will use the words *quaint* and *picturesque* many times in this book, since they apply to so many parts of the country, but nowhere more so than for the fishing villages of Newfoundland that are strung along every coast. Some of these towns have existed since the 1500s. Again we find the colourful wood-sided homes, usually going up a hillside surrounding a bay. Boathouses and docks, covered with neat stacks of lobster and crab traps, line the shore. Dories are tethered just offshore. We see these scenes on picture post cards or wall calendars all the time. They are real.

Of course, there is also the winter that will set in. Then much of the area will be grey and bleak, with icy winds blowing across the rocky landscape. The desolate scenes in the movie *The Shipping News* portray that reality very well; I felt cold just watching it.

Passing through one of these towns, we see Canada Post folks moving down each side of the local highway, delivering the mail to the homes stretched out along the road every hundred feet or so. It's another great Canadian compromise. If you live in "old" neighbourhoods you get mail delivered to the door, but in "new" areas you need to go to central boxes located every block or so. I experienced this in Calgary, where we had mail delivery to our home in an inner-city community, but family members who lived in the new subdivisions had to go to the corner. Canada Post claims to be a commercial enterprise, but I guess it just cannot shake those government roots and its funny logic at times.

A stop at the Bay Bulls/Witless Bay area is a must. Here we can take a boat ride out to see the offshore islands in an ecological preserve that are inhabited by a wide range of birds. There are a number of tour boats available, almost all run by Irish families. The last time I was here, all was pleasant and calm and they seemed to cooperate well. After our boat spotted and followed a whale for a brief while, the captain informed the other boats in the area and then broke away as they arrived so as not to crowd the whale. Later, however, we heard tales that there have been fights on the docks between the boats' crews over tour bookings, right in front of the customers.

There are many other tales and folklore we can hear from the boat guide as we travel along, including the one about a sunken ship in the harbour that is claimed to be the first war ship sunk in North America. The English captain scuttled his own ship here, while fleeing from French navy ships, to prevent it being captured. Then the English gunneries on the shore convinced the French to turn back to Argentia, rather than carry on to St. John's with their mission of plunder. Some of the old cannons are now used as gateposts in the fence of a local church.

Let's get back to the birds. There are literally millions of them around the area. They fill the sky in swooping flocks; they line the rocky shores wing tip to wing tip; and they scurry across the water surface diving for fish. There are gulls, gannets, murres, kittiwakes and, special for most tourists, the puffins. These short, plumpish, black-and-white birds with their broad heads and bright orange beaks and feet are so uniquely attractive. Again, we see them everywhere on post cards and as stuffed toys, but it is worth the trip to see them in nature.

Place names are also a special feature of Newfoundland. They are often a blend of various languages that have been used in the area or they reflect some local phenomenon. For example, in this area, Bay Bulls is said to be an Anglicization of baie d'bois, which is Bay of the Woods in French. That's plausible. Witless Bay is said to come from the history of a family named Whit that settled here long ago and called the area Whit's Bay. When they all moved away, the locals changed it to Witless Bay. Only in Newfoundland might I believe such a story.

One thing we can see in the harbour at Bay Bulls that is personally depressing is a cod-farm pen. It is a netted-off area in the water, about 15 or 20 meters across. The moratorium on offshore cod fishing means that, other than during a few days allowed for recreational fishing, the cod now needs to be raised on these "farms." What a sad commentary on the human race; we have harvested billions of cod from the Grand Banks but have not been able to preserve the population feedstock.

The locals also bemoan the fact that the seal population has been growing at a high rate, as they are voracious consumers of cod. Of course, this then leads to the issue of seal hunting, one argument they are not going to win easily, not with all those posters of the cute, white seal pups which are used so effectively by the anti-hunting lobbyists. Even with hunters allowed to take over 300,000 seals a year, the seal population has grown from under two million to over five million in the past 30 years.

In reality, it has been a mystery to the fishermen and to scientists why the cod population fell off so quickly. We have a lot to learn about nature. The newly-evolving sciences of chaos, which analyses changes that occur precipitously rather than in a continuum, and of complexity, which analyses situations where the interaction of independent events can create unpredicted results, are only beginning to help us understand many phenomena, whether they be physical, social or economic. Meanwhile, the cod disappear.

Moving west across the Avalon Peninsula, we next come to Placentia Bay, an area first settled by the Basques and then later used by the French as their base for battles with the English in the seventeenth century.

I can recall my first visit to Placentia vividly, again a tale of Newfoundland weather and the sea. In the mid-1980s I was on a trip by helicopter from St. John's to the Marystown ship yards on the far side of Placentia Bay. Our group was inspecting a heavy-duty work boat that was under construction for use in supporting the offshore oil exploration work. By mid-afternoon the weather started to turn cloudy and windy and the pilot urged us to return quickly. As we flew back over the Bay, we could sense that the helicopter was labouring and we seemed to be steadily losing altitude, down towards the choppy sea. As we approached landfall, near Placentia, the pilot said we needed to land immediately. He set us down in a schoolyard near the shore. When we were able to climb out, the problem was obvious. The helicopter was covered in a multi-inch layer of ice. The conditions of rapidly falling temperatures over the water had caused this to happen and the enormous extra weight had caused the helicopter to struggle. It was a sobering experience and it provided a personal perspective on the constant challenge from Mother Nature. As you will hear later, that was not to be my only encounter with weather and helicopters.

From the town of Argentia there is a summer ferry service to Nova Scotia. They are large boats that carry trucks and cars. They also have cabins and bunks that can be rented for the 15-hour trip. There are movies, arcade games and food services to pass the time and, according to their promotional brochure, "the sea and sun to enjoy." I am not sure the weather always cooperates.

As we travel back north from here, we encounter the shores of Conception Bay to the west of St. John's. Town after town is strung along the local, narrow, winding highways. Most of them are one house deep, off the side of the highway, so as to not require local street building and maintenance. Where roads do go off to the side, they are called lanes or coves or paths, again more descriptive than streets and avenues. The bay itself is a wide expanse of dark blue water, framed by high cliffs which are carved by many smaller bays and inlets.

Here, as elsewhere in Newfoundland, the roadside garbage containers at each home have become a local art form. They are about two meters long and one meter high and can be circular, hexagonal, octagonal or trunk-shaped in cross section. They are painted colourfully and can be decorated with outlines of animals, letters, names, or even the Canadian flag. It is entertaining to look out for the more elaborate ones as we drive through the area.

Along this route is the small town of Brigus, one of the many picturesque bayside communities we find across the province. This one even has a small creek that runs through it, which has been neatly rock lined. A two-story stone barn has been converted into a local museum. But the key interest for me is the Hawthorne Cottage, the home of Arctic explorer Bob Bartlett.

Captain Bartlett reached the northern latitude of $87^0 47''$ N. with the explorer Robert Peary in 1909, which is just over 200 kilometers short of the North Pole. This is arguably the farthest north anyone has ever reached on a two-way non-air-assisted trip, since the claims of Robert Peary and, later, Frederick Cook to get much farther, let alone to the North Pole itself, are in serious doubt.

Bartlett also was involved with the disastrous trip and dramatic rescue of the crew of the *Karluk* off Siberia in 1913, as well as dozens of other Arctic explorations over 50 years. He was a Canadian adventurer and hero that few of us know much about today.

The cottage at Brigus is full of Arctic artifacts and mementos that serve to remind us of the strong role that Newfoundland played in the exploration of the high Arctic through the nineteenth and early twentieth centuries. After all, this area was the most northern "civilized" base for many of those long, forlorn expeditions. As well, there were Inuit tribes that historically settled as far south as southern Labrador and northern Newfoundland. Thus, the many northern carvings and art pieces that can be found for sale throughout the province have a very legitimate heritage here.

North of Brigus is Bay Roberts, an active small town where I once managed to make five wrong turns in a row. Driving from there, across the northern arm of the local peninsula, we head for Trinity Bay. As we drive through the tree-filled hills of the peninsula we notice that all of the trees have a permanent lean to the east, even on a calm day, a testimony to the strong prevailing winds than habitually blow in Newfoundland. The ground is a blaze of colour with all of the wild flowers — white, yellow, purple, red. A few times we can spot a wild fox running through the roadside grasses.

I love to see creative names for things, especially small businesses. Back in St. John's I had seen a sign for the Crooked Crab Café, recalling that the tall colourful houses of the area are called crooked houses. Along here there is a flower shop called *Grandmother's Bloomers*. That's good.

Trinity Bay is another wide expanse of dark water, this time with significant waves and whitecaps that hint at the strength of the open sea. It is somewhere along here that I came to appreciate why Newfoundland is often referred to as "The Rock," even by the local inhabitants. Everywhere we have traveled has been characterized by steep-sided, rocky shorelines. The inland areas, covered by thick forests, are cut through with boulder-filled, fast-running rivers and creeks. In all of my travels across the province, I have never seen any significant farms, although I am told there is some farming at the south end of the Avalon Peninsula.

Driving down the Trinity Bay coast, the first town we come to is Dildo, I kid you not. The history of the name has been lost; historians say it might be an old forgotten town in Portugal, it might be an Indian name for a tree, or it might have been a joke that got out of control. In any case the local folks have resisted various attempts to change the name. As we drive in, there are signs directing the way to Dildo Island and so, as we drive along, I keep glancing offshore wondering if I'll see a tall narrow rock formation. Then we round a bend and there ahead of us on the side of the road is a grey, cylindrical, bulbous erection, perhaps ten meters high! I immediately think, "They can't be serious?" As we get closer, it becomes clear that it is a sculpture of a large whale rising from the sea. What a relief. I suspect the folks of the area get a fair bit of teasing at times. I wonder what kind of cheers the school teams hear.

South from Dildo, we soon join up with the Trans-Canada Highway and head northwest. Actually, here in Newfoundland it's just called "the TCH," a habit I haven't noticed elsewhere in the country. This transcontinental highway system starts in St. John's and ends in Victoria, B.C., or is it the other way around?

Traversing the narrow neck of land joining the Avalon Peninsula with the rest of the island of Newfoundland, we find ourselves between Bull Arm and the harbour of Come-by-Chance. Only a few kilometers separate these bodies of water, but the first one joins up with the Atlantic to the north and the latter with the entrance to the Gulf of St. Lawrence to the south.

There is one immediate indicator that this is a tough area. All across Newfoundland we will see signs and posters for various festivals, usually based on some local treat such as blueberries, strawberries, lobster or crab. In a local town here the annual event is called the *Fog Festival*!

Newfoundland, as does Canada, has its basic economy built on natural resources. Here it has historically been fish and timber, with mining and petroleum now emerging as significant factors.

There is the natural desire by the government and the people to diversify their economy and to benefit from enterprises that exploit the province's natural resources. These are admirable objectives, but sometimes they defy economic reality.

Newfoundland has had a number of industrial misadventures, including the story of the cucumbers that has become a modern day provincial legend. The government was convinced to invest in a series of greenhouses to hydroponically grow cucumbers. A lack of sun, the cost of energy, and the fact that cucumbers do not have enough inherent value to pay for an elaborate infrastructure all contributed to it becoming a total economic disaster.

Similar things have happened in the area around Come-by-Chance. First, there is the large crude oil refinery that was built in response to the oil crisis and international embargos of the 1970s. The concept was to build a refinery for making products for export to the United States in those tumultuous times. It was supported by tax and duty-free concessions to bring benefits to Newfoundland. But, the world settled down and then the facility became an economic white elephant. It became the biggest bankruptcy in Canadian history to that time, with a loss of some 500 million dollars. It is now operated for the local market.

Across the road from Come-by-Chance at Bull Arm there is another story. The large Hibernia oil field was discovered offshore Newfoundland in 1979. As I related earlier, there was a need to design a production system that could reliably operate in the difficult North Atlantic environment and be safe from the threat of icebergs. Based on the desire for local employment, the Newfoundland government insisted on a concrete structure that would be set down on the sea floor, creating a foundation for an upper deck that would contain the drilling rig, the operating equipment and accommodations for workers. This was a much more expensive concept than the more traditional use of floating facilities. However, it was done successfully. This marvel of engineering and construction took place at Bull Arm. The concrete structure was floated out to the Grand Banks, pulled by a large fleet of tugboats, and then ballasted down on the seabed. That occurred in 1997, eighteen years after the discovery! The design and regulatory approval processes, coupled with the cycling of world oil prices, had caused this massive delay in the benefits to Newfoundland from the project, but it did happen. The site at Bull Arm was then sold to the government for one dollar, probably never to be used again for such a project. The subsequent developments of other oil fields are using floating platforms, the only truly economic way to proceed.

More recently, the province was involved in another multi-year delay of a major project as the parties negotiated the employment and economic benefits for Newfoundlanders – the Voisey Bay mining venture. There seems to be a deal struck now and the project is going forward.

It is a difficult process to get such mega-projects to reality. This is especially true when the political election cycle is shorter than the project construction cycle. Exploration activities and early results can get turned into unrealistic expectations and then cause distrust.

Our next stop is at Port Blandford, beside the Terra Nova National Park. The lodge there has good facilities for an R & R break, including a fine golf course. It has some of the most spectacular backdrops anywhere, with the fast-flowing, tumbling, rock-filled rapids of the salmon rivers cutting through the area. I'll blame the scenery for the number of golf balls I have left behind here, especially on the par 3s that cross those streams. It is also fun to hit a good shot and hear someone say, "He be a good 'un, b'y." Just be sure to have repellant for the "chunk-removing" black flies.

A side road through the national park takes us out to the coast again where we find a small cove at Eastport. There are many cottages and tourist places, all near a nicely-sheltered sandy beach, a handy and quiet spot for a retreat from St. John's.

Farther up the road we find the harbour of Salvage (pronounced cell-vage, as in rage). It is somewhat different from other towns we have seen, in that it is tucked in behind high rocky cliffs that guard a narrow exit to the sea. There is a viewpoint high above the town that provides a great panoramic perspective on the village, which, as always, has colourful homes and lobster-trap covered docks. This is a private and protected little corner of the world.

Continuing north on the TCH, we come to Gambo, the hometown of Joey Smallwood, the leader who brought Newfoundland into the Canadian confederation in 1949. We often forget that it occurred so recently and that it was so controversial – our first example of a close Canadian decision. In this case the vote was 52% to 48%, and that was only on a second try after the first one was too close to call.

Newfoundland had been a colony under British oversight. The debate of the day was not just over independence from Britain versus joining Canada, but also about Canada versus the United States! Those who favoured independence also visualized the opportunity to develop some form of free trade with the Americans. It's all a matter of timing! It's amazing how history can be determined by small differences.

Traveling on north, we follow the shore of the Bonavista Peninsula with its many coves and villages. Once more we encounter numerous seaside villages with colourful houses, lobster-trap laden wharves and floating dories. Signs often remind us that some of these villages have been here for four hundred years. The local water bodies are called coves, arms, reaches, bays or harbours; we learn that if there is a narrow entrance it is called a tickle. Lobster ponds are frequently advertised. It's all fascinating for a prairie boy.

We next cross a series of islands connected by bridges, causeways and local ferries to our destination for the day, Twillingate, the self-proclaimed *Iceberg Capital of the World*. We are not disappointed in our anticipation, as we glimpse a shining white object out in the ocean through the narrow opening to the local harbour – oops, I mean through the tickle. Down to the waterfront we go and sign up for a two-hour boat trip to see the icebergs up close.

The icebergs are sourced off the glaciers of Greenland and take three or four years to reach this point, carried along slowly but steadily by the ocean currents. The large ones will sometimes reach south of the Grand Banks before they melt – remember the *Titanic*.

As we approach each iceberg, we can't help but recall that it is just floating ice and, like the ice cube in our drinks, it is mostly below water. And yet the boat comes up remarkably close. It's somewhat reassuring when someone explains that they erode and melt away as much by the warming water and wave action as by the sun and, therefore, they tend to hang down from the part on the surface rather than spread out at the waterline. Nevertheless, I keep a close eye on the water as we approach one of them.

I have seen many pictures of these floating ice sculptures, but they did not prepare me for the real thing. It is an awesome sight. The whiteness is so intense, magnified by the sunlight reflecting brightly off the glistening, melting surface. The surface is so smooth, only broken by the fault lines through the berg that add a bluish tinge to the image from their refraction effect.

A short distance away from the main berg we see smaller pieces floating in the sea, mere meters across. Our captain says these "bergy bits" had sloughed off the berg just a short time ago, since they were not there when he made a trip out here a few hours earlier. As we circle around, someone finds a fishing net and scoops out a piece. Up close, the ice is crystal clear and filled with small air bubbles, testifying to its origin as a packed snow glacier, perhaps thousands of years in the making. Naturally, along with most everyone on board the boat, we must get a picture holding the piece of iceberg.

As we look out to the horizons we can see other large icebergs to the northeast and southwest. They look like a navy flotilla of battleships strung out in a straight line, separated by miles of water, but heading steadily and determinedly in the same direction. I can stare at this for a long time, transfixed by the mixed sense of power and tranquility.

There is still more to be seen on this boat excursion. As we are returning to the bay, we spot the telltale spray of a humpback whale and divert off to have a look. After a number of sightings and seemingly interminable waits while the whale goes down to feed, it suddenly blows and surfaces very near the boat. What a magnificent animal. Its graceful motion through the water belies its huge size. After a few minutes of photo opportunities we break off and head to shore, feeling this has been a very special experience.

Driving back south to regain the TCH, we see a road sign that directs us to the N.W. Arm East Middle United Church. I suppose that if you sit in the south pew you will have covered all the bases. I love it here!

Our next stop is Gander. This is a place out of the history books for many of us, as we recall stories of early trans-Atlantic flights or the ferrying of wartime aircraft during WW II between here and the nearest spots in Europe, such as Shannon, Ireland. Gander appears as a basic town set up in the hills of northern Newfoundland, but, of course, that is exactly why it is here. It's as close to Europe as possible, but away from the low shoreline areas and the Avalon Peninsula with their high frequency of foggy days. Although there may not be much fog, Gander is the snowiest city in Canada, averaging 4 ½ meters annually.

Gander also becomes the unintended destination for flights that encounter some form of difficulty over the North Atlantic, whether it is a mechanical problem or a disturbance caused by an unruly passenger that forces the flight to land for assistance. The most momentous day for unexpected visitors was September 11, 2001, the day of the horrendous attacks on the New York World Trade Centre and the Pentagon in Washington, when all flights destined for the United States were ordered to land as soon as possible. Thirty-eight commercial jets, with 6,600 passengers, descended on Gander. This town of 10,000 people, along with the other towns in the area, received, billeted, fed and befriended all those people for four days, until flights could resume. What an inspiring story of help and compassion in that time of tremendous grief and uncertainty.

The history of Gander is captured by the displays in the air-flight museum just beside the highway. Old aircraft fill the lot outside, while inside is a wide collection of old flying gear, uniforms and equipment. But it's the photos that capture the historical sense of the place, whether it is the old Flying Clippers or aerial shots of the runways lined with hundreds of planes assembled for the war supply flights to Europe.

In the museum they have a poster describing "24 Rules of the Air." I cannot resist getting a copy for my pilot friends. Rules #14: "Try to keep the number of landings you make equal to the number of takeoffs you've made"; #17: "Helicopters can't fly; they're just so ugly the earth repels them"; and #21: "It's always a good idea to keep the pointy end going forward as much as possible," all catch my fancy.

West we go. We drive through rolling terrain, tree-covered on both sides. It is broken here and there by ponds full of reeds, lily pads and the occasional beaver lodge, or by fast-running rivers and brooks that glisten over their rock-filled beds. I realize that this is the physical reality of most of Canada. More than three-quarters of our trip will be through similar terrain, with only a variety of tree types to distinguish the areas. Except for the cities and the cleared farmland, the southern prairies and the very far north, this is what our country looks like. It's both awesome and humbling to realize just how vast and undisturbed most of it is.

Hardly a river or stream goes by without the sight of vehicles parked at the side of the road and the presence of fishermen beside or in the water, casting for the big catch. Along with the big, open country of ours comes the love to get out into nature. And what could be better to take home for the barbeque than a fresh salmon?

Grand Falls–Windsor is the largest city in the central region of the province. It has been a major centre for pulp and paper for almost a hundred years; it began to supply the British newspapers with newsprint in 1909. Still today, the highways and side roads in the area carry a steady stream of log trucks on their way to the local mills.

Carrying on down the TCH, we pass a number of large, inland, fresh-water lakes. We soon come to a key junction in Western Newfoundland when we reach Deer Lake. A number of cottage developments exist in the area, attracted by the lakes, the salmon-fishing rivers and the winter skiing on the local mountains. There are many people who come right across the province from St. John's for this getaway. It seems a long way, but, in reality, it's no different in distance than the folks in Alberta going to the interior of B.C. or the folks in Toronto going to Muskoka.

From here we can travel up the Viking Trail as it wanders toward the northwest end of the province. The first area that we come to is the Gros Morne National Park. The western coast has a broad range of mountains up to 800 meters high, intruded by deep fjords, reminiscent of the west coast of Canada in appearance (except for the height of the mountains). However, here in the park the fjords have a distinctive feature; they are separated from the open sea by a strip of land. Thus, they are isolated and filled with fresh water. This is the result of the land rising when the glaciers melted and retreated tens of thousands of years ago.

One of the most impressive and accessible "stranded fjords" is called Western Brook Pond. The approach itself is fascinating, as we take a 45-minute hike off the highway and through a variety of tree-covered ridges, open wetlands and peat bogs cut in many places by quietly running streams and populated everywhere with colourful blankets of flowers, including an amazing number of irises. The trail is well kept, with interpretive signs along the way to educate us on what we are seeing or to provide us with an excuse to take a rest.

Reaching the Pond, we face a large open lake with the rising mountains in the background. A local story is told to explain why these relatively large lakes are called ponds. It says that the early settlers were from central England, where there are no lakes and, thus, the only word they knew was pond. Again, only in Newfoundland could we believe such a story. In fact most of the lakes in the province are called ponds. The locals also like to say that a lake is just a pond with city-dwellers cottages on it.

A two-and-a-half hour boat tour of the inland fjord is a special experience of the journey. As we move from the broad open lake into the narrow valley, we can see high rocky cliffs, remnants of rock slides that have cascaded down the slopes, surging waterfalls that tumble over rocky outcrops into the lake, and even snow that lingers in the deep crevasses in mid-summer. This is a spectacular corner of Newfoundland, very different from everywhere else.

Back on the coast, we see that the western shoreline tends to be one of gentle coves with beaches covered in rounded, water-weathered rocks and boulders. The tree growth along the coast is also very different from that inland. The trees are short, stunted, gnarly spruce and fir that grow in thick groves with the perpetual onshore wind-swept tilt we have seen elsewhere in the province. They are called Tuckamore or just plain "tuck" by the locals.

I regret that I haven't had the time to drive the length of the Viking Trail to the northernmost point of the island or to cross over to Labrador. The remnants of the early Viking explorers and ancient Inuit settlements await a future trip. Friends who have taken the trip say it is fascinating.

At the town of Cow Head we turn back south. It was near here that I experienced a highlight of all my travels across Canada. There, beside the road, was a moose calmly grazing in a field of bright flowers. It quietly stayed put while I got out of the car and took a whole suite of photographs. I had been trying to do this for years! I love to photograph wildlife. Sure, I had seen a moose many times back in Alberta and other places, but they had always wandered off into the woods, calmly and majestically, just fast enough to avoid my camera. I have many photos of trees in which I pretend I can make out a moose. This has been made all the more frustrating by the signs along the highways in many places, especially in Newfoundland, which tell us to watch out for the moose; after all there are over 100,000 of them in this province alone. My wife has decided that moose are just the most introverted animals in the woods, avoiding socializing with strangers as a priority. One thing the signs do accomplish is to give us something to occupy our minds and pass the time on the long stretches of highway through the woods.

The moose signs in the Gros Morne Park are different from other places. They show a moose staring down at an automobile with the front windshield and roof caved in. They are a big animal set up on high legs, such that if you do run into one it will ride up over the hood and come right into the passenger compartment. I have seen cars beside the road that were just like the picture on the sign.

Something else we notice in this area is small garden plots along the side of the road. They appear to be carefully tended and are bordered with wire and brush, presumably to deter animals. Good soil is hard to find on these rocky shores and people are taking advantage of every opportunity.

As we pass back and out of the national park I realize that the local towns of Rocky Harbour, Sally's Cove, St. Paul's and Cow Head have been carved out of the national park, or at least the park was created around them. I wonder if this is not a solution to the perpetual conflict between development and preservation of natural areas in places such as Banff and Jasper. After all, parks, by definition, are for people to enjoy nature. Reserves and protection areas are something else again; there the flora and fauna should be protected from human impact. Why not divide these parks into two distinctive zones? It seems to work in Newfoundland.

Next down the western coast is Cornerbrook, the second largest city in the province. We approach it from high in the hills and see a city laid out on the hillsides along the various inlets of a wide body of water, the Humber Arm that connects to the Gulf of St. Lawrence. The Humber River, which runs into the Arm through the city, is known to be a great place for Atlantic salmon fishing, as are many other rivers in the western part of the province.

The central feature of downtown Cornerbrook is the huge lumber mill on the shoreline. It is claimed that this was the largest mill in the world at the end of World War II. It fills the city with its distinctive odour, both sweet and pungent at the same time. The local weekly newspaper is creatively called the *Humber Log*.

One of the local movie theatres is a single screen structure called the Majestic. It is adorned with a colourful set of murals on the outside walls depicting past explorers. There are quite a number of murals throughout the city. The theatre is run by a very friendly family that sells the tickets, makes the popcorn and runs the projector.

On a hilltop in Cornerbrook is a testimonial to Captain James Cook, which can only be found with perseverance and many wrong turns. In the mid-1760s, well before he undertook his explorations of the Pacific and the west coast of North America, he led a survey of western Newfoundland,

and the area around Cornerbrook in particular, for the British governor in St. John's. Such historical minutia can lead to things like the Captain Cook's Galley restaurant along the highway here today.

The drive out to the west of the city is spectacular, again with colourful fishing villages and pretty coves. There are hills as high as 750 meters here; at places, waterfalls tumble down from high perches.

Along here, as in many places across the province, there are many houses that do not have stairs up to their front doors. These look like bungalows that have been set on high foundations to provide for a lower level. There is a front door some two or three meters off the ground, facing out into open space with no steps or landings or railings! It appears time after time, on homes that looked very nice and finished in every other way. The only explanation I can get is that everyone enters through the back door; when they have company they all tend to gather in the kitchen. Thus, the front door is redundant. All I can say is that anyone who makes a mistake is going to experience a big first step when they leave. Don't drink too much screech. They are also called mother-in-law doors.

I can't help but reflect on the large number of towns and villages we have seen across the whole province with the same picture-book look. Some have had populations in the hundreds, if not more, but many have been small, with only a handful of houses. They all have seemed well kept and even have a sense of recent construction. There is a real sense of permanence. This conflicts with the knowledge that the population of the province is basically static and, as always, the big city is growing. It also contrasts with the reality that over 250 small towns were dismantled by government directive from the mid-'50s to the mid-'70s. I suspect it simply means that the sea does support a base load of people and the strong traditions of local communities and close families ensures that many of these villages have survived, albeit as small entities. I wonder what will happen with the next generation, particularly if the catches from the sea become permanently limited.

Stephenville is the next city along the west coast. As we approach it, we pass a wide bay with all of the trees along the shore growing in an extreme onshore direction. All of the branches spread that way as well, even if they started on the other side of the tree. Oh, the wind!

Coming over the hills, we can see the image of a town in the distance, or more precisely we can see huge hangar buildings and long wide runways across the flat landscape. This brings into memory that the U.S. Air Force had a big base here in the past as part of the continental defense system. As we approach, the image changes. We see that the buildings are all abandoned and the windows are mostly broken. The runways are cordoned off with chain link fences and there is grass growing through the cracks in the pavement. However, over the next hill is the real town;

there are nearly 10,000 people in the area and it seems to be bustling. The vestiges of the airbase are ever-present, with a USAF fighter jet mounted on display in the centre of town and the streets having names such as Michigan, Utah, Indiana and Massachusetts.

Leaving Stephenville, we continue down the valley into an area of high, tree-covered rocky hills, or mountains, as they are called locally, rising to 500 meters or more. Apparently the mountains of western Newfoundland are an extension of the Appalachians in the eastern United States.

The wind seems to blow constantly here. There are stories of trains in the past, and trucks now, being held back at times lest they blow over on their sides.

Port aux Basques is at the extreme southwest corner of the province. An old train is on display at the station museum as you enter the town. It has a huge snowplow blade on the front that reminds everyone of the winter realities. But the track stops a few feet ahead and there does not seem to be any other line. Asking around, we come to learn that there is no train service in Newfoundland anymore. The old narrow gauge system was hard to maintain and most communities were well off the main line so that the handling of goods onto trucks was required anyway. The labour issues of boat to train to truck made it impossibly expensive. Now it's just direct trucking, off the ferries from mainland Canada or loading out of cargo ships.

Another legacy of the railway is that the old rail bed has been converted to a provincial park and hiking/cycling trail from one end of the province to the other. It is a bit rough for any extended bicycle riding, but it is used extensively by walkers and people on four-wheeled quads. This must be the longest and narrowest park in the world; it is 1000 kilometers long and 10 meters wide! Even better is its creative name: *T'Railway Park*.

This is the embarkation point for the six hour ferry ride to Nova Scotia and mainland Canada where we will pick up on our trip.

Nova Scotia

2. Nova Scotia

Arriving from Newfoundland, the ferry enters the spacious harbour of Sydney and lands on its north shore. There are a few things that become quickly apparent.

The first is the nature of the harbour itself. Unlike the steep-sided, relatively narrow nature of the harbour we saw in St. John's, this harbour is wide and long with major arms off in a couple of directions. As we learn as we travel around, it is about 15 kilometers long and it is five kilometers wide in the centre. This is one of a number of large natural harbours along the shoreline of Nova Scotia that have a long history of shipping and of marshalling activities for navies and convoys in times of war. German submarines were detected in the harbour area during World War II, and a ferry traveling between Sydney and Port-aux-Basques was sunk in 1942, claiming 137 lives.

The second, as we are quickly reminded by everyone we meet, is that we are on the island of Cape Breton, part of Nova Scotia, but also an area with its own distinct history and heritage. So, although Newfoundlanders may talk of the ferry going over to the mainland, that will not be the best way to describe it to the locals of this area, who have a proud independence as "islanders" themselves.

Sydney is a city of contrasts. Entering the city, we can see some subdivisions and shopping areas that remind us of many other places in Canada. Along the harbour front there is a string of relatively new hotels and condominiums that face out over the wide channel. A long boardwalk winds along the shoreline, full of activity as people go out for walks, encounter the street vendors and entertainers, and partake of the nice restaurants in the area. The contrast is seen in the downtown commercial area and in many of the older neighbourhoods, where there is a tired, worn-out look.

The economic history of the area can be summed up in one word: coal. For over 250 years the coal mines have been the backbone of the local industry, starting with the French settlements of the early 1700s. As the mines were worked underground, they stretched out under the ocean floor.

Underground coal mining has to be one of the most difficult and dangerous occupations in the world. Deep and dark, with lung-filling dust in the air and the ever-present danger of cave-ins and gas explosions, the mines were a forbidding presence. A memorial at New Waterford commemorates the approximately 300 miners killed in the area operations. The Miners' Museum and Village at Glace Bay provides a good overview of the industry's history.

Now, the economic realities have finally caught up with the area. After decades of government-supported attempts to sustain the mines and other related industries, such as steel-making, the mines are now closed. As we saw with the outposts of Newfoundland and will see with the towns of the prairies and elsewhere, the pressures to move out to areas of greater economic opportunity are real, especially for the younger people. The difficulty is the angst of leaving families and abandoning communities to inevitable decline. It's hardest for those who are now in middle age, having started in the mines over the past twenty years or so. Perhaps the writing was on the wall as to the future, but there was the expectation that the government would continue subsidizing the operation. In fact, the news stories that emerged at the time of the closures were all focused on the anger toward the government for not doing so; the government minister certainly had to take a firm position.

The area is struggling. One initiative is to expand the tourist industry. There are a lot of appealing areas to visit in Cape Breton, and Nova Scotia in general. In fact, this province may be my favourite to visit.

One highlight for tourists in this area lies 30 kilometers to the east, at the reconstructed old town and fortress of Louisbourg. The buildings, shops and colourful re-enactments bring to life the times of French colonization in the early 1700s. We can easily spend a full day here absorbing the ambience and the history.

In the first half of the eighteenth century France dominated much of North America. They had control of the St. Lawrence River, the Great Lakes and the interior regions along the Ohio and Mississippi Rivers. They established settlements from Quebec City to Montreal, at Detroit and Pittsburgh (then called Ft. Duquesne), and down to New Orleans.

The British controlled the thirteen colonies along the Atlantic seaboard, eastern Newfoundland, and they were establishing themselves in mainland Nova Scotia. The French decided they needed a fortress and settlement on the south side of the entrance to the Gulf of St. Lawrence. As a result, a large and thriving presence was established around the large ice-free harbour at Louisbourg, built up over a quarter century beginning in 1719. This became a busy crossroad for the French navy, settlers, fishing fleets and trading ships. Some years saw over 200 ships pass through.

This fortress also marks the location of the initial British push to drive French control out of North America in the middle of that century. The British actually first captured Louisbourg in 1745 but it was returned to the French almost immediately by a treaty that ended a broader European conflict. The British then moved back south and started to establish a military garrison and settlement at Halifax. Shortly thereafter, the British and French were again engaged in war, the Seven Years' War from 1756-1763. It was a worldwide conflict. In the early years the French were the most successful in the battles in North America, generally held south of the St. Lawrence River and Lake Ontario (upstate New York today). However, in 1758 a force of some 12,000 British troops put to siege and finally captured Louisbourg. This was the preamble to the battles for Quebec City and Montreal over the next two years and the eventual British control of Canada.

The modern day reconstruction of Ft. Louisbourg and the settlements offers a fun opportunity to step back in time and to revisit some of our most significant historical moments.

Now we will return back through Sydney and drive the northern and western shoreline of Cape Breton, what's known as the Cabot Trail. This is one of the most spectacular drives in the country. There are steep cliffs over the sea, narrow winding roads through the wooded highlands, and remote villages and tourist havens to be discovered.

For example, at Ingonish there are high cliffs and coves with beaches to be explored. There is also a first class resort lodge, a challenging golf course carved out of the wooded hills and plenty of opportunities for hiking, boating and fishing. It's a neat place for a getaway vacation. I have to smile when we pass a rustic general store set back in the woods with a sign out front that says, "Provisions, Gear and Golf Balls."

I have driven the Cabot Trail a couple of times and have always marveled at the scenery, but there is no doubt it is extra special in the fall when the trees change to their autumn colours. The palette of reds, yellows and oranges in all their hues and combinations can be breathtaking, especially when you can see a panorama across miles of the rolling highlands with the colours undulating like waves in the ocean in response to fall breezes.

I have to believe that the slowest drivers in Canada are in Nova Scotia. Granted you should not be in a hurry when driving on a vacation through beautiful countryside, but it can still be very frustrating to trail a car going only 30 km/h along a winding two-lane highway for long stretches. Cars parked on the narrow edge of the road will sometimes start up and enter the highway right in front of us, apparently presuming that we are traveling that slowly as well. That can be scary. As we travel across the country I will note the drivers at the other extreme, i.e., fast and aggressive (clues: what province starts with Q or what big city starts with T?).

There is another highway phenomenon that I found disconcerting. Nova Scotia, like all the provinces, has many two-lane highways. It also follows the common practice of building a third, passing lane from time to time which allows traffic to decongest, especially in hilly or winding road areas. In many parts of the country, certainly in the west where I do most of my driving, the cars in the single lane are not allowed to use the new middle lane to pass other cars; you must keep to your own lane for that section of road. Here, in Nova Scotia, you can use the third lane "when it's safe to do so." I know I avoid the temptation, but I am still nervous using the passing lane even when I have the right of way, since I am never confident that someone coming the other way hasn't decided to use it as well. As we will see later, the only area with more bizarre, and I think more dangerous, use of these third lanes is Northern Ontario. Oh well, let's get back to the trip, carefully.

Coming off the highlands, the highway drops down to sea level and our drive along the western shore of Cape Breton encounters a string of fishing villages set in coves with rocky beaches. The underlying culture here is French, harkening back to the early settlements by the Acadians in the 1600s. It's fun to stop along here for a very good home-style meal in a quaint restaurant looking over the water.

Turning east into the middle of the island, we come to the shores of the Bras d'Or Lakes and the town of Baddeck. The Bras d'Or Lakes fill the interior of the island and, for all purposes, divide it in two. The Lakes are large, with long channels and narrow openings between segments. They are open to the ocean at the north end, causing the water to be somewhat brackish as the lakes are impacted by the tides. The south end was physically closed off by a narrow spit of land, but now there is a canal that allows boat traffic to transverse. Obviously this is cottage and boating country.

The town of Baddeck is a real delight. Its main street is full of interesting shops and restaurants, all with a quaint colonial look, many of which look out over the water. There are many talented artists in the area with shops in town or along the surrounding country roads. They include potters, painters, glass blowers, quilters and wood workers. Of course, there are also the more "touristy" souvenirs. I am always surprised at how many small leaded glass representations of lighthouses, boats, birds, flowers, children, dogs and cats can be found in every shop in the land; the market seems to be infinite.

A highlight for me is to visit the Alexander Graham Bell National Historical Site and Museum. Dr. Bell had spent a lot of his later life at his estate in this area and he is buried there. He had continued his research here in his many subjects of interest including aeronautics, medicine, genetics and working with the deaf. It was his interest in the deaf that had stimulated his research in sound which led to the invention of the telephone.

My faulty memory of history, or perhaps just the version presented in our history books, had left me with the impression that the invention of the telephone had a strong Canadian connection. In fact, Bell had moved from Scotland to Brantford, Ontario with his parents in 1874 and then had moved on to the U.S. a short while later, where the original telephone was created in 1876. When we read the fine print of the testimonials here, and later when we visit Brantford, it is clear that the Canadian connection is limited to: "He conceived some of the ideas while briefly living there with his parents." Somehow, over the years, I had convinced myself that the telephone was a Canadian invention! Next thing I know, someone will tell me that the Disney Corporation is in charge of marketing the RCMP.

Continuing our journey southwest to the end of Cape Breton, we can take the causeway across the Strait of Canso at Port Hawkesbury. Now we really are on mainland Canada, although we will be diverting onto many islands again as we travel.

It is about here that I suddenly realize that the major food group in Nova Scotia might not be seafood after all, but ice cream. I think that every corner store in every village has an ice cream freezer. They advertise that fact for miles in every direction with signs in the shape of an ice cream cone, with the distance to the next fix clearly stated. Sometimes the stores are just free-standing ice cream stands that boldly proclaim the dozens of flavours available. I should note that this is an observation, not a complaint, since I always sample my fair share.

Our first mainland stop is at the town of Antigonish, about 5000 people strong and self-described as the Highland Heart of Nova Scotia, which relates back to the early Scottish settlers who established the area. As we travel across the country we will note that many communities like to attach a motto to themselves, some serious and some not so. By far the most common theme will be the "Heart" of something.

Antigonish is pronounced in a lilting manner that is pleasing to the ear. I love to trip it off my tongue as I do with Merigomish, Tatamagouche and others. If you don't know the pronunciation, it's hard to describe, but basically it's said as one continuous sound with no emphasis on any specific syllable. Try "anta-gun-ish," but quickly without a break between the parts.

The town is old colonial, with lots of red brick and brownish stone buildings with white trim, all surrounded by big multi-limbed trees set on gentle hills. The centrepiece of the town is the St. Francis of Xavier University, simply called "St. F.X." by everyone. Here, we find a relatively small university, set in a small town setting, with a picturesque architecture, that has earned national attention both scholastically and athletically. The MacLean's annual survey always ranks it number one or two in the Primarily Undergraduate category. It is quite a success story.

From here, let's go down to the Atlantic shore, the east shore of Nova Scotia. I must digress and talk about directions in Nova Scotia. First of all, we need to recognize that the long dimension of the province runs much more east-west than north-south, which is not the intuitive orientation of folks from "away" who have been fooled by the projections on some Canadian maps. Then there are the local conventions to deal with. The shore along the Gulf of St. Lawrence, from Cape Breton to New Brunswick and facing Prince Edward Island, is the north shore. That seems O.K. The shore along the Bay of Fundy that faces New Brunswick is the west shore. Again, a look at the map tends to confirm this as logical. Now we come to the long, relatively straight Atlantic shoreline. To the northeast of Halifax, which is in the middle of this coast, it is the east shore. To the southwest of Halifax it is the south shore. Get used to it as you travel Nova Scotia and talk to folks or read direction on the road signs. Bring a map and shut off or ignore your car's onboard compass.

We now take the highway due south from Antigonish to the east shore (trust me on this). We travel through an area of tree-covered rolling hills, small lakes and local rivers, interspersed with a smattering of farms. Cottages appear periodically on the freshwater lake shorelines.

As we get near the ocean shore, we follow along the relatively wide, fast-flowing St. Mary's River. We get glimpses of kayakers skimming along the surface. Near the town of Sherbrooke we see and smell a salmon smokehouse operation and thus salivate our way to lunch in a local restaurant.

The east shore is dominated by wide bays and coves that come well inland from the ocean and have forested shores. A small village is situated in most coves, usually at the mouth of a river that flows down from the interior, sometimes with a small rocky falls at the end. Once in a while, there will be a bay with a more elaborate marina and a fleet of ocean fishing boats. Seafood farming is also prevalent; we can see the long lines of small floats that mark the underwater system of ropes and nets. Lobster and crab traps cover the many wharves.

The road along the coast runs past the head of these bays, so that we do not really see the open ocean. It is a relatively narrow and rough road with lots of sharp curves. The towns all seem to have names that end in Harbour, Cove or Bay. The headlands are called Point, Head or Peninsula. There are some unique names such as Ecum Secum, Necum Teuch and East Quoddy. (Yes, there is a West Quoddy, but it's not on the maps.) There are also some larger bays with more substantial towns and industries such as the pulp and paper plant at Sheet Harbour.

By the time we reach Oyster Pond the sides of the road are becoming more populated and commercial enterprises start to appear, as we are closing in on the greater Halifax-Dartmouth area.

Halifax is one of my favourite cities to visit in Canada. Coming from this direction, we enter the area through the sister city of Dartmouth, somewhat more industrial than Halifax, but showing growth with some new upscale neighbourhoods set in the tree-filled rolling hills of the area.

The entrance to Halifax is via the high MacDonald Bridge that crosses the wide harbour just where it narrows to enter the huge interior Bedford Basin. This is a world class harbour with its immense size, many docks and wharves, and total shelter from the open sea. Railway yards, refineries, shipyards, naval facilities and container terminals line its miles of shoreline.

Greater Halifax has a population of over 350,000 people, making it, by far, the largest city in Atlantic Canada; in fact, it is larger than St. John's, Saint John and Charlottetown added together, and, unlike those others, it is showing some growth, albeit small.

For visitors, the focus of the city is on the downtown area, which spreads out from the shoreline of the inner harbour up to the Citadel, which sits high on the hill above the city centre. The Citadel, a stone-walled, star-shaped fortress surrounded by defensive dry moats, is a key vantage point from which to get a panoramic sense of the whole area. It is also an interesting site to visit to learn the history of the area and, in summer, to observe re-enactments of fortress life in the centuries past.

The town clock, with its four faces, sits on the corner of Citadel Hill and can be seen from across the city. For 200 years there has been the firing of the noonday cannon to coordinate the time for ships in the harbour. It is long past being a functional role, but it is a great tradition. This happens in harbours worldwide, mimicking the daily event at Greenwich, England, the "centre of time."

The streets are very steep as they head down to the waterfront. Walking through the downtown can be strenuous, although we quickly learn to go along the parallel streets and search out the narrow alleys with steps, or work through shops that allow us to enter on one level and use a stairway to exit on the street above or below.

Halifax has undertaken an impressive renewal of its downtown area and, in particular, the waterfront area. On the streets are a number of new office buildings and hotels. The wide boardwalk along the water has a new enclosed marketplace, lots of interesting shops, a maritime museum and many restaurants. It's a treat to sit in a waterside restaurant, eating a fresh seafood dinner and watching the busy harbour at work. There are ocean-going freighters, cruise ships, navy vessels, work boats, sightseeing tours, high-mast sail boats and fishing charters. Often there will be live music playing familiar local tunes.

At times, there will be an offshore drilling rig in the harbour for refurbishing. These large floating platforms can operate in the deep water of the Atlantic continental shelf where they explore for crude oil and natural gas thousands of feet below the sea floor. This is a new industry for the province that has the potential to make a significant impact on its economy, although the more recent exploration results have been disappointing.It was my involvement in this business that brought me to visit Nova Scotia in the 1980s, when I first gained my appreciation for the area.

There is a plaque along the waterfront that describes the Halifax explosion of 1917. A munitions ship, the Mont Blanc, collided with a relief ship in the harbour, setting off the largest explosion in the history of the world until the advent of the Atomic bomb in 1945. The city was devastated and 1600 people were killed.

Along the streets of Halifax there are a number of bookshops that always catch my interest. One used book store here has an appropriate name, Back Pages. There are also some impressive arts and crafts galleries. One shop in the market area offers the fine Nova Scotia crystal that is made locally.

The street names reflect the origins of the city in the second half of the eighteenth century, when British settlers and the loyalists from the American colonies arrived. King, Queen, Princess, George and Charlotte are all here, as they are in almost every city and town throughout the Maritimes and Ontario.

In the centre of downtown, on a small quiet square, sits the provincial legislature, the 1819 Provincial House, which is the oldest "local" legislature in the British Empire. It is a stately three-story, columned, sandstone structure surrounded by an iron-pike fence.

In the courtyard is a statue to the famous politician-orator-statesman-journalist-poet Joseph Howe, the father of Nova Scotia and a somewhat reluctant father of the Canadian Confederation.

The inner legislative assembly hall, modest in size with an overhanging balcony, is impressively decorated with white trim, plaster columns and arches, and a series of very large paintings of the early leaders.

Most impressive and reassuring to me is the quiet ambience and trust shown here in these times of turmoil and terrorism. I was able to wander through the legislative chamber and other key rooms at my leisure, with just a nod from the attendant, in the summer of 2004, well after the events of 9/11 in the U.S., near the time of the Russian school bombing, and during the ongoing problems in Iraq and the Middle East.

Down near the south end of the city wharves, actually in the working area of container terminals and loading docks, is Pier 21. This is the site where over a million immigrants entered Canada between 1928 and 1971. It is now a historical museum that includes powerful displays, entertaining videos and interactive stations. The set-up is dramatic, as we can relive the entry and processing of all those people who came from around the world to set up a new home and to help grow this nation. We can also relive the journeys they took as they dispersed across the country; the audio-video effects make us feel like we are on a train passing through the ever-changing countryside.

It was a very moving experience for me. Like those who came through Pier 21 later, my grandparents arrived from Scotland in 1913 with my infant father in tow. They entered through the port of Montreal and then took a train to southern Manitoba. The experiences and images for them would have been very similar to those portrayed here. I once spent quite a while here absorbing it all on a rainy day. The heavy rain and fog that lay over the harbour that day just seemed to emphasize how momentous the decisions were for families to pick up and leave for unknown futures half way around the world.

This facility is now the terminus for large cruise ships that bring many visitors to the city. That creates a very different atmosphere of busy, high-energy tourists flocking along the waterfront and heading off to tour the sights.

On the way back from the pier to the city centre, we can stop and tour the Alexander Keith's 1820 brewery, the oldest operating brewery in North America, and then go on to have lunch and a pint. It's impressive how all of the various regional and local breweries have had a renewal over the last decade or so. Now there is a super variety of styles and flavours to be found everywhere.

In the local Halifax bars it does take some adjustment to their classifications of beers. In one pub, "domestic beer" included Keith's, Canadian, Blue, Budweiser and Coors, while "imports "included Heineken, Corona, Sleeman's and Kokanee. I guess that describes the local feelings toward Ontario and B.C. Other pubs are more discrete, using labels such as Here and There or Home and Away, rather than Domestic and Imports.

We need to be aware that there is no general Sunday shopping in Nova Scotia. When you travel a lot you forget that there will be local anomalies like that and can get surprised. Many people I talked with on my more recent visits here thought that this restriction would change soon but a plebiscite in October, 2004 kept it in effect by a 55:45 ratio.

As we move out of Halifax to head "west," we can see some of the old established neighbourhoods with stately homes and nice parks with large spreading trees. The good news, as we leave, is that the routes are labeled "inbound" and "outbound" rather than by direction. The bad news is that the signs that indicate a critical turn are sometimes lost in the branches of the heavy foliage on the boulevards. Again, I manage to go the wrong way a couple of times.

One little tidbit of trivia we learn here is that they drove on the left side of the road, English style, until the 1920s. That was also true in the other Maritime Provinces and British Columbia. Newfoundland did not convert to driving on the right side until it joined the Canadian Confederation in 1949. Granted there was not as much inter-provincial travel before the 1920s, but it must have been confusing to change sides of the road as you moved between various provinces.

Anyway, we are now on our way out of the city and traveling down Highway 103 West. (That's official.) Immediately, we can sense a change from the area east of Halifax. It becomes hillier and rock outcrops appear along the road. The land is generally forest-covered with small lakes and inland rivers to be seen.

Our first side trip is out to the oceanfront at one of the most picturesque and most photographed spots in Canada – Peggy's Cove. The cove itself is a very narrow, short inlet between enclosing sides of smoothly-worn rock. There are a few weathered docks along the inlet, usually piled high with lobster and crab traps. Some colourful fishing boats are tethered alongside. On the ridges along the road sit a small cluster of the colourful, but basic, wood-sided homes of the villagers. A few shops sell souvenirs, crafts and cozy warm knit sweaters and waterproof slickers — this is the North Atlantic coast after all. However, what sets it apart from the other coves is the imposing granite headland that juts out into the sea with the tall, white lighthouse capping its presence. As we stand there and watch the ocean waves pound on the shore and spray sea water high into the air with a loud roar, it is quite an awesome experience. The lighthouse serves as a post office and so we, along with the busloads of people there with us at any time, can send the impressive picture postcards to friends and family.

Just outside of town there is a memorial to the 229 people who perished in the crash of Swiss Air Flight 111 in 1998. The response and support to the families by the people of Peggy's Cove was outstanding and has been recognized widely — a very similar story to the one about Gander and the events of September 11, 2001.

As we carry on down the coast, we notice that the bays and coves are narrower and have higher shorelines than "up east." Often, there is a sandy beach at the head of the bay. The area is more populated, both with villages and towns and with homes and cottages in the woods along the shore. This is an area for getaways by Haligonians as well as being the permanent home for many others. (Okay, admit it, did you really know that the people from Halifax are called Haligonians?)

The good-size town of Chester comes next, set on a large inland bay with some secondary inlets. There are some impressive homes on the hillsides and waterfront, many set on wooded acreages. Shops sell arts and crafts, fused glass, antiques and various collectibles. Let's stop for lunch at a pub with an outside deck looking over the water. A cold beer and a lobster-and-shrimp pizza make it perfect. The view over the docks and boats and across the blue water to the various white-sided homes and buildings is vivid in its intensity and contrasts.

One other thing that dramatically stands out to me is that almost every home and shop along the harbour has a flag pole and the red and white Canadian flag fluttering with the onshore breeze in the bright sunlight. It's my sense, totally unscientific, that the folks in Atlantic Canada in general and Nova Scotia in particular fly the Canadian flag more than anywhere else in the country.

Our next stop is Mahone Bay. Entering the bay area, we find another picturesque corner of the province with a quaint town. The architecture and décor of the buildings have been well-coordinated to represent an old-fashioned, colonial-style town. What quickly catches our attention though is the large number of church steeples that pierce the tree-backed vista. They form a unique and distinctive scene.

One shop that catches lots of attention is the pewter store. It's full of the usual interesting and even amusing articles — goblets, picture frames, small animals, etc. — but the real appeal is watching the process of pewter being poured into forms. Pewter is a tin-based metal mix that becomes molten and easily pourable and formable when heated, but it sets up as a solid very quickly when cooled to room temperature. This leads to fun demonstrations by the staff at the store, as they pour the molten pewter on slabs and quickly manipulate it into shapes before it hardens. I was going to say that it's fun for the kids in the crowd, but I admit that I can be entertained by it for a long period as well.

Our next stop along the south coast is Lunenburg. It is similar to a number of the towns we have visited, but here the history and the architecture have been preserved even more, with some of the buildings and homes dating back to the founding days of the mid-1700s. In fact, Lunenburg has been declared a Canadian National Heritage District and the United Nations has designated it as a UNESCO World Heritage Site.

There is an excellent Fisheries Museum on the waterfront, complemented with real fishing boats that can be toured. The main streets run parallel to the waterfront on a very steep hillside. It is quite usual and very convenient to enter a building off one street and then to exit on another from an upper or lower storey. It's similar to the experience in Halifax, but even more so here, since the hill is steeper and the streets and buildings are narrower.

Most Canadians probably relate Lunenburg with the schooner Bluenose. Lunenburg had a shipbuilding industry that was world class and many schooners were built here to harvest the Atlantic fishing banks. It was only natural that the sport of boat racing became part of the entertainment and rivalries between the various fleets. In the 1920s and 1930s the Bluenose was the undefeated champion of the North Atlantic and four-time winner of international challenges. We see a picture of this boat every day on our dimes. There is a replica that was built in the 1960s that can be visited when you find it in port, here or in Halifax; the original ship sunk off Haiti in 1946 after it hit an underwater reef.

Back on the highway we pass through Bridgewater, the largest town on the south shore with over 7000 people. It describes itself as the Main Street of the South Shore, which becomes apparent when we see the large stores, distribution warehouses and dealers for farm equipment and automobiles, as well as the hospital, medical centre and schools.

Next, we come to Liverpool, the Home of Privateers. Here, they particularly honour one ship, the Liverpool Packet, which captured over 100 "enemy" vessels. Now, we need to learn the difference between pirates and privateers. It's basically a matter of legitimacy. Pirates were bad guys who robbed and plundered ships at sea. Privateers were good guys who did the same thing, but they did it under the sponsorship of the king or the government and, thus, only attacked ships from other countries. In other words, privateers were pirates who paid taxes. You can probably think of some modern-day equivalents.

Liverpool is set on the bay at the mouth of a river. A nearby town, Milton, is the site of a scenic set of rapids and a small waterfall with a fish ladder for migrating salmon. The river is the Mersey. Can there be any doubt that the early settlers here were English? You might think that we will come across a tribute to the Beatles, but, no, this is Canada and this is the hometown of Hank Snow, the country and western music legend. The local exhibition centre pays tribute to him and other Canadian country music performers.

We can also take the side road out to Moose Harbour and Mersey Point. It comes as a surprise and a bit of a shock when we get to the coast line and see huge waves breaking over the rocky shore, sending a big spray and a loud roar into the air. Although we have been traveling along the Atlantic coast for long distances, we have only seen quiet coves and quaint villages. The ocean has been hidden and we can forget that it's there, over the hills. There are some large homes in this area with panoramic ocean views.

There is an impressive variety of signaling equipment at Mersey Point. Along with a tall white-and-red lighthouse, there is a high radio tower and a large light array, all designed to warn ships of the dangerous coast. I have to confess that I once jumped high into the air when I was standing very close to the lighthouse and its loud, deep-toned horn bellowed unexpectedly.

We could cut across the province from here to the west shore, taking Highway 8 north (or is it still west, even if we turn right?). It's a relatively narrow, winding road through forested countryside that's full of isolated rivers and lakes. It is a popular area for camping and fresh-water fishing. The folks who live in that area must really like it, as they gave their towns names such as Harmony and Pleasantville.

But we are going to stay on the coastal route, passing many more beautiful coves and towns, reaching the junction of the south and west shores at Yarmouth. Although there is no real corner in the shoreline here, we know it has happened because the highway changes from 103 West to 101 North.

Yarmouth has a long history of shipping and fishing. Located at the mouth of the Bay of Fundy and being the closest point in Nova Scotia to New England, it has been the crossroad for a lot of traffic. Ferries run from here to Portland and Bar Harbor, Maine, bringing lots of tourist traffic. There is much to see and visit, as the area was settled at different times by the French, the English, the Acadians and the Loyalists in the 1600s and 1700s.

The Bay of Fundy is huge, being 300 kilometers long from the mouth to the upper arms and over 50 kilometers wide most of the way. It is a totally Canadian body of water as it divides the west shore of Nova Scotia from the south shore of New Brunswick. From Digby, N.S., a small town on the bay, a ferry service runs to Saint John, New Brunswick.

Digby is set inside the opening to a long, narrow, protected bay that runs parallel to the main shore and the Bay of Fundy proper and provides access to the Annapolis Valley. This area was first visited by Champlain in 1605 and attracted some of the earliest settlers to what is now Canada.

The Digby harbour is home to one of the world's largest scallop fleets. Also in the bay we can see a large array of wide-mesh, metal cages that hang down in the water from an elaborate above-water system of connecting walkways and boat moorings. These are salmon pens. Salmon is now extensively farmed, as with cod in Newfoundland, due to the depleted natural stock.

Moving up the valley, we come to Annapolis Royal, one of the oldest settlements in North America. Just across the local inlet is Port Royal, where the earliest European settlement north of Florida was established by the French. Annapolis Royal today looks sedate, with its wide, treed streets and gracious homes. There are many historic buildings, including the oldest remaining wooden building in Canada, a house built in 1708.

At a narrows in the inland bay there is a small power plant that generates electricity from the force of the tides that surge in and out of the area. It is modest in size, but it represents the ongoing search for lower-cost, renewable energy forms. The informative displays at the visitor centre give us our first sense of the magnitude of the Fundy tides. We can anticipate learning a lot more about the tides as we move around the bay.

The Annapolis Valley is excellent farming country. Stretching out for miles between the surrounding hills, the valley is filled with fruit orchards and vegetable fields, plus extensive corn and hay fields that support the numerous dairy farms. The town of Berwick declares itself to be the Apple Capital, a bold claim in this fertile area. New Minas is satisfied to be the Shopping Centre for the Valley. Driving through the region in the fall, we can see large fields filled with orange polka dots – pumpkins ready for the Halloween-time harvest.

As we leave the valley and enter the area along one of the upper arms of the Bay of Fundy, Cobequid Bay, we come to the town of Wolfville and the nearby Grand Pré National Historical Park.

Wolfville is set at the end of the wide bay, below a big headland. Although it is relatively small, there is a prosperous look to its homes and farms. It is the home of Acadia University, again one of those small-size, small-town schools that rank well nationally. It is the location of the Apple Harvest Festival and major antique shows. The local micro-climate supports vineyards and wineries as well. The town also boasts some outstanding restaurants that feature seafood and French country dishes. I am always surprised when I talk to people in other parts of Canada before a trip to Nova Scotia and they volunteer the advice to be sure to go to eat in Wolfville.

The Grand Pré historical site presents a testimonial to the Acadians, who were the first Europeans to settle this area. A small but impressive stone church sits on a well-maintained site with large, spreading trees in the yard. Paintings in the church depict the life and trying times of the Acadians. In the yard is a statue of the fictional Evangeline, who was the heroine in Longfellow's epic poem by that name that honoured the plight of the Acadians. Out in the surrounding fields we can see signs of the elaborate and impressive dike systems that they constructed hundreds of years ago to keep the brackish water of the bay from their fertile, low-lying fields. You can tell that all of this is a significant tourist attraction by the upscale souvenir shops that line the road in from Wolfville and the large parking lot designed for big buses.

It is heartening to be in an area of trusting and, therefore, presumably trustworthy people. Driving by this area in October, I saw a farm wagon beside the road, at the end of a long lane to a farm house, which was loaded with pumpkins. A small sign simply said "$1.50/$2.50/$3.50." On the wagon was a box with a slot for money. That was it, a true honour system.

At the upper end of one of the arms of the bay we find the town of Windsor, set in a valley among rolling hills. The area is surrounded by a large tidal marsh, which is crossed by a long causeway. For a small town, it has a lot of claims. First, and most importantly to most Canadians, it claims to be the birthplace of hockey. Apparently students at a local school played the first game on a local pond in the mid 1800s. Montreal also claims to have had the first "real" game in 1875, with rules, boards, etc. Recent researchers found that the famous northern explorer John Franklin noted in his journals from 1825 that his crew played the game of hockey on the ice of Great Bear Lake to amuse themselves in the winter. The debate about who invented hockey will never be resolved as, in reality, the game evolved from one of straight sticks and a ball with people running and sliding on the ice to one where there were curved sticks, a puck, skates and defined rules. It makes good fun for the communities involved in the debate, although you sometimes hear that they take it too seriously and even threaten legal action over the claim to be first.

Windsor is also the home turf for the Dill pumpkin variety that grows to over 1000 pounds and is featured in those contests that always briefly turn up in the news each fall.

Finally, this is the hometown of the author Thomas Haliburton, who created the character Sam Slick, who, in turn, is the namesake of the local annual festival. Be sure you don't get this all mixed up and conclude that Sam Slick played the first hockey game at a local party using a pumpkin for a puck. Or maybe he did.

Now we are going to move on to the northern part of the province. A look at a highway map would show a four-lane highway system going down from Windsor to Halifax and then reversing to the north towards Truro. As an alternative, there is the secondary route, Highway 14, which is much more direct from Windsor to Truro. This seems like the logical thing to do, and it would be on a nice clear day, as we could wind our way through rolling hills and picturesque farmland.

However, the time I decided to take the route was on a dark fall evening. It started out fine, but the weather turned into a hard-driving rain storm. The road is very narrow and full of sharp curves. There is no shoulder to speak of. I was feeling my way along the route, admittedly going slow so as to avoid missing one of the corners and catching my tire on the steep edges. The intensity was not helped by signs warning me to watch out for cows, horses and wagons at unseen crossings. That was the longest 60-kilometer, 1½-hour shortcut I have ever taken. The 100-kilometer "long way" on the major highway would have just been a boringly easy one hour or less.

At least when I got back to the main road and saw the town of Shubenacadie I could distract myself with all of those great sounding names again, although I am not sure I wanted to know the name means "the place where wild potatoes grow." It sounds grander than that.

Our next stop is Truro, situated at the upper end of Cobequid Bay and our gateway to northern Nova Scotia. More officially, it is known as the Hub of Nova Scotia, being the crossroads of the major east-west and north-south traffic routes.

Truro has over 10,000 people, making it the third largest city in the province after Halifax and Sydney. To me, Truro represents those great old cities of the east. It is full of large multi-story brick or wood homes on large lots; the streets are lined with large trees with massive, overhanging branches and big leaves; the downtown streets are lined with solid two- and three-storey brick buildings; and there are a number of good-sized parks with small lakes and fountains. Of course, there are some old industrial areas and modern malls and subdivisions on the outskirts, but the overall image is one of historical substance.

Truro has created a unique art form, driven out of a big problem. Truro has many stately elm trees that are being attacked by Dutch elm disease. The city is fighting back by carefully managing what they call their urban forest. This requires the careful monitoring of all the trees, the culling of diseased ones, and the planting of new ones. The unique dimension is that the diseased trees that need to be cut down are then carved into interesting figures and returned to the boulevards around town. These sculptures are large and impressive in their detail. They depict many figures – fathers of confederation, Indian chiefs, highland pipers and dancers, sportsmen, community leaders, family figures, Mounties, priests, animals; you name it. There are over 30 of them so far and the number continues to grow. It is a creative solution to a problem and a nice attraction for the city.

All of the rivers in the area experience large tidal surges throughout the day and thus offer good amusement opportunities for observation and high energy boat rides. Be prepared to get wet.

Our first destination on the north shore is the New Glasgow and Stellarton area. As the name indicates, we are definitely back in Scottish heritage land. We saw some of this on our way south earlier, through the town of Antigonish, some 50 kilometers east of here.

Stellarton is in the centre of another coal mining region. The area was mined for almost two hundred years, but, as with other areas in the province, the mines were closed as they became marginal and uneconomic. Again, there are monuments to those lost in the mines, including 26 lost in an explosion in 1992. This is also the site of the Nova Scotia Museum of Industry, which has a large collection of heavy equipment and presents a learning experience about industrial life, using actors and interactive displays.

New Glasgow sits on the hills lining a river that feeds into Pictou Harbour. Like Truro, New Glasgow is a regional centre that has maintained its historical appearances as it added more modern amenities. We do know that we are in the "New Scotland" of old times when we see that the town centrepiece is a large, white Presbyterian church on the hill and that the street running into the town centre is called Temperance.

Farther down river we come to the town of Pictou on Pictou Bay. (It's pronounced pick-toe, not pick-too.) This is the site of the original landing of Scottish settlers to the province. In 1773 a boatload of "highlanders," 33 families and 25 single men, arrived to build a town and settle the land. In the harbour at Pictou there is a replica of the ship Hector that they came on, which can be toured, and a museum with Scottish historical and seafaring displays. Along the waterfront drive there are banners of the various clans who first settled the area.

Of course, one of the legacies of these Scottish settlers is the highland game festivals; you know, where they throw boulders and toss telephone poles, accompanied by bagpipes. These festivals seem to happen everywhere in the country. Pipers are also the rule, rather than the exception, at formal or political events in Canada. You either love them or you hate them; it's either a stirring sound or just a high-pitched screech to your ears. With a name like Stewart, I do have a certain appreciation for them, at least for a short duration; there was a piper at some of my children's weddings. It's all harmless fun, unless it involves haggis.

The Pictou area has a number of quaint small hotels and B&Bs, restaurants that look over the water, and an active marina full of power and sail boats. Some very large homes and acreages can be seen along the shoreline as we move away from the town centre. Again, this area seems like a great getaway place, this time with access to the Northumberland Strait rather than the open Atlantic.

The drive along the north shore, with rolling hills and open valleys, is scenic, but not as dramatic as the south shore. The shoreline tends to be flat and relatively straight, with some low cliffs here and there.

We move on through Tatamagouche, the village with the great name. A unique feature here is that the railway station has been converted to a hotel/restaurant with an old dining car being the dining room and colourfully painted converted cabooses being the guest rooms.

Next we come to Wallace, another small village set at a river mouth on a local bay. Around the area is a large marsh and natural woodlands. The nearby Wallace Bay National Wildlife Area has a wide network of hiking trails, where they apparently have seen 168 different bird species. I think I could take up bird watching as a hobby. It would add an extra focus to my travels and my learning.

In the area is one of the Tim Hortons Children's Camps, an exciting place for children from less fortunate backgrounds to come and have fun and learn new skills with new friends. And to think, it all derives from Canadians' insatiable craving for doughnuts.

Also in the area is a new golf resort called Fox Harb'r, which is located on a spit of land across the bay from Wallace. It is a challenging course that roams over the local hills, through the woods and along the rugged cliffs of the Northumberland coast there. It is already being called one of Canada's best courses. I am glad it was sunny, warm and calm the time I golfed there. I can only dread the thought of my score when it rains and the wind blows in off the open water

Next we come to Pugwash. You can be sure we are still in a Scottish land as the street signs are in Gaelic with English subtitles. Sraid An-Righ is King Street; Sraid Mhic Ille Dhuibh is Black Street; Rathad Garradh Na Breic is Brick Road, and so on.

Again, there is a large marsh and major conservation area near town. This time we are on the lookout for blue herons, eagles, osprey and foxes.

Two enterprises in town are well known to all. The Seagull pewter factory and shop is full of all the items we see in every mall and gift shop we ever visit: picture frames, candlesticks, animal figures, flowers, goblets, pins, boxes, napkin holders, thimbles, decorations, you name it.

The Windsor salt factory turns out over a million tons of pure salt a year. It is a little disconcerting to see your future table salt going by in a huge dump truck and being stored for processing in a mountainous pile in an industrial yard. All in all, this is an enterprising little town.

This small town has also become internationally famous as the original site of policy conferences that are attended by leading thinkers from around the world. Organized by Canadian industrialist Cyrus Eaton, the original Pugwash Conference was held here in 1957, when leading scientists and academics came to discuss the Bertrand Russel – Albert Einstein Manifesto that was concerned about weapons of mass destruction in the nuclear era. "Shall we put an end to the human race or shall mankind renounce war" was their catchphrase. More than fifty Pugwash

Conferences on Sciences and World Affairs have been held world-wide since then, spawning hundreds of other seminars and workshops.

Traveling inland a bit, we come to the town of Oxford, the Blueberry Capital of Canada. Over one-half of the country's blueberries come from this area. A large processing plant sits just outside the town. In town there is, what else, a large, blue, blueberry sculpture. As we go across the country we are going to encounter all sorts of weird and wonderful tributes to local pride.

A little farther down the road we come to Springhill, another old coal mining town. Again, the mines are closed and the town is suffering as it struggles to find a new economic base. It does offer old mine tours and has a museum, but it's a tough sell in a province with so many outstanding attractions. This is also the hometown of Anne Murray, the well-known pop singer. There is a bright new Anne Murray Centre on the main street that has memorabilia and displays about her career. In a way, by contrast, it seems to emphasize the difficult shape of the rest of town.

I have noted the very difficult and dangerous nature of coal mining as we visited Sydney and Stellarton. It is all driven home by the memorial display to fallen miners in Springhill. The centrepiece is a high statue of a miner with a testimonial to the 125 men killed in an explosion in 1891. There are also major stone testimonials to the 39 killed in 1956 and the 75 in 1958. To me, the most telling element is the array of stone tablets arranged around the back of the memorial. All of the others who had been killed in the mines from 1876 to 1958 are listed there chronologically. There were only a couple of years without a tragedy and the rest averaged about three per year for more than 80 years. On top of that there was a grim repetition of the same surnames, such as McLeod, Ross and MacDonald. The memorial creates a very strong and lasting impact.

Going back to the main road and carrying on west through the last corner of the province, we come to the regional centre of Amherst. The local terrain is one of gentle hills and forest interspersed with farmland. Over by the shoreline there are a series of cliffs, an area where ancient fossils can be found. It all flattens out as we reach the border and say farewell to Nova Scotia, a province with a rich treasure of natural beauty and a strong heritage.

Our next destination is Prince Edward Island. We will cut across the corner of New Brunswick, following the Nova Scotia border for 50 kilometers, and cross the new Confederation Bridge into the land of potatoes and Anne of Green Gables.

Prince Edward Island

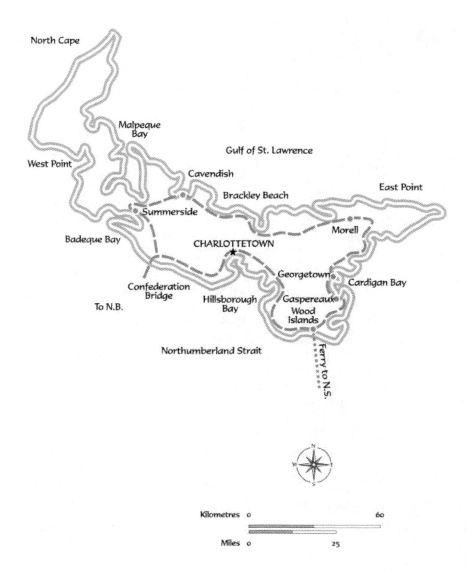

3. Prince Edward Island

The bridge is an awesome sight. I have traveled across the Confederation Bridge a number of times since it opened in 1997 and I am always amazed by it. In fact, on one of the trips to PEI my wife was convinced I only wanted to go so I could see the bridge again; perhaps there was a grain of truth to that.

It appears as a long, white ribbon stretched across the 13 kilometers of the Northumberland Strait, perched up on its dozens of narrow pylons. It arches high over the water to allow ship traffic to proceed beneath unencumbered. Statistics, and even photographs, do not adequately portray its majestic presence and breathtaking art form. To appreciate its strength and resilience, we need to visualize the wind, wave and ice pressures that it must withstand through the seasons. On one of my trips across there was a reasonable wind present, perhaps 30 or 40 km/h, and, as a result, the car was significantly shuddering and swerving in response. There was a steady spray from the sea in the air and the windshield wipers had to be run constantly, even though it was a clear and sunny day. Traffic slowed down well below the posted 60 km/h and you paid strict attention to staying in your own lane on the narrow two-lane road.

Once when driving through a heavy rainstorm back in Nova Scotia, I heard a radio report that said the storm was also blowing across the northern strait at speeds up to 140 km/h and that this bridge had been closed to traffic. I would guess so. That would be a terrifying experience. I know I would be twisting the iron ring on my little finger and hoping that the engineers had done all of their stress and fatigue calculations correctly. (An iron ring is presented to all professional engineers in Canada when they graduate to remind them of their professional responsibilities and their oath to design and build facilities that will be safe for the public. The ring ceremony is a stirring one, which includes the recitation of a poem written by Rudyard Kipling specifically for this event. The symbolic ring represents the remains of a Quebec iron bridge that failed in a storm.)

We could have crossed the strait by ferry from Pictou, Nova Scotia. It can be a good plan to enter the island one way and leave by the other.

Of course, before 1997 all traffic used ferries. They can also be a wild ride in stormy weather or when the channel becomes ice-filled in the winter. I am told that the service would be unavailable for only a few days a year, when conditions were very bad or the icebreakers could not keep the way cleared.

The first image we get of the island as we exit from the bridge is of a wide, flat shoreline, backed by gentle hills, and a landscape filled with open farmland. The soil is distinctly red in colour. The farm homes, buildings and yards all seem particularly neat and tidy. This will become an often-repeated scene and a lasting image of Prince Edward Island as we travel around.

There is a large visitors' centre, a museum and numerous quaintly decorated shops right after entering the island. It's well worth the stop, as we can get a good overview of the island's history and geography from the informative displays. We also will then see the first of the many larger-than-life statues of "Anne." If you haven't been to PEI, you probably think of Anne of Green Gables as a fictional character from a series of entertaining children's books. Not so! Here she is a legend — a true icon and economic force for the province. The provincial map in the travel centre refers to a large part of the province as *Anne's Land*. We'll discuss this more a bit later.

Our first destination on PEI is the city of Summerside. It's some 15,000 strong and PEI's second largest city. Actually there are only two cities here — the other one being the capital, Charlottetown. Summerside is a neat place, with a "historic" downtown that has an early-colonial architecture and ambience. There are new subdivisions and some nice homes and gardens along the shoreline of Badeque Bay that connects with the Northumberland Strait and the expected marina full of boats.

One time I was in the middle of town looking toward the main harbour when I looked back in the rearview mirror and saw water as well. This confused my sense of direction, especially when I drove over there and encountered another definite shoreline. On checking my map I realized I was looking at Malpeque Bay, off the Gulf of St. Lawrence, and, in effect, I had been looking at both sides of the island at the same time. Prince Edward Island is small. We know that, intellectually, but it does not really sink in until you see it. The province is less than 200 kilometers long and maybe 30 kilometers wide on the average.

There are a couple of interesting things that catch our attention in Summerside. One is the College of Pipery. I guess this means there will be more generations of pipers for all those highland festivals and banquets.

The second is a sign for a community bingo centre that says in big, bold letters, "Your Friendly Bingo Centre." Can you imagine that there is an unfriendly bingo hall here? Perhaps lying below the calm and quiet surface image of PEI lurks a dark side: a mean and aggressive bingo players' underground.

Another thing to notice here, which we will see in a few other provinces later, is that the street lights are shaped as well as coloured. They are round for go (green), diamond shape for caution (amber) and hexagonal for stop (red). What a good idea. I am sure it helps people that are colour-blind and I know it helps all of us when the sun is shining brightly on the lights and you can't distinguish the colours, just the relative brightness.

Malpeque Bay carves its way deep into the north shoreline of the island and has its entrance to the open water protected by a long, narrow sand spit. The name just calls out the image of fresh plump oysters. They are a must for a meal here, at least for those people who love oysters. I am one of them, and it does not matter whether they are raw, smoked, or gussied up as a member of the Rockefeller family.

Driving out in the countryside east of Summerside, there are long gentle hills with periodic patches of trees. Fields of hay and corn surround farmyards full of patterned dairy cows and long, neat, white barns with green trim. Modest-sized farm equipment sits on the lanes — seeders, pickers, fertilizer spreaders and augers. We come to anticipate this scene repeating itself over and over as we crest each hill on the quiet back roads.

Along the roads there are uniform marker signs that identify everything and anything we might want to visit: not only B&B's, lodges, restaurants, craft shops, flea markets, coffee shops, golf courses, cheese and syrup stands, but also gas bars, auto body shops and the like. This is a user-friendly place.

There is one caution, however; if we stop at one of the stores to get a drink of pop or some beer to take back to our hotel, don't look too long for cans or plastic bottles. There aren't any. An inquiry as to why not will receive the universal answer that it is for environmental reasons. It's a curious answer, since many other jurisdictions are also very environmentally active and, yet, it is only here that these items are prohibited by law. I know the debates about which is better for the environment are always complicated, e.g., cans versus bottles, paper bags versus plastic ones and gasoline versus electric motors. By the time you analyze direct emissions, the energy of making the items, the logistics of distribution and the ease of recycling, the answers are often hard to determine. The only real answer is to use less and to reuse, recycle and recapture the materials afterward. As to the PEI situation, further queries determine that the only plant on the island is limited to using glass containers. Coincidence? Such a suggestion only elicits a wink and a grin.

Traveling along the north side of the province, we enter *Anne's Land* proper. I am sure almost everyone has heard of Anne of Green Gables, the fictional creation of Lucy Maud Montgomery. It is the story of a poor orphan girl who comes to a farm family and community on PEI in the early 1900s. There are some 20 books in the series. Well, she has become real on the island now. The farm house that inspired the author, plus all of the countryside around the town of Cavendish, have become dedicated to this theme and the commercialization of it. Tourists come by the busload, year round. For some reason, it has become a particularly attractive story and destination for Japanese visitors.

There is "the farm" to see, of course, but there are also many other Anne-theme attractions and even an amusement park. The Green Gables golf course is a legitimate layout, originally designed by the renowned Stanley Thompson. The image of Anne is on everything you can imagine and some you can't: dolls and accessories of course, but also cups and glasses, towels, napkins, stationery, quilts, ceramics, posters, jams, cordials, clothes and shoes. There are many versions of the books and various DVDs of movies and television shows that have been produced about her. As well, there is a musical that is presented in the Charlottetown theatre. If we don't have time for that, we can always go to an "Annie" dinner, where a local performer dressed as Anne will appear and sing. A favourite souvenir of mine is an Annie straw hat: you know it, round and relatively flat, with a colourful ribbon and a red wig with bangs and braids. My granddaughter loves it. Anne is big business for PEI and also an enduring symbol of the province and its lifestyle.

Some of the finest art shops anywhere are located along the local roads in this area of the province. The paintings, carvings and glass pieces come from talented local artists and from others throughout the Maritimes.

The north coast line of PEI is a natural treasure. There are long, wide, sandy beaches, stretching out in front of wind-swept sand dunes covered in sea grasses. The beaches are accessible and well-used by the locals and visitors alike, although it is recognized that the dunes and sea grasses are a fragile ecological preserve. Passage through those areas is carefully controlled. Walking the beach, picking sea shells and driftwood, or just sitting on a sand hill to watch children play in the sand and surf can pass a very pleasant afternoon in the summer sunshine.

Potatoes dominate farming on the island; this reflects the combination of the fertile red soil that is ideal for growing potatoes and the potato-growing Irish settlers of the late eighteenth and early nineteenth centuries. They came together to create a successful economic base for the island, coupled, of course, with its natural fishing location. The soil's distinctive red colour is most noticeable when you see it in the low-angle sunlight of the early morning or late evening, which also accentuates the long furrows and mounds in the fields. Red dust soon covers our car and everything we wear if we decide to venture out in the fields and watch the action at harvest time. The fields are a beehive of activity, as the ponderous picking machines fill the trailing dump trucks for their trips to the large processing plants that exist throughout the island. Here, when we see those truck-crossing signs on the side of the road, it's not to warn us about construction traffic but about the large potato-hauling trucks that constantly enter the highway from the surrounding fields.

The eastern end of the island is perhaps a little more rugged and forest-covered, but the basic scenes of sea coast and farm land repeat themselves in one picturesque setting after another. There are some local rivers, ponds and small lakes in the interior that break up the landscape.

Everywhere on the island we seem to encounter a golf course. There are at least thirty of them. I know some people who come to PEI just for a golf vacation. Well, that may be a bit of an exaggeration; they just happen to golf every day and work the scenery, beaches and seafood dinners around their tee times. The gently rolling hills, surrounding forest, local streams and rivers, and the seashore coastlines all provide ideal sites for golf course architects to apply their creative skills. With names like Clyde River, Belfast Highlands, Glasgow Hills and The Links at Crowbush Cove, we can imagine ourselves on the links of Ireland or in the heather of Scotland, the homeland of golf.

When we see the various names of towns and landmarks around the province, we realize that they reflect the rich heritage that combines the early French settlers, the relocating Loyalists from the post-revolution United States, and the early immigrants from Great Britain and Ireland. Thus, we can find Georgetown and Gaspereaux near Cardigan Bay.

On the southeast coast is the town of Wood Islands, the PEI terminus of the ferry to and from Pictou, Nova Scotia. The specific site is a grassy marsh area situated below tree-covered hills. The Nova Scotia shoreline is easily visible, some 20 kilometers away, or at least it is on a calm, sunny summer day, which is the only time I have seen the spot. However, as we noted earlier, there are some stormy, foggy, icy days when this is not a fun place to take a boat ride.

Heading back west along the south shore, we follow Hillsborough Bay to an inland harbour at the mouths of the Hillsborough and Yorke rivers. Here, we come to the provincial capital city of Charlottetown, one of the tidiest and most historic cities in the country.

The city centre is situated along the sheltered harbour. The harbour-side street is Water, backed by King Street, and both are crossed at 90° by Queen Street, the main commercial avenue. Tell me you are surprised by the names.

Along the waterfront is a marina full of pleasure boats, a wharf with a range of work boats alongside, and a terminal for the cruise ships that stop in here as they carry visitors up the St. Lawrence River to Quebec City and beyond. The Coast Guard has a regional office building on the waterfront looking out on all of this activity.

Inland a few blocks, we find some impressive stone and brick buildings. The provincial legislature is a three-storey stone building with a portico in front. The grounds have a large and impressive memorial statue showing soldiers in action. The court house and big old churches all add to the historic feeling of the city. A little farther out from the centre are the brick buildings of the University of PEI campus.

One attraction in the downtown area is the Confederation Centre of the Arts. A modern structure, it contains a museum, art gallery, library, a memorial hall that can accommodate major events, lecture halls, performing arts theatres, a restaurant and an upscale gift shop. This is obviously the centre of cultural activity for the city.

Queen Street is the one wide street in downtown; it's wide enough that parking is perpendicular to traffic, not along the curb. Thus, even in rush hour, when a car wants to leave its parking spot, traffic just stops and waits.

But, what am I saying; what rush hour? Remember, this is PEI. The city has a population of 32,000 and the whole province has only 135,000 people. This means that the city is not even in the top 100 cities in Canada by size.

On the other hand, although I don't know which city has the highest ratio of pubs to people, my unofficial, non-scientific observation would give that title to Charlottetown. The guide books and signs in hotel lobbies all advertise pub tours in the evening. It's worth doing, just to check out the old buildings' architecture and décor of course. The pubs along Queen Street, and the area in general, have the old look of brick and stone with small pane windows. They all have old-country sounding names, such as The Olde Dublin Pub and The Merchantman Pub. It does seem kind of unnecessary to say that the tours are walking ones. I should also note there are daytime walking tours of the historic districts, the grand buildings and the waterfront, complemented with guides and performing troupes you encounter along the way.

We can always stop on the way at one of the many seafood restaurants. The names often emphasize the local specialties of oysters and lobster. I wasn't sure about Fishbone's Oyster Bar and Seafood Grill. I will say I was overwhelmed one evening in the dining room of my hotel when I ordered an appetizer of mussels, priced at about $7.00. There must have been six dozen large mussels served in a huge bucket — enough for a whole party of four or more as a meal starter, but I was by myself. With my main course to follow, I was there for quite a while. No surprise, they were delicious.

Another indication of the homey, community nature of the area is the conference on quilting being held in my hotel the last time I visited. I must admit it; I took a walk by the display areas and was very impressed with the large, intricately-patterned quilts and other items such as comforters, pillows, and wall hangings. They are true pieces of art.

When shopping you quickly become aware of the taxes. The provincial sales tax is 10.7%, the highest in the country. They claim it is 10%, but they apply it after calculating the 7% federal GST. At least in other provinces, such as Newfoundland and Nova Scotia, they harmonize the two taxes; i.e., they do not double dip. It certainly adds up. I know there is a process for getting refunds on sales taxes if you are from other jurisdictions, but that is cumbersome and has never made any sense to me. Visitors use the highways, parks and government-funded facilities, such as museums.

A major highlight in a visit to Charlottetown is the Founders' Hall, located on the waterfront wharf. Here, we can go back in time and relive the history of the country through impressive displays and very effective, short, audio-visual presentations. A unique dimension of the video presentations is that they report on the historical events as they would be covered on television today. This means they include headline stories, interviews with key figures, man-on-the-street reactions, late-breaking news interruptions and background reports on the political and social dimensions. It is extremely well done and easily holds our attention as we move through time.

Charlottetown played a key role in the early creation of Canada. It was the site of the initial conference of the leaders from the various colonies to discuss confederation. The presentations here make you realize just how fragile and uncertain the process was.

In 1864 there were seven separate British colonies in what is now Canada: Canada itself (what is now southern Quebec and southern Ontario, then being the provinces of Canada East and Canada West with a common capital city in Ottawa), New Brunswick, Nova Scotia, Prince Edward Island, Newfoundland, Vancouver Island and British Columbia. There had been a lot of unrest in "Canada" over the previous decades as the French and English factions competed for power; as the pressures from the independent republic of the United States clashed with the feelings of the British loyalists; as there were increasing demands for more local independence from Britain and its appointed governors and councils; and from all the economic and logistical growing pains of the burgeoning new colonies. The civil war was in full progress in the U.S., which caused some anxiety for the Canadian colonies since they feared retribution from the likely-victorious North; Britain had been supporting the Confederacy.

The leaders of Canada, Nova Scotia, New Brunswick and Prince Edward Island met in Charlottetown in September 1864. They chose this location because PEI was so uninterested in a confederation that they would not send a delegation anywhere else. Newfoundland would join the second set of meetings, held the next month in Quebec City. The west coast colonies were not yet in their thinking.

Out of these meetings came the framework for the country which defined the nature of the new government structure, i.e., an elected House of Commons, an appointed Senate, and administration by a Prime Minister and his Cabinet. It also defined the powers and relationships between the provincial governments and the federal government. All of this is the basic system we still have today.

The colonies of Canada, New Brunswick and Nova Scotia decided to form the Dominion of Canada, with Ontario and Quebec now identified as separate entities. The name Canada was adopted after considering a range of possibilities including Britannica, Borealia, Victorialand, Efisga and Tuponia! Oh, to think we could all be Efisgans or Tuponians now. The term "Dominion" was invented; it had no defined political meaning then, nor does it now, although New Zealand also adopted the term in 1907.

They also adopted the purpose of the confederation as being to provide "peace, order and good government." This is very Canadian in its tone, as compared to the French "liberty, equality, fraternity," or the American "life, liberty and the pursuit of happiness." To compete with "fraternity" and "happiness," they could have at least mentioned our many three-day summer weekends.

The various colonies then went back to "ratify" the deal, which took almost three years and involved a lot of political maneuvering. For example, New Brunswick voted "No" in 1865 and then "Yes" in 1866. Finally, on July 1, 1867, Canada was proclaimed as a single colony. Only in the first half of the twentieth century did we really become an independent country, having final authority over our laws and constitution and our independent presence in international decisions.

In any case, based on these early meetings, Prince Edward Island came to identify itself as the "Birthplace of Confederation." Of course, there is one little problem with that, if you noticed. PEI did not agree to become part of Canada at that time. In fact, when it joined up in 1873, due to economic and railway problems, it was the seventh province; Manitoba and British Columbia had already signed on. As we discussed earlier, Newfoundland did not join until 1949.

The first order of business for the nation was to deal with separatism. It seems some things are ingrained Canadian processes. In the federal and provincial elections of 1867, separatist supporters won overwhelming support in Nova Scotia. This led to long and intense negotiations for more than a year to appease their concerns and to keep Nova Scotia in the confederation. A second serious separatist movement also occurred in British Columbia in 1873. The federal government had been threatening to back off on its commitment to a transcontinental railway, but, again, the threat was resolved; the railway was built.

A significant step for the new country was to purchase the Hudson's Bay Company's rights to their lands in North America in 1869. This would allow the later expansion of Ontario and Quebec to the north, the creation of the Prairie Provinces and Northern Territories, and lead to disputes with the Americans about boundaries in the west. The displays in Charlottetown's Founders' Hall go on to describe the growth of Canada to the west and north and many of the other later political events, but I'll save most of those tales until we visit those areas later during this trip of ours.

Charlottetown also played a central role in the later constitutional events of the 1980s and 1990s.

The first Quebec referendum on independence, or at least on the thing they called "Sovereignty Association," was held in 1980. Prime Minister Pierre Trudeau rallied various forces in the province which resulted in the defeat of the Parti Quebecois initiative led by Premier Rene Lévesque.

That, in turn, led to the initiative to repatriate the Canadian constitution from Britain, which Trudeau thought would help appease Quebec. However, after a couple of years of negotiations, Supreme Court decisions and last minute political brinksmanship, the federal government and all the other provinces could not get Quebec onside. Even so, they went forward and, in 1982, the constitution became truly Canadian. They also added a Charter of Rights and created an amending formula that recognized provincial involvement. Lévesque called this a betrayal of Quebec and continued to use this to his political advantage in later campaigns.

We have learned since that Lévesque was determined not to agree to any deal to bring the constitution home because he saw some element of political leverage for Quebec while it was still controlled by the British. He was hoping to convince other premiers to opt out as well, for various reasons of their own. We also know from their writings that Trudeau knew this; that Lévesque knew that he knew this; and so on. Thus, Trudeau had to act without the government of Quebec being onside. Since he was from Quebec, as was the Minister of Justice who drove the process, Jean Chrétien, and the provincial referendum had given its pro-

Canada message just two years earlier, it's hard to say Quebec was really not in agreement; just the hard core sovereigntists resisted.

One really bizarre element of the Canadian constitution is the "notwithstanding clause," which allows provinces to override key elements, such as the Charter of Rights, if they conflict with provincial laws. An irony of all this is that the only significant use of the notwithstanding clause has been by Quebec to negate the Supreme Court ruling that its language laws violated English Quebecers' rights.

Anyway, we had the constitution, but still had the issue of Quebec not being truly aligned. So, along comes the next Prime Minister, Brian Mulroney, also from Quebec, and his desire to solve the problem. He met with the provincial premiers at Meech Lake, Quebec, in 1987.

The Meech Lake Accord that they created was an amazing concept in many ways. It created extra powers for the provinces, invented the concept of opting out of programs *with* compensation, gave regional vetoes on constitutional amendments, and changed the way the Senate would be appointed. Most critically, it recognized Quebec as a "distinct society." Although Quebec had been saying similar things for years, and used phrases such as "two founding Nations," there was nothing in history or law to support that. Think about it. When Canada was formed, and, later, when it was expanded, independent colonies joined together. British Columbia, Prince Edward Island and Newfoundland joined Canada, not just the English half of Canada. Manitoba, Saskatchewan and Alberta were created by Canada as fully independent provinces, not appendages of Ontario and Atlantic Canada.

The leaders set a deadline of June 1990 for the Meech Lake Accord to be ratified by the federal government and all of the provinces. And it was quickly ratified by many of them, including Quebec. There was opposition however. Trudeau, and others, strongly opposed the weakening of the federal government and the concept of Quebec as a distinct society. Other groups, such as the aboriginal community and women's rights organizations, felt they had been left out. Then, in the middle of all this, there were new governments elected in Manitoba and Newfoundland who were not as committed to the process as their predecessors.

In the final analysis, time ran out. Manitoba had delayed so much that it required unanimous agreement in its legislature to proceed. However, in his famous stand, the aboriginal member Elijah Harper refused to allow it. With Manitoba unable to proceed, Newfoundland just sat back and did nothing as well. Meech Lake was dead.

It is amazing to me today, well over a decade later, how much anger you can still find in some Quebecers over this, especially since the story had not completely played out. There was the Charlottetown Agreement that followed in 1992.

Before we leave Meech though, it is worth pointing out that eight of the provincial legislatures, including "redneck" Alberta, "centralist" Ontario, "truly bilingual" New Brunswick and "free thinking" British Columbia, did ratify Meech, and thus agreed with the distinct society concept for Quebec. We often forget that.

So, back to Charlottetown they came. This time, everyone was consulted and involved. The Charlottetown Agreement took "Meech" and added: more refinements on provincial-federal rights; even more regionalized constitutional amendment and Senate election processes; recognition of aboriginal rights; and, of course, the distinct society concept. Everyone seemed to be onside: federal, provincial, aboriginal, women leaders, all. And this time it would not be left to the whims of the legislatures to approve it; there would be a national referendum when all the people of Canada could show their support. What a great Canadian compromise and success!

There was only one problem. In October 1992 the voters of Canada defeated the Charlottetown Agreement by a margin of 54% to 46%. The specific vote in Quebec was essentially the same.

It is hard to say what happened, even now. It just seems people were more concerned about what other groups were gaining than what they were getting themselves. An elected senate and regional vetoes didn't offset Quebec's distinctiveness, and *vice versa*. People didn't trust their leaders who had so strongly supported the deal. So, we were left with the status quo.

The status quo itself has all sorts of compromises and balances, of course. Here in Prince Edward Island may be the best place to illustrate that.

Let's compare two islands, PEI and Vancouver Island. To do this, we will need to recognize that Vancouver Island has about 1/6 of the population of British Columbia and so it will, on average, have 1/6 of the B.C. seats in the House of Commons and the Senate.

First of all, let's look at the federal government processes.

The make up of the House of Commons starts by assuming there will be an allocation of seats by population. You simply take the target 282 seats, divide by the total population of the country, and assign seats to each province accordingly. But, then, there are a few adjustments based on history and precedents which are designed to minimize the loss of seats in areas that are not growing as fast as the country. This means that every province except Ontario, Alberta and British Columbia, which are growing the fastest, gets extra seats. The extras range from two for Newfoundland to seven for Quebec. Nowhere is it more significant than in PEI where their basic allocation of one seat is increased to four.

The Senate seats are allocated regionally: 24 from each of Ontario, Quebec, Western Canada and the Maritimes, six from Newfoundland, and one from each of the three territories. PEI receives four of the 24 Maritime seats.

So, how do the two islands compare:

	PEI	Vancouver Isl.
Population (000's)	135	660
Members of Parliament	4	6
Population per MP (000's)	34	110
Senators	4	1
Population per Senator (000's)	34	660

What a difference! Vancouver Island has three times as many people per M.P. as PEI and twenty times as many people per Senator. Vancouver Island was a separate colony until 1864, when it joined up with the mainland colony of British Columbia; then they joined Canada in 1871. Perhaps they should rethink the arrangement.

You may recall that there is some flexibility in the total number of Senators that can be appointed at any specific time. Brian Mulroney appointed eight extra senators in 1990 in order to get the GST legislation passed. The number then reduced back to the normal level as individuals retired or died over time.

The Supreme Court is somewhat more balanced with population, having three members from each of Ontario and Quebec, two from Western Canada and one from Atlantic Canada.

The other dimension of the federal equation is the redistribution of monies between provinces through the federal transfer payment equalization program. This is intended to help the below average or "have-not" areas. In 2002 seven of the provinces and all the territories received equalization payments. Only Ontario and Alberta paid out. British Columbia was a small beneficiary, essentially break-even. If we go back to the comparison above, under this program PEI received about $2,000 per person and Vancouver Island nothing.

Also, with the desire to have regional representation inside the government itself, PEI always gets at least one cabinet minister, as long as they vote in a member of the winning party. They have almost always managed to do that. They only missed out in one election over the past thirty years: the 1988 Conservative victory in the midst of controversy over Meech Lake and Free Trade.

PEI also takes its role in government and from government very seriously. I happened to be in PEI once when its cabinet minister was fired over patronage and conflict of interest issues. While the national media focused on the details of the "scandal," the local media seemed to just emphasize what a good job the minister had done for the province. His replacement assured everyone that he would look after PEI interests well, never mentioning the problems of his predecessor.

But the system does work reasonably well, primarily due to the good will of most Canadians. We need compromises to make a federation work; we just need to ensure they do not get out of control. As a whole, we tend to reject those who try to polarize and divide us.

As I mentioned earlier, I have traveled and worked extensively around the world; I think that it is fair to say there is a widespread admiration of Canada. I recall making a presentation to a conference of all of the foreign ambassadors and high commissioners to Canada a few years ago. It was a three-day workshop on Canada — sort of a primer on Canada for outsiders. Time after time, an ambassador would speak out in amazement, even disbelief, about some of our internally divisive issues. They saw Canada as a great country with so much energy and goodwill and saw our problems as minor compared to the poverty, disease and political repression in so many other places.

Wow! Look what a trip through the Founders' Hall in Charlottetown can stimulate: a whole discussion of Canadian history and the evolution of our fundamental government structures and processes. I wish that the contents of the hall could be shipped in truck-transportable modules across the country. Every student should experience it; it would be so much more interesting and alive for them than history books filled with names and dates.

Let's get back on the road, but there is one stop we must make before we leave the island — at one of the community lobster dinners. There are many of them, usually located in small towns. The eating hall can be large, often capable of seating hundreds of patrons. There is a lot of food, down-home and basic, from salads and breads to homemade pies and cakes. But the centerpiece is the lobster, always fresh and absolutely delicious. The only big decision we will have to make is whether we want our lobster hot or cold, and, if it's hot, is that boiled or broiled? Such decisions! The only sensible choice is to stay on the island long enough to try it every way.

So, with our car full of Anne of Green Gables memorabilia, beach sand and red soil in our shoes, and our stomach full of lobster, we head back to the bridge and on to New Brunswick, the officially bilingual home of fiddleheads and Mooseheads.

New Brunswick

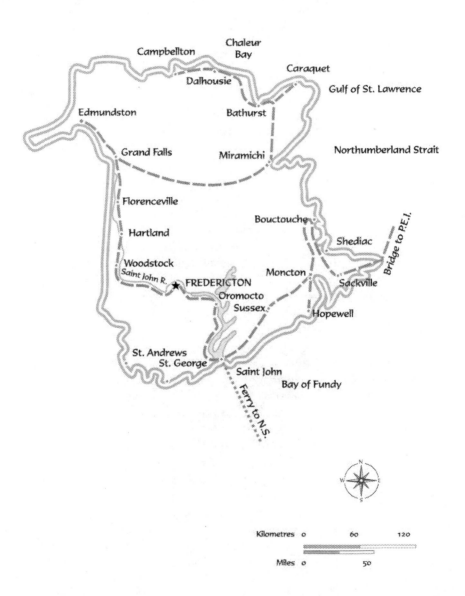

4. New Brunswick

Having returned to the mainland, we now return back along the New Brunswick–Nova Scotia border, traveling through a landscape of mixed forest and flat farmland. As we pass the first service station and general store enroute, we see a sign in front that proclaims that pop is available in cans and plastic bottles. Obviously, folks from PEI, or knowledgeable visitors on the way there, stop in to buy some before they cross the bridge.

As we approach Sackville, our first stop in New Brunswick, we can see a large field full of metal towers, radio antennae and communication dishes. A sign informs us that this is the base for Radio Canada International. From here they apparently broadcast Canadian news and entertainment by short wave and satellite to listeners around the world. You will note that I used the word *entertainment* for CBC radio. I just could not think of another word or phrase; perhaps *talk* would be better.

Often, while traveling across Canada by car, the only radio station that can be picked up is the CBC. Thus, I have listened to it a fair bit. It is amazing how quickly you know when a station is the CBC. I started to test myself on one cross-country trip and discovered that it did not even take a fully spoken sentence. One word was usually enough for absolute identification and, at times, even the silence before a word was adequate. Even "nothing" on the CBC is profound and ponderous.

As I said, I have listened to the CBC frequently and, therefore, have heard some fascinating reports by very serious reporters and interviewers. Often there are long interviews with people you have never heard of about some obscure hobby or book they have written, which can be captivating. The interviews, the story tellers, the background pieces, the comedians…they all create a unique Canadian mosaic for the listener.

On my last trip two stories stood out. One was about problems with rats in some downtown neighbourhoods in Toronto. The reporter gave us a background report and expressed concern about health issues. This was presented in the context that the reporter had gone out in the streets of the affected neighbourhoods one night with some government inspectors. The item probably lasted ten minutes. At the end of the report, when asked how many rats they had seen in the dark alleys and garbage bins, the reporter simply said they had not actually seen any. The piece ended.

The second story was a local report in Newfoundland about an upcoming marathon race in support of a charity. The reporter took us on-site to a warehouse, where all of the paraphernalia for putting on the race was stored — you know, the signs, banners, water cups, running bibs and reporting tables. A race organizer was introduced to describe the logistics of organizing the race. The opening question was, "So, this is where you store all the materials?" The answer was, "Yes, but as you can see, it is empty now since everything is out onsite for the race tomorrow." Of course, being a radio report, we could not see that. The reporter was not to be distracted from his "on location" news item, however, so he went on, again for probably ten minutes, to elicit what would have been in the warehouse if it wasn't empty. You can't make this stuff up!

I do not intend to appear critical of the CBC. One thing it does exceptionally well is the production of documentaries, particularly historical docu-dramas. The television mini-series, "Canada, a People's History," is truly a masterpiece. I wish every student, even every Canadian, could watch it; it's available as a twelve-disc DVD set. We need a better understanding of ourselves and our past to best shape our future.

Anyway, let's get back on track and move on into Sackville. It's a basic town of about 6000 people, old but tidy. It is located at the upper end of Chignecto Bay, which is one of the far-reaching arms of the Bay of Fundy. Similar to the area around Grand Pré in Nova Scotia, much of the farmland here has been reclaimed from the tidal marshes by an elaborate set of dams and dikes, all going back to the time of the early Acadian settlers.

A distinctive sight in the town is the campus of Mount Allison University, which was founded in 1843. The buildings are faced with dark, reddish-brown, rough-hewn rock. The grounds are very well maintained, with large trees and quiet ponds spread through grassed yards. Again, this is an institution that excels in academic and athletic achievement in spite of its small size and remote location.

From here we can drive up to the east coast, which faces the Northumberland Strait and PEI again. The town of Shediac is similar in size to Sackville, but quite different in appearance. It is situated around a local bay, edged with parks, beaches and a marina. The waters here are said to be the warmest on the Atlantic coast north of Virginia.

A tourist focal point is the World's Largest Lobster, a sculpture which dwarfs a man-sized fisherman figure on the rocky shore. In July a week-long Lobster Festival attracts many visitors to this town that proclaims itself as the *Lobster Capital of the World*, no less.

I offer one word of caution. When you are traveling in Atlantic Canada, always remember that the best lobster comes from the province, even community, where you are at that moment. When you are unavoidably caught in a "discussion" between folks from PEI, Newfoundland, Nova Scotia and New Brunswick about the quality of their lobsters, all I can advise is that you suddenly develop an urge to go for another beer. At least have a prepared conversation diverter such as, "How about those Blue Jays!" or something less controversial such as capital punishment or abortion.

Another interesting debate also occurs about the best way to eat a lobster, not just the hot-cold, boiled-broiled options we discussed earlier, but whether you eat just the flaky white parts in the claws and tail or eat all of it including the "green stuff" in the body. My sense is that the locals savour the latter while inlanders limit themselves to the former.

Slightly farther north along the coast is the small town of Bouctouche, set on the edge of a long, narrow inland bay. Outside the town and all along this coast of the province there are single-file rows of houses that face the water over the shoreline roads. They range from small-and-old to large-and-new.

Near the town is the Irving Eco-Centre, a preserved natural area of sand dunes, sea grasses, native plants and local birds and animals. We can walk through this isolated and relatively undisturbed habitat on an elaborate network of elevated wooden walkways. There is an interpretive centre to help us understand the area ecology. I would like to come back and see more of this area; the day I was last here the winds were howling and a driving rain storm was blowing in off the strait. It was great weather for ducks, I guess, but not for the waterfowl watchers. I should use the singular *watcher* since I was the only one present; even the staff had gone home.

Driving along this coast, I realized that I had traveled along the seashore of the Atlantic Provinces a fair amount and had seen a lot of the signs and trappings of the seafood fishing industry, but, in reality, I did not understand much of what I had seen. I happened to stop in a village and had a chance to talk to a local fisherman and ask some questions.

The fish farms (remember we saw cod farms in Newfoundland and salmon farms in Nova Scotia) start with small fish being developed in fish hatcheries and then being transferred to the pens in the sea for maturing over a few years. Harvesting is fairly straightforward in that controlled environment. Fish farming has become much more significant than I realized; one-quarter of all the fish harvested in the world now come from farming operations.

Oyster and mussel farms (remember our noticing the array of floats in the harbours of Nova Scotia) are simply seeded and matured on sub-sea arrays of ropes and nets suspended from those floating buoys. This reflects the fact that oysters and mussels are immobile and grow in tightly-connected colonies. They are harvested in their shells since the food is the internal animal itself.

Scallops are quite different (recall the fleet of scallop schooners in Digby) since they are mobile. Although scallop farming has been tried, it is difficult. They are slow-growing compared to oysters and mussels and hard to contain, since they do not fix themselves to an underwater surface. They are caught with drag nets that are pulled along the sea floor by the boats. Also, their harvest is very different. Since the food part is really the muscle that connects the two halves of the shell, they are opened and cut out on board the schooner. The shell is then simply thrown back into the sea.

Clams tend to be found on the sandy seashores near the water line. They can be harvested by hand, but often need to be chased underground as they bury themselves in the soft beaches. All of this makes for fun beach parties, where the big decision is whether to have a clambake or clam boil along with some cold beer.

Lobster and crab are caught in traps set on the seafloor. The traps are made of wood and netting, specifically designed with openings that allow the animal in, but not out again, as it pursues the bait placed inside. We have seen these traps piled high on the wharves in every village along the coast in all the Atlantic Provinces. They are a fixture of the picturesque scenes that are captured with every tourist's camera and on the many postcards we buy.

Because of its relatively high value and the fact that short-term prices can vary significantly with supply and demand, lobster fishermen sometimes keep their catch in underwater pens to wait for specific market strengths. The lobster and crab are shipped live to processing plants or directly to good seafood markets and restaurants everywhere.

I also learned that access to many of the salmon-fishing rivers in the region is privately controlled. Individuals, fishing clubs and commercial services own the rivers. As an outsider, you can rent a cottage, some fishing equipment and a river if you want to try your luck.

As we have all learned more recently, there are emerging issues related to fish and fish farming. The food chain in the rivers, lakes and oceans can concentrate chemicals and diseases in the seafood, and the controlled farming operations can impact the general dynamics of the sea life environment. Concerns about this have caused a dramatic decline in seafood consumption recently – general seafood sales are off by 25% and salmon sales are off by 50%. This is distressing to the economics of the industry and disturbing to nutritionists who recognize the general benefits of seafood in our diets. Solutions are not obvious.

Now you know as much about seafood fishing and farming as this prairie-based tourist. I am sure that some of it was an oversimplification.

The other thing I have noticed is that with today's refrigeration methods and air cargo distribution you can get excellent, fresh seafood just about anywhere you go. The industry has done a great job to make this happen. This was highlighted when a seafood restaurant in Calgary, which is 1000 kilometers from the nearest ocean, was recently chosen as the best new restaurant in Canada.

Turning back inland to the south, we can head for Moncton. This is a city of some 60,000 people, situated on the Petitcodiac River at the point where it widens out and enters a long, narrow bay off the north end of the Bay of Fundy.

The city itself is the typical eastern blend of old, established neighbourhoods and new subdivisions and malls. The downtown exhibits this with a mixture of older-looking brick and stone buildings and new high-rise hotels, office buildings and condominiums. We get the sense of a modern, well-functioning city with a touch of down-east history. Stretching out from downtown, impressive parkland runs along the river.

Our first impression of the river, and the view from all those new hotels and condominiums, totally depends on what time we arrive on any particular day. I know that when I first saw the view of grassy marshes and reddish mud flats I was somewhat perplexed as to why that was chosen as the prime vista for the city. Sure, it was natural and rustic and all, but, still, is this the best location?

Before we can answer that, we need to learn more about the tides of the Bay of Fundy. To do this properly, we need to drive along the local bay to the shore of the Bay of Fundy at a spot called the Hopewell Rocks.

Here, there is a visitors' centre that explains "the highest tides in the world." From there, a peaceful walk of about one kilometer, through the woods full of birch, pine and aspen trees and a groundcover of moss and lichens, takes us down to the shoreline, where we can see the tides in action.

Twice a day, due to the gravity pull of the moon and the sun, the ocean tides rise and fall. The intensity varies through the month due to the relative positions of those two bodies. Also, since the moon orbits the earth once every 28 days, its relative position to the surface of the earth slowly changes from day to day. As a result, the times of day for the tidal peaks change steadily.

On top of that, there are the local coastline effects. The Bay of Fundy is wide and deep at its opening to the ocean and, most importantly, it reduces down to narrow and shallow bays and river openings at its upper reaches. When the tidal waters enter the Bay of Fundy they cause a rapid and high-rising water flow into those upper sections. Thus, we have the forces available for the tidal power plant at Annapolis, the surges necessary for the exciting river rides at Truro, and the rising waters that turn mud-flats to riverfront views in Moncton.

At the Hopewell Rocks, which are tall towers of rock beside a steeply-cliffed section of the coast, the tides average 11 meters (35 feet) in height and have been as much as 17 meters (55 feet). The rock formations that have been carved by the surging tides are impressive to see. We could observe all of this by spending at least six hours watching a half-cycle, seeing both extremes of high and low tide if we time it perfectly. We could also come and go over the day, spending time visiting the centre, the restaurant and other local sites.

When we don't have all that time available at a tidal site, we need to pick a specific period during the day. Since most local papers in seacoast regions report the times of tides each day, this is no problem. Of course, I don't usually remember to do this. The first time I specifically set out to see the big tides I arrived at the exact time of the extreme low tide according to the posted signs. "Great," I thought, "I came to see the world's highest tide and there won't be any!" The word I used might have been something other than "Great."

Was I ever wrong! If you only have a brief time to see tidal effects, you must go at the time of low tides. Think about it. At high tide everything is full of water. The shoreline will tend to look natural and undisturbed, whether it is a cliff side, an open marsh or a sandy beach. At low tide you can see the far-out or far-down surface of the water and what has been left behind. In this case, it will be carved rocks, mud flats and long expanses of hard, wet sand. It is only at low tide that you can truly see the full extent of the tidal impact. I was lucky. Of course, to really see and feel the forces of the tides, you should stay through at least a half-cycle.

Now we can return to Moncton with a much better appreciation of the salt marshes and mud flats along the river and the dynamic but fragile ecosystem they represent. Also, we now understand that the views from downtown are of the dynamic changes that occur as the tides rise and fall.

We also learn that twice a day the incoming tide causes a wave to advance up the river – it's called the Tidal Bore. Depending on specific tide and weather conditions, it can be as much as two feet in height as it leads the surging waters inland, churning the river bed such that the disturbed muds and clays turn the river brown. Even when the wave is only six inches high it is an impressive sight; creating a sense of awe about nature that causes the tide to ebb and flow twice a day, every day, forever.

Along the road back to Moncton, we pass a railway museum and a collection of old industrial equipment near the town of Hillsborough. In that collection there is a small, old, oil-well pump jack. This may seem strange and out of place, but the fact is that crude oil was discovered and produced in this area in 1859, the same year as it was in Titusville, Pennsylvania. Publicity from the Americans would have you believe that Titusville had the first oil well in the world, but that achievement really happened somewhere else in 1857. No, not here in New Brunswick, but elsewhere. We'll visit that site later during this journey. And no, fellow Albertans, it wasn't out there either.

Natural gas was also discovered in this area in 1909; by 1912 it was being piped into Moncton for consumption, making it one of the first cities anywhere to have a functioning natural gas system.

As we leave Moncton we must make a stop to see the Magnetic Hill. I think everyone has heard of this phenomenon; we simply park our car in neutral at the bottom of the hill, take our foot off the brake, and then sit there and watch in amazement as our car rolls back up the hill!

Naturally, it is all an optical illusion. In reality, we are rolling downhill in an area where the surrounding land slopes away at a greater angle, which creates the illusionary effect. It is an experience that I have all the time when I am playing golf on the courses in the Rocky Mountains. There, I often target a putt two feet to the right of the hole, to allow for the apparent slope, and then watch it curve two feet farther to the right as it breaks "uphill." Optical illusions, coupled with bad eyesight; I know.

Off we go, along the south end of the province, parallel to the Bay of Fundy. It's also parallel to the west shore of Nova Scotia, but we don't want to revisit all that, especially since we do not plan to take the ferry from Saint John back to Digby. The countryside is mostly gently rolling forest with intermittent dairy farms.

Driving along the highway again, I realize that there are two different ways that highway exits can be numbered. They can be sequential, i.e., 1, 2, 3, or they can relate to distances traveled in kilometers along the highway from some reference point, e.g., 10, 37, 82, 123. The first system does not convey much information and has a problem when new exits are added. The second system allows us to anticipate the distances to key exits or destinations based on the various highway information signs we see. It also is totally flexible for the addition of new intersections. I prefer this second type. That is what is used here, but with a twist. I guess they have rebuilt and rerouted the highway in places, which has resulted in some changed distances. Therefore, we can see signs that say something like, "Exit 450, formerly 465." If they make more changes, will it say, "Exit 440, formerly 465 and for a while 450"? I haven't seen this habit elsewhere. I guess New Brunswick just has a stronger honesty-in-highway-information ethic.

At times I manage to find radio stations other than the CBC, but much of the time this results in a steady dose of country music. Boy, they really do cover all the dimensions of grief and sadness, usually related to lost love. I guess that song of some years ago about "another somebody did somebody wrong song" said it all. Driving along here today we get a song about some fellow who had to choose between his wife and fishing. He said he would miss her.

On one trip along this road I heard a sports report that was lamenting about the Flames still looking for their first win of the hockey season. I thought it odd that the Calgary hockey woes would have such prominence here. Then I realized that the Saint John team, also called the Flames, was Calgary's number one farm team and they were also having problems. Anyway, it made me feel like I was at home. Of course, all those attitudes changed with the amazing performance of the Calgary Flames in the 2004 Stanley Cup and the enthusiastic support they drew from their fans at home and people all across Canada.

The approach to Saint John is quite impressive. In general, this shore of the Bay of Fundy is fairly rugged. The city sits along a large harbour at the mouths of the Saint John and the Kennebecasis Rivers, which also lead to deep bays inland from the city itself. We approach all of this from the hills high above the city centre. Our first view is of the large port, populated with many ocean-going ships and lined with an extensive working area of rail and truck terminals, which are full of containers and warehouses. This is obviously a busy place.

Saint John is the largest city in New Brunswick, with a metropolitan population of about 120,000 spread over a wide area. (The province has a total of 730,000 people. New Brunswick, as with all four of the Atlantic Provinces, has been slowly but steadily shrinking in population according to the last census figures; the region shrunk by four percent between 1996 and 2001.)

The downtown area sits on the sides of steep local hills, really knobs, which slope down to the harbour shore, where new shopping facilities, markets and restaurants attract the tourists and locals. The city streets themselves are very narrow and curved as they work around those hills. Near downtown there is a maze of bridges to cross the rivers and inlets. A good place to view all of this is the Fort Howe lookout, a small hill slightly inland from the centre.

I use the word *lookout* for a spot, usually near the road, that offers a good panoramic view. Most often there is a sign to identify the location as we approach. As we travel, it will be apparent that the term varies from place to place across the country. Sometimes it is a *lookoff*, other times an *overlook*. I haven't seen *overview* or *view point*; I guess those words are saved for writers and commentators.

At the upper end of the outer harbour, just where the Saint John River terminates, is another natural phenomenon that attracts all the tourists, the Reversing Falls. A narrow river gorge with high rock walls creates a drop of about five meters for the outgoing river flow. But, now that we are experts on the Bay of Fundy tides, we realize that this height can be overcome with the tidal flow during the high cycle. That is exactly what happens. At low tide there is a fast flow out of the river into the bay. At high tide the water backs up through the gorge. The flows both ways are rapid. Boaters who want to move in and out of the river must do it just before and just after the peak tide, when the flow direction is right and the water depth is adequate.

All of this is fairly impressive. What is somewhat irritating is the tourist promotion that creates the impression of a waterfall that actually "falls" in both directions. Of course that is physically impossible, but, nonetheless, there are brochures and postcards that convey this image by overlaying a reversed photo of the river rapids on a base picture of the normal low-tide rapids. Based on conversations that I have overheard, some people expect to see a reversing waterfall! You can't even explain the ridiculous expectation that has been created for them without pointing out their gullibility.

Leaving Saint John, we travel inland by following the Saint John River upstream to the north. The land is hilly and heavily forested. The road is a narrow two-lane highway, without shoulders, much of the way until we intersect the Trans-Canada Highway again near Oromocto. The nature of that stretch of road is surprising to me since we are talking about the route from the province's largest city and major port of Saint John to the provincial capital of Fredericton.

Yes, Fredericton is the capital of New Brunswick. Apparently this is not a secret; it's just that nobody knows it. I know I had forgotten that on my first visit to the province. When I poll people about provincial capitals there are always some who confuse Calgary with Edmonton, Saskatoon with Regina and, more often, Vancouver with Victoria. However, when it comes to New Brunswick their uncertainty always seems to be between Saint John and Moncton. Fredericton gets mentioned about as often as Bathurst or Edmundston! I do not know why this is the case.

Fredericton is a pleasant city of about 50,000 people, set on a big bend in the wide Saint John River. Downtown parallels the river on King and Queen Streets. The provincial legislature and Lord Brunswick hotel, as well as the nearby university, all create a sense of history and permanence. The city hall is an impressive structure of red brick on a stone foundation. Nearby, there is an old, long, low brick-and-stone military compound that now houses an arts and crafts college. There are many well-preserved, grand old homes with turrets and balconies along the river, and an abundance of parks and squares populated with a multitude of statues. The park downtown even has its own lighthouse on the river.

One anomaly that quickly seizes our attention is the art gallery in the city centre. It is a solid brown-stone structure in an early colonial style, but on top is a large white panel with bold red, blue and yellow lines drawn at apparently random angles. It's eye-catching and definitely different from anything else in its surroundings.

Reading about the industry in New Brunswick, I discovered that the province is becoming a significant base for data processing and telephone call centres. With today's technology and long distance communications links these activities do not need to be located close to the major commercial hubs. The lower cost of doing business here makes these activities economical. Next time you are speaking with a commercial telephone caller ask them where they are located; it could be New Brunswick.

There is a discernable emphasis in Atlantic Canada on what the government can and should do. The expectation for government involvement in the economy is high. For example, in the last provincial election in New Brunswick the previously popular Conservative government almost lost over the failure to control insurance rates.

The expectations from government vary tremendously across the country. To be terribly overly simplistic, Alberta wants less government; Ontario is similar, except with a greater emphasis on the role of public utilities and general regulations; Quebec seems to focus more on local community benefits; the Prairies' main expectation is for support when natural disasters strike agriculture; British Columbia is more protectionist about local jobs and the environment.

Atlantic Canada expects more than just disaster relief and utilities management. I mentioned this around the Nova Scotia coal mines and in the replacement of a federal cabinet minister from PEI. New Brunswick has lobbied Ottawa to give it preferential access to Nova Scotia's natural gas, meaning subsidized prices. This attitude is further illustrated by the Newfoundland government's recent successful protest, which included lowering the Canadian flag at the provincial legislature, over the inclusion of their oil royalty revenues in the equalization calculations for transfer payments, much to the angst of other provinces such as Saskatchewan, which counts its royalties, and Ontario, which supplies most of the funding.

These differences in perspectives and priorities cause many of the political disagreements across the country and have been responsible for the emergence of more regionally based political parties. The old PC Party had become quite regionalized in Atlantic Canada. The Bloc Quebecois represented much of Quebec. The NDP had its main support in pockets on the Prairies, the west coast of B.C. and the labour areas of the Maritimes. The Reform/Alliance Party dominated in Alberta and the B.C. Interior.

The Liberals have been able to appeal to the large population base of Ontario as well as pick up some general federalist support across most of the rest of the country, thus forming the government for more than a decade. The new Conservative party is trying to create a new national consensus of their own.

The challenge for effectively governing the country is to find ways to blend and balance the various regional expectations. I have observed that, in spite of all the differences, there is a tremendous amount of goodwill across the land to make the country work.

Carrying on up the Saint John River, it continues to be amazingly wide, spreading out periodically into lake-like proportions above local dams, such as at Mactaquac. There are also small lakes off to the side, often populated with modern cottages. At times, the woodland is interrupted by open farmland.

At various towns we can spot a pulp and paper mill. As we drive right across Canada, we do come to appreciate just how extensive the forestry industry is and how many towns and villages are centred on a plant. This is true in every province, but especially noticeable here and in eastern Quebec, northern Ontario and British Columbia. The smell of the air in all those towns is very distinctive; earlier I described it as pungent but sort of sweet in a way. As we notice the details at each plant or town, we also come to appreciate the specialization that takes place, from newsprint to corrugated cardboard to fine papers. This is all in addition to the lumber mills, which are also very significant, especially where the trees grow largest.

These same forests also provide the glorious show of colour in the fall as the leaves turn to red, orange and yellow. The lookouts where we can see long expanses of rolling hills can be breathtaking.

As we move on through Woodstock and continue north, the farms become a blend of dairy operations, with their grazing herds, big barns and silos, and the emergence of potato farming again. One clue to the latter is a roadside shop called *Potato House Antiques*.

The town of Hartland boasts that it has the longest covered bridge in the world. It is a single-lane structure that spans almost 400 meters across the Saint John River. The cover shields the decking from rain and sun and thus prolongs the useful life of the planks. It is a quiet, even quaint, operation in that there is no traffic control mechanism, just courtesy and common sense as the flow alternates in direction every few cars. A couple of prim gift shops at the end of the bridge confirm this is a local tourist attraction. We will notice a number of such bridges around the province, but most of them are much shorter.

The next village we come upon is Florenceville. It is tiny, set on the mouth of a small river that connects with the Saint John, complete with its own covered bridge. What makes this place so significant is that it is the headquarters for the McCain food company.

A McCain advertisement in the New Brunswick tourist guide book states that McCain produces one out of every three french fries consumed in the world! Can you even imagine how many that is? I can't.

On the main street of the village, almost the only street, there are a couple of small frame buildings. One of them has a sign that says "McCain Produce Company Limited" and the other says "McCain Traffic and Distribution." I once stared in disbelief that this could be the centre of such a large enterprise. It turns out it isn't, but a nostalgic remnant of times past. Outside of town there is a large plant with a modern, but modest, brick and glass building identified as the "World Headquarters." Their local day care facility in town is appropriately called "L'il Spuds."

Our journey carries on through similar countryside and towns. As I have mentioned, my most recent personal trip across the country was in the fall. Just when did October become a month-long preamble to Halloween? This seems especially true in rural communities.

As I have driven through villages and farm communities, I have seen some amazing displays. There are large collections of pumpkins, both carved and simply displayed; yards full of clothed human figures with pumpkin heads; ghost-like figures swaying in the wind from tree branches; rural mail boxes decorated as witches and goblins; and harvest displays of hay bales and produce. I always seem to sense a big smile on my face when I spot one of these creations.

At that time of year we also often see swerving flocks of birds or high-flying V-formations of Canadian geese, honking their way south for the winter, which somehow seems to complete the image of fall.

Grand Falls is a town of about 5000 people. There is a large power dam built on the river with impressive rocky rapids below. The reservoir behind the dam creates a central focus, with the downtown and commercial development in a crescent shape around the water. The main street has a treed boulevard. There are some light industrial developments and a large potato processing plant; not far away are a large lumber mill and a paper plant. This town, in a way, represents much of the provincial economy. All that is missing are the fishing and shipping activities of the coastal areas.

It is also here that you can get a real sense of that other dimension of New Brunswick, truly functioning bilingualism. It becomes apparent that French is the background language of the area but everyone you encounter seems to easily switch to English; no fuss.

This province is the only one that is officially bilingual. The population is very mixed, going all the way back to the original French settlers and the British loyalists that followed in the eighteenth century.

Signage is quite diligently given in both languages everywhere we look. Street names always show both designations: rue & street, chemin & road, promenade & boulevard. It is convenient for the sign makers that linguistics dictate the designation comes before the name in French and after it in English, e.g., Rue King Street.

There is a series of falls along the river which can be effectively viewed from a walkway constructed over the water at a narrow gorge. It is quite a scenic view, attested to by the frequent presence of wedding parties having their photos taken on the bridge. The path to the falls is called Lover's Lane Trail. I guess that a walk down that trail precedes, and perhaps foretells, the walk down the aisle.

There is a local Indian legend about a pretty maiden who lured enemy warriors to their doom over the falls. I'll leave it to you to draw the link to today's lover's lane and wedding ceremonies.

Having a meal here in New Brunswick should include fiddleheads and Moosehead beer. Fiddlehead, as I expect you know, is a green vegetable that grows in a narrow stalk with a distinctive flat spiral shape at the end. This resembles the shape at the top end of a violin, and, thus, we have the origin of the name. I guess its real appeal to the natives and early settlers was that it was one of the first edible plants to appear in the spring after the snows disappeared, and so it was much anticipated and appreciated. It has become associated with New Brunswick in the minds of many. It definitely adds a bit of colour and "shape" to a meal's presentation.

Moosehead is one of the most successful regional beers in the country. It has developed an international presence, often found in pubs across the United States and as far away as Europe and Australia. In fact, I have noticed that for some international patrons it is the only Canadian beer they know.

Before we turn back across the province to the eastern coast, we can divert up to Edmundston, the largest city in the northwest part of New Brunswick, having about 17,000 people.

It sits along the Saint John River in the area where the river defines the border with the United States. As we enter the city from the surrounding hills we can see two large pulp and paper plants in what appears to be the centre of the city. When we get closer, we realize one of them is in Edmundston and the other is across the river in Maine.

Historically, the location of this border was very controversial. At the time of the American Revolution in the late 1700s, many loyalists moved north to remain with the British. Some of them settled in the forest and lake country around here. However, when the border was finally set in the treaty that ended the War of 1812, many of them ended up in Maine, often separated from other family members who lived across the river in New Brunswick. There was actually an armed battle over this some 25 years later, called the Aroostook War, but the conflict was short and the border was left unchanged.

Being a border-crossing location, there are the normal customs and immigration facilities at the entrance to Canada, in this case just before the bridge that crosses the river. Once during my drive around the city to take in the views and look across the river at the opposite town, I somehow managed to get in behind the Canadian entry point and then drive back through without stopping. When I realized the situation, I stopped my car and walked back to the window on the side of the building to explain. Although the officer looked perplexed as I approached on foot, he accepted my explanation readily and wished me a good day. He even offered to give me directions on how to get out of town by a direct route. I didn't take that as an order, so I turned onto the main street, nicely called Rue Canada Street, and continued with my tour. Maybe my sense of direction isn't as good as I think it is, or else I am just easily distracted when I am touring.

Now we want to backtrack a little and take the route across the province to the city of Miramichi. Right off the mark I need to admit that before my recent trip I had never heard of Miramichi, and, even when I saw it on the map and read the signs, I had no idea how to pronounce it.

It is located at the mouth of the Miramichi River where it enters the relatively large Miramichi Bay on the Gulf of St. Lawrence. This gives us a clue as to the origin of the name of the city, which was created in 1995 with the merger of Chatham, Newcastle and eight other villages.

This region has a history of fishing and ship building which makes sense given its location and nearby forest resources. The city lines both sides of the wide river with a very high bridge to connect the shores. There are some old neighbourhoods and impressive churches, but I have had trouble finding a real city centre, probably reflecting its history as a number of distinct communities. There are some nice new developments along the shore in what was Chatham. Farther up the river is a large plant with a sign out front that says it makes oriented strand board, whatever that is.

Well, how do you pronounce Miramichi? Recall I had fun rolling around names like Antigonish in Nova Scotia. Well, the basics are the same; say it quickly and smoothly with no distinct emphasis on any syllable, except perhaps the last one. Think *mihr-am-mis-she*, and remember continuous and without breaks or emphasis. Do not even think of a pause between *mira* and *michi* or make any sound that comes close to Meech! When I first heard the pronunciation on the local radio station I did not realize they were referring to this city, but, after hearing an ad for the local car dealer a half dozen times, it sunk in.

Now we are heading for the northeast coast, the last corner of the province for us. Bathurst, and the area along the shore to the east, is the site of some of the oldest French settlements in North America. Jacques Cartier first arrived here in 1534. The town of Caraquet has become the "capital" of the Acadian community. How did this come about?

The history of the Acadians is a complicated one. We have experienced parts of it during our trip through Atlantic Canada.

From the early times of Cartier and Champlain through to the early 1700s, the French explorers and settlers controlled the Gulf of St. Lawrence and the St. Lawrence River areas. The French settlers who became identified as Acadians populated the Bay of Fundy areas of Nova Scotia (then called Port Royale), Cape Breton (Ile Royale), Prince Edward Island (Ile St. Jean) and western Newfoundland. The British were only located in eastern Newfoundland and the thirteen colonies on the east coast to the south, which would later become the United States.

The British and French were at war off and on throughout the 1700s and naturally it impacted their North American possessions. Early in the century the British had been most successful and they captured Port Royale, Annapolis Royal today. In the treaty of 1713 the French conceded Acadia to the British, which was then defined as the Bay of Fundy areas, PEI and western Newfoundland.

The next forty years saw relative peace, during which time those French communities grew under British control. It was during this period that they developed the elaborate dike systems we saw at the communities of Grand Pré and Sackville on the northern end of the Bay of Fundy. However, the French were still active in the Gulf of St. Lawrence and it was then that they built Louisbourg on Cape Breton Island.

War flared up again from 1740-48. Louisbourg was captured by the British in 1745 but returned by treaty to the French in 1748. This led to the British deciding to build a garrison and settlement at Halifax in 1749. The French still controlled the Gulf of St. Lawrence and the river however.

The next war would be the last one, from 1756-63. That resulted in the French being defeated at Louisbourg, Quebec City, Montreal and St. John's. They then finally relinquished all their North American holdings except for the two small islands of St. Pierre and Miquelon near Newfoundland.

It was during the build-up and duration of that last war that the problems for the Acadians became acute. The British in Nova Scotia and the thirteen southern colonies treated the Acadian colonies as a buffer from the French to the north. They expected and demanded that the Acadians swear allegiance to Britain and fight for Britain in any war. The Acadians agreed to the first but refused to agree to the latter condition. They would not agree to fight with the British against the French, a state of affairs that seemed to be inevitable and perpetual in those days.

As a result of this impasse, in 1755 the British declared the Acadians to be traitorous. Their position was that loyalty is not something that can come with conditions or, to use the vernacular of today, "either you are with us or you are against us." They set about confiscating their lands and possessions, destroying their buildings and deporting them far and wide: to England, the American colonies and the Caribbean. Many escaped into the backwoods of what is now New Brunswick and Maine.

One little piece of history that we often hear is that some of the Acadians who went to England later moved on to France and from there to the Louisiana colony along the Mississippi River. These "Acadians" became "Cajuns." Although the French culture was well-established there, their link to France was soon lost as the area became controlled by the Spanish in 1763. France did regain control of the huge area by treaty in 1801, but then they almost immediately sold it to the Americans in 1803, the famous Louisiana Purchase.

Anyway, back to the Acadians in Canada. After the war ended in 1763 they were allowed to return to the Gulf of St. Lawrence area. They did so over time, but their old lands and structures were gone and they had to compete with the inflow of British settlers. By the 1770s they also faced the migration of British loyalists from the newly-independent American colonies. As a result, many of the Acadians then tended to move farther north, into the areas that are now New Brunswick. Caraquet, which had seen fleeing Acadians arrive since 1755, became their new focal point. And it is here that we can visit their history. There is a historic village and museum that portrays the residents' life of the late eighteenth century.

Now we are on the final leg of our Atlantic Canada travels as we approach Campbellton. This whole area from Bathurst to Campbellton displays the signs of active fishing, farming and forestry. The highway itself at this point is two lanes through relatively heavy forest. There are some noticeable characteristics to the road. One is that there are third-lane passing zones quite frequently, but they are very short. If you are behind slow traffic, you need to anticipate the opportunities and use them aggressively if you actually want to pass someone.

A second characteristic is that the pavement is quite rutted, due to long term use and heavy trucks. When we see the roadside signs that warn us to be careful when it's wet, we must pay attention. When it rains the ruts fill with water and this causes two problems. First, the puddles are uneven, so our vehicle feels like it is constantly hitting a wall of water, but unevenly on the two front tires, causing us to swerve from side to side. Second, when we pass an oncoming vehicle we are drenched in a wave of water and are blinded for a few seconds while the windshield wipers clear it all away. It's great fun! As we experience all of this, there is an announcement on the local radio station that effectively says, "It's raining; cars are in the ditches; be careful; and have a good day."

Let's talk about moose again, remembering our earlier experiences in Newfoundland. Here there are also signs warning us about the dangers of moose on the highways. They are not as graphic as in Gros Morne, but they do show a walking moose and a car. They are certainly better than the stationary, solitary moose figures on signs in most provinces.

Other signs tell us to report any "moose spotting" and provide a phone number to call. I should mention that on the trip that I have been periodically referring to, I was traveling in the other direction. It was October and I had just driven through northern Ontario and Quebec at the start of the moose hunting season. I had seen many hunters and dead moose. I will tell you I was in no mood to report any moose that I might see. Instead, I would have been more likely to get out and alert any moose to the dangers that were lurking about.

Of course, all of this is academic since I hardly ever see a moose, and if I do, it disappears into the woods faster than the speed of my camera's shutter.

Finally, we reach the city of Campbellton, having passed the nearby towns of Dalhousie, Balmoral and Dundee. I'll bet you have guessed that the area was settled by Scots. It is a pleasant area, stretching along the narrowing Chaleur Bay and the wide mouth of the Restigouche River. On the waterfront is a huge silver-coloured metallic sculpture of a salmon. The area has been a centre of the salmon fishing industry for a long time.

This ends our adventure through New Brunswick and, for that matter, Atlantic Canada, with all of its history, culture and scenery. Everyone we have met has been friendly and welcoming, always willing to answer the naïve questions of this prairie-born traveler. I will be back for sure.

We have traveled less than 25% of our expected distance, even with all of the diversions that we have taken in each of the four provinces. Our drive from coast to coast, not taking into account our planned flight to the Far North, will be about 20,000 kilometers in length.

So, let's cross the bridge, set our watches back one hour to Eastern Time, and start our travels through Quebec, a whole new adventure and culture.

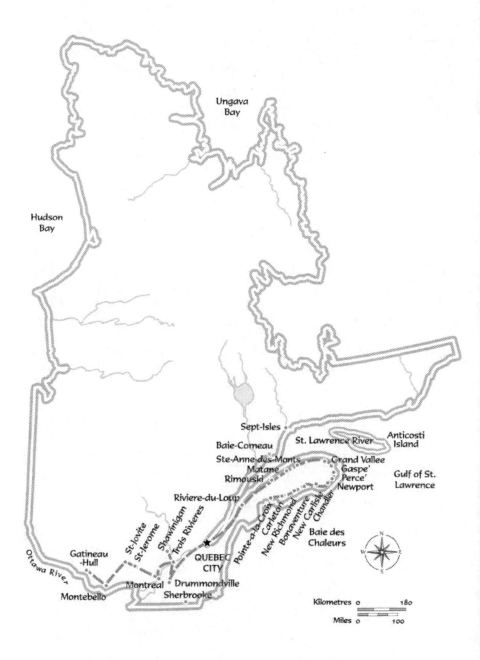

Quebec

Ungava
Bay

Hudson
Bay

Sept-Isles

Baie-Comeau   St. Lawrence River   Anticosti
                                               Island
Ste-Anne-des-Monts   Grand Vallee
         Matane   Gaspe'
Rimouski   Perce'   Gulf of St.
                                     Newport   Lawrence
      Riviere-du-Loup

                                                   Baie des
                                                   Chaleurs

      St-Jovite
         St-Jerome
             Shawinigan
              Trois Rivieres
Gatineau   ★
 -Hull   QUEBEC
                          CITY
Ottawa River
                 Montreal   Drummondville
Montebello   Sherbrooke

Kilometres 0   180
Miles   0   100

5. Quebec

Leaving New Brunswick, we cross the bridge over the Restigouche River at the point where it flows into the expansive Chaleur Bay and enter the village of Pointe-à-la-Croix, which has a large stone cross at the head of the bay to mark the town site.

The south shore of the Gaspé Peninsula runs east from here for about 300 kilometers to the town of Percé. This coastal drive is through gentle hill country, with some low cliffs rising above the shore in places. Higher hills can be seen in the interior. The road and a railway line tend to run very close to the water, with most development being located on the inland side of them.

There are many small bays and coves, usually at the outlets of rivers running from the inland hills. Signs indicate that essentially every river is a salmon river and thus the site of spawning and fishing. In the bays we usually see signs of the offshore fishing industry — boats, wharves piled with traps and nets, and wooden racks on the shore for drying the fish. Some of the wharves are anchored with large rock-filled cribs to withstand the force of the sea.

The land near the shore is a mixture of farm and woodland, which turns to heavier forest as we look inland. Periodically we will see a lumber mill or pulp and paper plant. Corn and hay fields are prevalent on the farms, as are herds of dairy cattle.

For the first 100 kilometers or so, the population is relatively continuous. That is, there is a steady line of homes, acreages and small businesses. What is so noticeable is that, in most places, the development is just one building deep on the one side of the road. At times, it all widens out slightly into a village, where there may be a general store and certainly will be a church.

One of the mysteries is how they have determined the speed limit on the road. It changes constantly and, it seems, randomly, between 50, 70 and 90 kilometers per hour. Yes, the little villages are obvious, but in many places the limit changes without there being any apparent difference in the population or housing density. I expect it reflects a combination of history and influence by local residents on local authorities. A suspicious person might wonder if it is just a series of speed traps for visitors to augment the local coffers.

The bay on our right becomes progressively wider as we proceed east. When the wind is blowing we can see significant waves and breaking whitecaps. By the time we pass New Richmond, the bay is over thirty kilometers wide and we can no longer see the New Brunswick shore on the other side.

There are many signs that this area has been settled by a variety of European groups over the centuries: the early French, the later Acadians, American Loyalists and direct arrivals from Britain and Europe. The town names range from St-Omer, Anse-aux-Gascons and Grande Rivière to Carleton, New Carlisle and Newport. The churches that are present in each village include Roman Catholic, Anglican, Presbyterian, Lutheran and Baptist.

Of course, all of the signs are in French, not one of my strengths. Most highway signs and directions are obvious in their meaning, although there are some detour directions that can turn me around. As I look back over my comments about driving in the five provinces we have visited so far, I again realize that I get diverted on the wrong path more than I like to admit.

Quite often at detours, construction zones or just narrow, steep or winding sections there will be signs that say "En nom de la vie: Ralentissez!" Since I don't travel with a dictionary, I loosely translate this as "For the love of life, Slow Down!" I think that is an effective message, definitely one with more impact than "Slow Down – Construction" or the threatening "Slow Down-Fines Doubled in Construction Zones." In the summer of 2004 I noticed some new signs at road construction sites in Calgary that are also very effective – they show a photo of a young child and have the message "Slow Down – My Dad Works Here." Either way, the job of being a flag-person in construction zones is one of the most dangerous anywhere; people do not slow down.

On the other hand, my loose translations can badly miss the mark. I saw signs in a couple of towns on my last trip that said "Centre Silenceux." I had the positive thought that this meant a quiet rest stop, or perhaps a community retreat. Wrong! It means a shop that fixes automobile mufflers.

I mentioned earlier, in New Brunswick, that my last trip across the country was in the fall moose-hunting season. Often I saw hunters dressed in bright orange standing along the road or sitting in their trucks with guns hanging on racks in the window. However, I was not prepared for a sight I saw near Bonaventure. Coming at me was a pick up truck with a moose head on top of the cab and the hide and legs spread over the back cargo bed. I guess it was meant to convey the image of a moose riding in the back of the truck. It was hideous.

Bonaventure itself is a nice-looking town. It is set in a relatively flat area with a lighthouse at the water's edge to aid navigation. As with a number of locations along this route, it is a resort town with attractive facilities and the ever-present golf course.

Each town along here has some local attraction. New Carlisle has a statue of Rene Lévesque, who was born here. Port Daniel has a particularly attractive railway station. Newport appears to be the home base for a large fishing fleet. It also has a popular bingo hall (traffic was congested and backed up there on a Sunday afternoon when I drove through). Chandler seems to be the regional centre, with a hospital and schools. Many of the towns have a local cove, with a sandy beach, nicely-developed parks and sheltered picnic facilities available. All in all, the south shore of the Gaspé is a quiet and pleasant area to visit.

Reaching the eastern end of the peninsula is defined by our arrival at the town of Percé. Its "rock," an offshore, round-profile island with a distinctive arched opening in the middle, is one of the most recognizable natural sights in Canada; I know almost everyone has seen a photo of it. A designated park and wildlife sanctuary, it can be visited by using local tour boats, paddling a canoe, or by walking along a narrow path and through a shallow pool at low tides. It is quite dramatic in its setting, just offshore from the quaint town and local high cliffs that face out to the Gulf of St. Lawrence.

Make no mistake; this is a definite tourist attraction. There are an amazing number of motels, gift shops, restaurants and organized tours here. There are also extensive RV parking areas, campgrounds, parks and rocky beaches. I agree that the sight of the rock is impressive, but this is a long way to come for the view. We have just driven 300 kilometers from Campbellton, hardly the centre of population itself, and the drive back across the northern shore of the peninsula to Quebec City will be another 700 kilometers. The narrow, winding roads are inevitably very busy, and very slow, in the peak summer season.

The whole eastern shore of the peninsula is characterized by high cliffs and rocky coves. We can sometimes spot hardy individuals in sea kayaks, making their way through the surf. I admire them for their skill and adventurous spirit.

The city of Gaspé, set on the hilly shores at the head of a large natural harbour, is the largest community on the peninsula, although, like most rural areas, its population is slowly shrinking over time.

It was here that Jacques Cartier first landed in 1534 to claim the area for France. He called it New France, but he also later heard the Indian word "Canada" that referred to their home place, the name that obviously stuck in history.

It's amazing when you think of the early European explorers and the vast claims on lands they made as they circled the world. Those claims were widely acknowledged and recognized between the various nations, which would then concede them or trade them to each other as they settled their many ongoing wars and disputes from the sixteenth to the twentieth centuries.

This was the start of the original French control and settlement of the whole St. Lawrence region. There is, as you would expect, a local monument to commemorate that historic landing.

There is also a notable cathedral in Gaspé. As I mentioned earlier, every town and village has a church. Usually they are central and dominant, being by far the largest building in most communities. They are always impressive in their design and construction, with their towers and spires and facades of stone, brick or wood siding. The church of interest here is very different. Its basic shape is modernistic, in that it has geometric angles of wood and glass. The outside finish is rough lumber, actually narrow planks with knots and branch stems still protruding out, all in a weather-stained brown colour. It takes a moment to appreciate just what it's all about, but it is intriguingly attractive in its uniqueness.

From here we start back west along the north shore of the Gaspé Peninsula and into the mouth of the St. Lawrence River. I should note that you need to be careful in giving directions out here since Highway 132 in effect circles the whole peninsula. Thus, leaving Gaspé, 132 West is the designation for the route going along both the north and the south shores of the peninsula, one leg leading back to New Brunswick and the other to Quebec City.

The north coast is more rugged than the south one. The high hills run right to the shore. The road usually runs right along the water's edge, diverting inland and over the hills at places where cliffs define the shore. The road becomes particularly steep and winding near Grande Vallee, where, as you would expect from the name, there are deep river gorges to cross.

Again, there are many narrow, small towns and villages along the shore, located on small bays or points where interior rivers emerge. The village homes tend to have white or brightly coloured siding and the central church always stands out with its high steeple. The hills and steep cliffs provide a strong backdrop and the wide expanse of the open water provides a sharp contrast. There is much less settlement between the towns, making them seem more isolated. There are few, if any, farms in most stretches, but always signs of fishing.

Most of the towns here have built picnic areas along their sea walls, some of them very elaborate stone structures with partial walls and roofs to protect people from the sun and rain. These facilities are well used in the summer by the local folk, as well as the many people traveling out to visit Percé.

As we are driving along the water, we see some highway signs that I have never seen before. They depict a car skidding as it is swamped by a wave of water from the sea. I am glad it's a calm day today. These signs are even more attention grabbing than the Gros Morne moose warnings.

On one stretch of road near the town of Marsoui there are hundreds of inukshuks, made with the rocks from the shoreline, ranging in height from very short to over two meters. They have been built on the berm between the road and the water. I interpret them as being a welcoming greeting for visitors.

Inukshuks were created by the Inuit people of the North. They are human-image figures made out of piled rocks that served many purposes: trail markers, cache identifiers, caribou herding helpers and artistic symbols of friendship and welcome. Their use in the south as art work and as location markers has been growing steadily. The folks who made these inukshuks at Marsoui have done a lot of work, but I expect it was fun for them.

The highways in Quebec are patrolled by the provincial police, the QPP, as they are in Ontario by the OPP. For those of us who live in other provinces this is a different experience, since the RCMP provides the provincial policing everywhere else. An exception is the wonderfully named Royal Newfoundland Constabulary which provides the general policing for the more populated parts of that province. I wonder if there is any real difference in their policing methods, but I seem to notice the QPP presence more. Some friends who have lived in the province suggest that the QPP does maintain a higher visibility in order to temper the tendency for fast driving here.

I tend to drive with the prevailing traffic in an area, making the assumption that the local drivers know the area and what is tolerated as an acceptable speed, and believing that going with the flow is the safest practice. But, I find Quebec drivers to be more aggressive and to be traveling faster relative to the speed limit than in most other places. Thus, when driving here I tend to drive slower than average.

As I was driving along the seashore road in this area on a quiet Sunday morning, however, I rounded a bend and saw a QPP cruiser coming at me. Almost immediately it flashed its headlights and then it passed on by, going around the corner behind me and out of sight in my rearview mirror. I naturally quickly checked my speedometer and saw that I had been going somewhat over the posted speed, but well within the tolerance I had experienced in Quebec. Nevertheless, I slowed down and watched expectantly in the mirror for the cruiser to reappear with its red lights spinning, but nothing happened. I took the headlight flashing as a warning to slow down and pay attention, which I did; I guess the stories are correct.

I stopped for a night on my most recent trip at the pleasant town of Ste-Anne-des-Monts, situated on a small bay at the mouth of a river. The local beach, golf course and facilities all looked good. Local signs indicated that there were agate mines in the area and, for sure, agates are available at many roadside shops.

The staff members at the motel where I stayed and in the restaurant where I dined were very friendly and welcoming. I was a little surprised that few of them spoke any English. They were all relatively young men and women. My bad French was better than their non-English.

I must confess again that I really do not speak French at all, having just a few words and phrases that I have picked up over the years. I wish I could. For reasons that are hard to understand today, I studied Latin in high school, not French. My only serious involvement with a second language was with Spanish when I worked in Colombia, South America, for a couple of years. In fact, when I try to communicate with someone who speaks French I will often switch to Spanish, somehow believing that this will help. All this really does is further confuse people who have being trying to understand my English-French garble.

I do understand and appreciate the desire of Quebecers to maintain their French language and culture, and the huge effort this requires in the face of the Canadian and American English presence everywhere around them. I just think it's a shame that any young person has not been given the opportunity to learn English as a second language. Those who haven't done so have been left at a serious disadvantage in competing for jobs and economic opportunities in the world. I know it's not easy when the everyday language at home and on the street is French.

ESL, English as a second language, is prevalent everywhere. I have seen this on every continent I have visited. For example, it was a huge desire of the young people I saw in Colombia, the classmates and friends of my children. Also, when I visited mainland China on a cruise, I was very surprised to find engineers, doctors and local professors at a luncheon reception. When I asked if their presence there was to show us how important the tourist business was for them, they answered, "No, it is to allow us to practice our English. This is our biggest need in China. We must be able to speak and read English so that we can learn and communicate technical and commercial matters."

Nevertheless, everyone I have met in eastern Quebec has been helpful and tolerant of my poor attempts at French; I always seemed to be able to muddle through. I would go back anytime.

Back to our journey. As we pass Cap Chat we can see a wind farm up on the hills. The huge windmills seem to turn so slowly, almost mesmerizing an observer. Wind power may be the most economic alternative form of power generation that does not have the environmental issues associated with fossil fuels; I think that could be the case in a few decades. I must also admit that although the facilities have fewer emissions they create serious visual pollution; a project can encompass mile after mile of the high rotating blades. They are best located in remote locations, out of sight.

Matane is a larger centre, farther west along the river. It is from here that the most easterly ferries depart for the north side of the St. Lawrence, connecting to Baie Comeau and Godbout.

It is not obvious where the Gulf of St. Lawrence becomes the St. Lawrence River. Maps seem to make the change at a line that would extend from the east end of the Gaspé Peninsula north to Sept-Iles. At that point the water is 125 kilometers across! Here at Matane it's still 60 kilometers wide. In fact, approaching Quebec City, some 350 kilometers farther inland, it is still over 20 kilometers wide. Tidal effects are felt all the way to Quebec City and beyond.

We cannot really see across the St. Lawrence until it narrows to about 25 kilometers in width, and that's only on a clear day when there are hills on the other side to spot. Often, the river is shrouded in a haze. From a practical viewpoint it seems to me that the "River" really starts at Quebec City. I guess I should say it ends there, since it does flow east from the Great Lakes. For comparison, Lake Ontario and Lake Erie average only about 60 kilometers across.

Whale watching is prevalent all the way. Halibut, cod and shrimp have been the mainstays of the area fishermen. Salmon migrate up the brackish St. Lawrence to spawn in the local tributary rivers.

As we continue west from Matane, the general terrain becomes less rugged and the area becomes somewhat more populated. The near-shore section of the river is often very flat, sometimes rocky, but usually muddy. This is most visible at low tide. In places, there are impressive clusters of homes and attractive seafood restaurants along the shore, facing out over the water. In one section there are a number of very distinctive houses: some are small and very narrow, but with four stories; others just have high towers on top of the narrow bases. These are recreational properties; the height is for river watching and whale spotting, both good pastimes on a hot summer day with a cold brew or glass of wine in hand.

Rimouski, with over 30,000 people, is the largest city we have seen since Fredericton; in fact, it's twice the size of anything else since then. It is set in an area of large rock outcrops along an incoming river. If we look carefully, we can probably see some people hang-gliding off the cliffs. With its size, and its role as the administrative and distribution centre of eastern Quebec, it naturally has larger buildings, shopping areas, a substantial hospital and a golf course. Ferries run from here, both across the river and down the river to the outer communities of Sept-Iles and beyond. Farmland is also noticeable now and will become more prevalent as we continue west.

At Rivière-du-Loup the incoming river contains an impressive series of falls and rapids. The local legend says that the name of the river, and thus the city, comes from the sea lions, *loups marins* in French, which used to frequent the area. Today there are many whales that visit the area and there are plenty of sightseeing boat tours to view them; a half dozen different varieties can be found.

This city is spread out along the river with a mix of old and new areas. There is a pulp and paper plant here and other commercial developments. Farm equipment dealerships indicate that we are truly back to more significant agricultural country. The ferry terminal juts out into the river from the end of a long point of land populated with some grand old homes. Here we can readily see the hills on the north side of the St. Lawrence.

We are finally back on a four-lane highway as we continue west on the Trans-Canada Highway toward Quebec City. We pass the villages of St-Andre, Ste-Helene, St-Pascal, St-Denis, St-Aubert, St-Vallier, etc. I do not know how many saints there are in the Catholic Church, but, if I were one, I would feel really left out if I did not have a village named after me in Quebec. My map shows almost 400 communities named for saints.

The farmland in Quebec is distinctive. Dairy cattle seem most common and the fields are generally hay and corn. Large barns with tall silos dominate the yards. Yet the scene appears very different from Ontario or the west, which is more familiar to me. It takes some time to sink in. Then I realize that the individual fields are long and very narrow and that the farm houses and buildings tend to string out in a row along the riverfront road. Therefore, the buildings of any given farm are relatively close to their neighbours. I have come to learn that this reflects the original land grant system of New France. The land was divided into long, narrow farms so that everyone could have access to the river. This was the case along all the rivers in the region, not just the St. Lawrence.

The ownership structure of those days was a feudal one, called the *seigneurial* system, which disappeared in the 1800s, but which caused the land to be divided into narrower and narrower strips as it passed through generations of descendants. This contrasts with the generally rectangular or square shape of farms and the larger distances between farm houses elsewhere.

One remnant of the seigneurial times is the identity of the people. The original tenant workers on the farms were called *habitants,* but as they became more independent they identified themselves as *Canadiens.* Thus, to this day, we have the fans of the Montreal Canadiens shouting, "Go, Habs, Go!"

Approaching Quebec City from the south side of the St. Lawrence, the first image we get is of the many high, steel-structured bridges that cross the river and funnel the traffic in towards the city. As we progress through the outer suburbs we see the homes, shopping centres and all the fast food and big box stores that are associated with any modern city. But that is not what attracts us. We are headed in to the heart of Old Quebec with its unique ambience and history. This is my favourite Canadian city to visit.

The old city is situated on high bluffs that hang over the St. Lawrence River at the point where it narrows down to just a couple of kilometers in width. It looks more like an actual river now. The inner core of the city is surrounded by a high stone wall.

Entering through the Upper Town district, impressive stone and brick homes appear, the streets become tree-lined boulevards and handsome parks abound. There are restaurants with sidewalk patios and colourful umbrellas, hotels with canopies and turrets, and official looking buildings with small parks and statues in front; they all contribute to our anticipation of a new experience.

Just before we reach the inner-city wall we see the provincial legislature and many government buildings, again large and impressive stone edifices. The Provincial Parliament, as it is called, looks more like a stately European palace than the domed rectangles we see in most North American capital cities.

The stone wall that surrounds the inner city and the narrow rounded arches that define the entry points immediately draw our attention. As we pass through, we get a sense of how Alice felt when she fell down the well and entered Wonderland.

Now the streets are even more narrow and winding, lined with solid three- and four-story buildings that touch each other. Single-file sidewalks run along the sides. Canopies, shutters, flags and bright red roofs all provide a blaze of colour against the background of grey stone buildings. The ground level of every building is occupied by shops that have a wide range of offerings, from souvenirs to fashions.

I cannot describe the specific layout of the city since there is no semblance of order. With constantly curving streets, corners that go off at random angles and little side alleys and curving passageways that interconnect, we can easily and quickly become disoriented; that means lost! Be sure to have a map.

At the edge of the cliff, in the middle of the old city, sits the dominant building of the area, the Chateau Frontenac, the historic railway hotel from the late nineteenth century. It is a castle-like structure with a high central tower, an inner courtyard and surrounding accommodation wings. The red stone walls, white stone trim on the windows and corners, and copper-green, high, turreted roofs make it stand out sharply against the sky.

In front of the hotel, along the top of the steep cliffs, runs a long and wide promenade boardwalk. In good weather this area is full of tourists and families, walkers and joggers, and street vendors and entertainers, making it a fun place to spend time.

The view from the edge is spectacular. Some 100 meters down below is the St. Lawrence. The community of Lévis on the far banks and the large downstream island of Ile D'Orleans are clearly visible. We will usually see many freighters, container ships and workboats on the river and in the harbour. Often a bright white cruise ship will be along the wharf. This is a busy seaport and very popular tourist attraction.

The other thing we will see is the top of the roofs of the buildings in the Lower Town and the old port. We can use the funicular, an inclined-rail gondola system, to get there or we can walk via the side streets that wander their way down the hill. I think most people use the funicular the first time because it is a novelty, and the cliff does look high. However, it really is more picturesque and adventuresome to take the walk through the narrow, walled streets and alleys. It's not that steep because of the way they wind down the hill. It's a good idea to go down one way and up the other. Because of the initial novelty of the funicular, I always seem to first ride down and then walk up. Better planning would probably reverse that.

The Lower Town is impressive. It is small, being only one or two streets deep against the riverfront harbour. The streets are very narrow, maybe three meters wide. They are lined wall to wall with shops. There are a few tourist souvenir places, but mostly it is upscale: fashions, furs, jewelry, paintings, sculptures and carvings, as well as nice restaurants, bistros, pubs and *choclatiers*. Old, stone harbour-administration buildings and a grand stone church on a cobblestone plaza add to the sense of history. Be sure to bring your wallet.

There are a multitude of sites to visit in Quebec City: museums, churches, parks and historic buildings, all within walking distance of the old city core. There are also quite a few old, small hotels in the area. The rooms are small, the amenities basic and the price not cheap, but they are well worth staying in for their charm and sense of history. Book ahead; in busy times they are filled well before the larger modern places

Back on the upper level again, we can walk along the promenades above the cliffs and visit the Citadel, which is positioned just inside the city wall. It is a British-built nineteenth-century walled fortress, with towers, cannon positions and a moat, all focused for defense on the inland fields and the river below. Tours and demonstrations are available. An interesting side note is that this facility serves as a second official residence for the Governor General of Canada.

The Citadel is located on the same site as the early fortifications that were built and maintained by the French in the seventeenth and eighteenth centuries. The view to the west is over the most famous field in Canada, the Plains of Abraham. Today it is designated as the National Battlefields Park. It is a well-maintained area of gently-rolling grass fields interspersed with rocky outcrops, stretching out before the city walls and looking down the steep cliffs to the St. Lawrence River. There are statues and interpretive plaques to inform the many visitors to the site about its history. There is also an incongruous tall concrete building with a revolving restaurant on top that provides a panoramic view of the battlefield and the city.

Of course, as we all know, this is where English Canada defeated, and thus conquered forever, French Canada in 1759. They did it by sneaking down the river and climbing up the cliffs in the middle of the night. They then won the conclusive battle in a short confrontation on these fields. Victory was theirs.

It's a great story, even today, for many English Canadians as they debate various constitutional or government policy issues. The battle of the Plains of Abraham has become the defining moment for many English Canadians. It's too bad that most of what I just wrote about it in the previous paragraph isn't true.

First of all, there were no English Canadians in the mid-1700s. France controlled the St. Lawrence Gulf, the St. Lawrence River, the area along southern Lake Ontario and Lake Erie, and the Ohio and Mississippi River basins. The British presence was limited to western Newfoundland, which joined Canada in 1949, southern Nova Scotia, which joined with Canada in 1867 and then tried to secede in 1868, and the thirteen colonies to the south, which separated from Britain in 1776 and then attacked "Canada" over the next 30 years. The British also had a couple of trading posts on Hudson Bay, but the Indian traders came to them; they were not yet seriously venturing inland. The only Europeans in "Ontario" were at a few French fur trading posts. There were no settlers on the western prairies. The British Columbia coast had not even been discovered, or, at least, was not understood.

Secondly, the battle at the Plains of Abraham was just one part of a larger campaign. The British had captured Louisbourg a year earlier. They had also been attacking Quebec for months before the decisive battle, using cannon fire and blockades. Furthermore, a second battle was fought at Quebec City again the next year, as the French tried to recapture the city. It was also during that next year, 1760, when Montreal was captured by the British in the truly definitive event. I don't think I mentioned this when we were traveling through Newfoundland, but the final battles actually took place two years later on Signal Hill above St. John's, finishing off the French attempt to re-establish a presence.

The final settlement of land control was not determined until the British-French Treaty of 1763. British military control and governance of Quebec began then. Only after that did English settlers and traders begin to arrive. As for Ontario, and even much of the Maritimes region, English settlers did not appear in significant numbers until the American War of Independence and the resulting migration of British Empire Loyalists, almost two decades later.

This pattern of migration and settlement explains why the original residence of the British Governor General was in Quebec City and why it is still maintained today for its historical significance.

Today, some people wonder why the British governors allowed the defeated French settlers to keep their language, culture and civil laws, which created the legally unique French-Canadian, but the reality of the numbers in those days made it necessary to maintain peace and to integrate the residents into the new colonies. The alternative would have required an armed occupation force – something that never works for long.

The treaty of 1763 had another far-reaching clause which stated that any lands that the French had not actually controlled or purchased reverted to the Indians, not the British. Thus were planted the seeds of many of today's land claims.

Anyway, that's enough history. We must reluctantly move on from Quebec City, being sure to at least drive slowly through the outer parts of the city; there are many fascinating districts and local sights.

Two thoughts come to mind as we leave Quebec City. One is that it is a travel destination dominated by man-made sights. This will be true of only a few places on our trip; Ottawa is another. Many other key tourist destinations have some natural attraction as the dominant feature: Vancouver has the ocean and mountains; Calgary has Banff; Niagara Falls is obvious; the shores of Nova Scotia and Newfoundland create their magic. Other cities, such as Toronto, Montreal, Winnipeg or Edmonton, are more places to go for specific events or activities, such as a play, concert, ball game or shopping.

The second thought is that my travels to most places have been in the summer. I am not really a winter person; remember, I grew up in Winnipeg and probably feel I have had enough winter already. But, Quebec City has a fabulous Winter Carnival; I must come back and experience that some time.

We have a decision to make. Shall we go north or south of the St. Lawrence River? We will juggle it a bit by starting out on the south side and then crossing over at Trois-Rivières.

The trip south of the river passes through more gently rolling landscape with big farms and lots of houses, barns, silos, sheds and bins. There are many small, narrow villages. The north shore would have more hills and forest and fewer farms.

Drummondville is the major centre on our southern route, with almost 50,000 people. It is situated on the significant St-Francois River at the site of some fast-running rapids. Driving around here, we observe a lot of greenhouses, many of them dedicated to growing roses. Away from the river the general landscape is very flat. For some reason the whole area and city reminds me of Brandon, Manitoba, for those who are more familiar with western communities. Of course, there are many differences in the details, one being the many flat-roofed houses here.

From Drummondville we can turn north and return to the St. Lawrence River, crossing it via a very long, high bridge with an elaborate iron-lattice superstructure to reach the city of Trois-Rivières. The first thing we find out as we drive around and read the maps is that, despite the name, there are not three rivers here; there are three separate channels defining the mouth of the large Saint-Maurice River. The city and surrounding area has well over 100,000 people; it's substantial with a noticeable blend of old and new. The city was founded in 1634 and there are homes and buildings that date from the 1700s.

Today it is a major centre for the pulp and paper industry. In past times it was a base for fur trading and home for many of the early explorer/fur-traders such as Radisson and Grosseilliers.

Canada was explored by canoe and snowshoe. The canoe was an Indian invention, quickly adapted by the early fur traders. Made of saplings and birch bark, it was light, durable and easy to repair en route. It could carry large loads but be readily hauled over land portages.

It was here, at Trois-Rivières, that the large transportation canoes were built. They came to symbolize the traders and explorers and are depicted in many familiar paintings of the activities of that era. They were amazing in their range and capacity. By the late 1700s, North West Company traders would leave from here or Montreal each spring to paddle these large canoes loaded with trade goods as far as Fort William at the western end of Lake Superior. They would then paddle back before winter with the canoes laden with furs from the interior. Imagine the trip: along the St. Lawrence, up the Ottawa River with its many rapids, across mid-"Ontario" via a series of rivers, lakes and portages, and then across Georgian Bay and Lake Superior; and back. Even today, storms on the Great Lakes can threaten modern ships. Those early traders were a hardy bunch; can you imagine their huge biceps and shoulder muscles?

Thirty kilometers north of Trois-Rivières, up the Saint-Maurice River, is the *City of Energy*, Shawinigan. The city itself is not fancy; this is a working town. The central area has low commercial buildings on a wide, very neat main street. A number of impressive churches are situated near downtown and a large church complex sits high on a hill looking over the whole area. There are also many eye-catching, three-story, brick multi-family homes that have outer balconies and entrances, all accessed by elaborately-curved, iron-railed, external staircases.

The general terrain is rugged, with many steep rocky outcrops. At the falls on the river here is a large hydro-electric generating complex. Pulp and paper plants and an aluminum plant are dominant fixtures. There is a very extensive visitors' centre that explains all of the development and history. It includes a very high observation tower that looks over a lake and down on the Shawinigan Falls. There are nice parks, picnic areas, boat rides and walking trails through the woods.

On my recent trip I took a walk through the woods to get a view of the falls from below. It was very peaceful and pretty. Being in the fall, the maple trees were in full colour. I had not realized just how big the leaves could be; some were very much larger than my hand. I gathered up a selection of red, orange, yellow and blended-colour ones to take home for my grandchildren in Calgary to see. I especially wanted them to see the large red ones and relate them to our flag; we don't have these hard-maple trees out there. They were excited with them and took them into their school classes to "show-and-tell."

Shawinigan is also the hometown of former Prime Minister Jean Chrétien. This makes me think about the history of our PMs and the rather dominant role played by Quebecers, certainly recently.

Since 1867 we have had twenty-two Prime Ministers, but only fourteen of them were elected as such, i.e., they actually led their party to victory in a general election. The others were transitional figures, filling in for a PM who had died, retired or who was forced to resign. Recent examples in the transitional category would be John Turner as PM for two months and Kim Campbell for four months. They both replaced a retiring PM and then lost the general election shortly thereafter.

Six of the fourteen "elected" Prime Ministers have come from Quebec, but since 1968, over thirty-five years ago, there has been only one elected PM from somewhere else, namely Joe Clark and his minority government that lasted less than one year in 1979.

In that same period we have elected Pierre Trudeau, Brian Mulroney and Jean Chrétien. They all won significant national majorities more than once. And yet, how different they are from each other: Trudeau, the *bon vivant* intellectual lawyer-writer from Montreal who drove so many social, nationalist and centralist programs (constitution, National Energy Policy, federal-provincial confrontations); Mulroney, the corporate labour lawyer from Baie Comeau who drove economic, trade and decentralization programs (GST, NAFTA, Meech, Charlottetown); and Chrétien, the lawyer-politician from Shawinigan who as "the little guy" focused on general administration and pragmatism (rebalanced social and economic programs, eliminated budget deficits and low-key responses to separatist threats).

Contrast that with Ontario. Until recently, the last Ontario-born elected PM was Lester Pearson, born in 1897. He led minority governments for only four years, 1963-67. Before that, we had John Diefenbaker, who was also born in Ontario but whose personal growth and political evolution all took place in Saskatchewan.

Prime Minister Paul Martin and Stephen Harper, the leader of the new Conservative party, were both born in Ontario, but that has not been their political identity. Harper completed his education and developed his political career in Alberta, which has a political image consistent with his philosophies. Martin was quite explicit during the June, 2004 election campaign; as he worked to hold on to the Liberal's base in Quebec, he declared, "I am a Quebecer; this is my home."

What has caused this fascination with Quebec politicians on the national scene? They take politics more seriously? The country believes they can deal with constitutional and separatist issues better? The country looks for an offset to Ontario's economic and electoral strength? There is the need to be truly bilingual? It is just a coincidence? It's probably a combination of all these factors. But think about it: Montreal, Baie Comeau and Shawinigan, not Toronto, Halifax, Winnipeg or Vancouver.

Let's go back to the main highway now and head west from Trois-Rivières along the north shore of the St. Lawrence. The hills start to recede to the north and the terrain becomes flatter with a mixture of farmland and forest. After we pass Bertierville the farms start to blend into new residential subdivisions and light commercial developments. The signs tell us we are now only 100 kilometers from downtown Montreal.

As we get closer in, we cross onto the series of large islands in the middle of the river that make up the city. First, we pass the heavy industrial section of east Montreal with its refineries, chemical plants and factories. Then we are into the heavily populated sections and the very busy multi-lane freeways, filled with the aggressive Quebec drivers I mentioned earlier. Driving here reminds me of the familiar saying, "Lead, follow, or get out of the way!"

Many of the residential districts we pass are characterized by homes and apartments that are rectangular in shape and have the flat roofs that are so distinctive in Quebec. I know it can rain very hard here. Either they have much better roofing skills than I have found in the various cities where I have lived or they have a lot of wet possessions.

Montreal is a big city. In the last census there were over 3.4 million people in its metropolitan area, continuing its trend of slow growth. Comparisons with Toronto would show that they both had 2.8 million people twenty-five years ago, but that Toronto has now grown to 4.7 million. Montreal has a solid foundation but has not experienced the booming growth of centres such as Ottawa, Toronto, Calgary and Vancouver. Business figures show similar results. Most observers attribute these differences to the political situation, in particular the laws regarding language and schooling, plus the concern about the future value of homes and small businesses. People who would have been willing, even excited, about moving to Montreal in the past, haven't come lately. Perhaps that will change in the new political climate.

However, none of that distracts from Montreal being an exciting place to visit, with its multicultural population, great shopping, fine restaurants, and many interesting sights. I love it here.

There is no doubt in my mind that for people outside of Canada it is the most recognized city and desired place to visit in the country. In my travels outside Canada, whenever I introduce myself as a Canadian or am caught out due to our unique speech habits, "eh," the conversation inevitably leads to some reference to Montreal.

Its functional bilingualism makes it easy for a visitor, and the overwhelming French ambience makes it intriguing. I swear that there is a distinctive sound to the laughter in the streets and in all the bistros, bars and sidewalk cafes. Part of the uniqueness is that there is a lot of laughter; I don't hear the same sounds walking the streets of Toronto or Calgary.

There is so much to see. Let's start with a general overview from high up in the park on top of Mont Royal. This is the big hill in the middle of the main island where Jacques Cartier first surveyed the scene in 1535 and bestowed that name. It is said that the Italian version of the name, Monte Real, is what led to today's spelling and pronunciation, although early French spelling often used Real as well as Royal and Royale.

The first thing to realize is that there are many islands here, ranging from the two large ones that contain central Montreal and Laval to many small ones. There is a serious series of rapids at Lachine, located at the west end of the complex. These rapids defined the end of navigable waters from the Atlantic and thus determined that this was the natural place to establish a new inland centre, which Champlain did in 1611. Today, a canal with a series of locks bypasses the rapids.

We do not tend to revisit history here as much as we do in Quebec City. There are so many other things to see and do. But remember, the definitive battle between the British and French occurred here in 1760. Also, I don't think most of us remember that the Americans attacked and occupied Montreal for the better part of a year in 1775. This was a pre-emptive attack to protect their northern borders in the anticipated battle with Britain for independence. They were driven back only after a later defeat at Quebec City, a hard winter, and the need to return home to fight for the independence that they officially declared in 1776.

The Americans had presumed that the conquering of Canada would be easy. They expected that their arrival would be happily greeted and supported by the French-Canadian population, anxious to be rid of the British control and ready to embrace American democracy. However, the French just passively stood back to start with, and then joined in to defeat the Americans. Hasn't that pattern repeated itself, again and again, around the world? No one welcomes an outside intruder, even a well-meaning one; nationalism and regionalism are powerful forces.

From the hilltop we can scan the outer parts of the city. We can see the sites of Expo '67 on the smaller islands to the south, an area with a large casino today. To the east, there is the infamous Olympic Stadium, the "Big O," "Big Oh," or "Big Owe," depending on your perspective about this structure created for the 1976 Summer Olympics, with its huge cost issues and malfunctioning roof system. Nevertheless, both Expo and the Olympics greatly increased Montreal's profile on the world's stage and made all Canadians proud.

On the lower slopes of Mount Royal are some of the most prestigious residential districts in all of the country, filled with stately mansions and impeccable landscaping. Down below that are the busy avenues and boulevards of the city centre. I can walk for hours along the streets to take it all in.

Running just below the hills is Sherbrooke Street, with its modern hotels and office structures, all mixed in with substantial stone museums and galleries. McGill University sits nestled between the street and the backing hills, its ivy-covered stone buildings and tree-lined walkways filled with a rich mixture of Canadian and international students. It is distinctive, in that it has much of the grand external appearance of Queen's or Western, but it is located just a few blocks from the centre of a large cosmopolitan city.

Heading for Saint-Catherine Street, Montreal's main commercial avenue, we can either go down Crescent Street for a fancy meal in one of the upscale restaurants which are located in converted old mansions, or we can move a few blocks east and find a corner deli, with those fabulous smoked meat sandwiches and huge dill pickles. I usually choose the latter.

Saint-Catherine is always busy: people, cars, music, all at a fast pace. There are shopping malls, fashion centres and department stores such as Les Ailes de la Mode, Compagnie de la Baie d'Hudson and Centre Eaton.

Signage in Quebec has become a big issue with the language laws. French must be used and be dominant. Brand names and logos can be used, sort of. Some companies will stick to their "brands" while others translate. These are big marketing decisions I am sure.

We can have McDonald's, as a logo with golden arches for the "M." We find the brand Burger King, but the translated PFK (Chicken Fried Kentucky). Home Depot is here but Staples has become Bureau en Gros. We see office buildings reflecting different decisions, e.g., London Life and Manu Vie. Bell and CN are OK. Petro-Canada is allowed because of the hyphen. Canadian Airlines created a neat solution by inserting their logo for the final *a* and the *e* in Canadian/Canadien. Hot dog and hamburger signs are everywhere; I haven't figured out why those are legal.

The English apostrophe for possessive is not allowed, except in brand names. Thus, we have Eaton, not Eaton's. As an aside, isn't it amazing how many cities in Canada still have an Eaton's Centre, long after the company has disappeared from the market?

I have also noticed a trend to eliminate the apostrophe more broadly, even in English parts of Canada. For example the old brown signs that said "Tim Horton's Donuts" now are bright and stylish as "Tim Hortons." The donuts have gone from the name, presumably to reflect the wider menu of soups and sandwiches, but so has the apostrophe. Look around. Where have all the apostrophes gone?

Back to the streets. More and more we are seeing artistic sculptures on downtown streets in many cities. Montreal is no exception. One of the most captivating pieces that I have ever seen is here. It is called "Illuminated Crowd," by the artist Raymond Mason. It depicts fifty or more life-sized figures made out of a cream-coloured resin, all huddled together looking at some unknown event in the distant sky. The range of characters and emotions depicted is amazing. I have walked around it and stared at it for the longest time, becoming somehow both intrigued by the figures and also drawn in as a silent participant, imagining what we might be looking at.

Below Saint-Catherine is Boulevard Rene Lévesque, or Dorchester Avenue if you have an old map. Here the big office towers and underground shopping complexes are centred on the grand old railway station and the very traditional Queen Elizabeth Hotel. I think the QE was the first place where I was charged more than ten dollars for a single drink, but the ambience is priceless.

I seem to recall that Place Ville Marie was the first office complex in Canada that was filled with lower-level retail outlets in underground passages that connect the various buildings. Today, Toronto has taken this sunlight-free, burrowing approach to civic development to new levels, heights or lows, depending on your perspective.

A few decades ago, the centre of Montreal was humming with new developments such as these complexes. Then everything seemed to stop due to the economic and political uncertainties. Now there seems to be a renewal. The building cranes are back and new complexes are emerging, such as Place Victoria and Place de la Cite Internationale.

One eye-catching sight is the Palais du Congres, the new convention centre. It breaks from all of the traditional architectural designs and stone-brick look of almost everything else here. It is very modern, with its geometrical shapes, and very bold, with coloured outside wall panels in yellow, green, blue, red and purple. It is so out of place that it fits in! This is Montreal.

We have now wandered down far enough to enter Old Montreal. This is a step back in time, perhaps not as quaint as old Quebec City, but much grander in scale. Horse-drawn carriages can carry us through the streets. There are many old, brown weathered-stone buildings with multiple pillars, turrets, towers and carvings. Chiseled names, like Molson's Bank, appear over arches. Foundations of old ruins, such as the hospital of 1693, remain. There are open squares and cobblestone streets, the customs house, the old courthouse, the first fire hall and City Hall.

The look of this area may be old, but the reality behind the walls is modern. Very upscale restaurants, bars, galleries, shops and newly converted condos fill the space. This is the "in" place to be.

Along the riverfront are the many large wharves, warehouses, elevators and cranes of the Port of Montreal. Remember, Montreal is a seaport and many large ships are always present when the ice is gone. With the canal system around the Lachine rapids and the upgraded St. Lawrence Seaway system in operation, this is a very busy place.

We can spend a lot of enjoyable days in Montreal, walking or using the efficient Metro subway system. There is no mystery as to why this is a favourite place for Canadian and international visitors.

As we leave the city and drive out to the north, well away from the city centre, we pass Mirabel Airport. This was intended to be Montreal's international airport, built to relieve the heavy demands on Dorval (now Pierre Elliott Trudeau Airport), the convenient airport at the west end of the Island of Montreal. Mirabel's remote location has made it a white elephant and a laughing-stock symbol of government decision processes; today it primarily handles cargo flights. It is almost as badly positioned as the Edmonton airport. We'll have more on that later.

As I was leaving Montreal last time, I was listening to the news and sports on the car radio. The announcer finished the report with, "All is well in the Centre of the Universe; the Toronto Maple Leafs won a hockey game last night." I loved it. That sentiment will keep Canada together long after the politicians have finished debating constitutional issues.

The busy, multi-lane highway north takes us to a region of recreational hills and lakes. The terrain becomes much more rugged with steep-sided, rounded-top, tree-filled hills. We pass ski hills with their lifts snaking up the slopes. It's not the Rockies, but it is handy and they do get lots of snow; this is one of the snowiest regions in Canada. The highway curves sharply through the area, and, although it is at least four lanes wide, we must slow down to the posted 75 km/h or less. In the fall, all of these hills display the full palette of colours — red, orange, yellow, rust, purple, brown and green. Therefore, we are happy to slow down and take it all in.

St-Jovite is the logistics centre of the Mont Tremblant area, one of the most popular recreational areas in the country. This town of some 5000 people, which does not count the hordes of visitors, is pleasantly situated on a fast-running river. It has a large selection of shops, restaurants and motels. The surrounding area, with the ski hills, trails in the forest and recreational lakes, has many cottages, hotels and fancy multi-star resorts. You can find everything you need here for a get-away vacation in every season.

From here we go southwest through the hills to encounter the Ottawa River at Montebello. The highway is very narrow and winding, so that when we go over each local hill we feel like we are on a roller coaster ride. We pass a number of small villages and forest-rimmed lakes on the way; great cottage country again.

The Ottawa River is surprisingly large. This is partially due to the presence of many dams that now exist along the river, including one downstream of here. The river does look like the highway of the voyageurs of centuries past. At a number of villages along the river there are local ferries to transport people and vehicles across. We will not see a bridge until we get to the Ottawa area. There is one at the mouth of the river, where it joins up with the St. Lawrence near Montreal, but we avoided that when we headed north into the hill country. The main multi-lane highway from Montreal to Ottawa is on the Ontario side of the river, but we will continue to follow the local two-lane route on this side.

Montebello is a quiet town on the river. The big attraction is the resort, Chateau Montebello, a member of the "railway-hotel" network.

It is totally different from all the others; this is not a stone castle with a green copper roof. Approached through a gated, forested parkway, it is a huge log cabin set in an isolated woodland setting. Now, *cabin* is not the right image; it is a multi-storey structure with many long wings. The lobby, in the centre of the main section, has a domed ceiling that is four stories tall and a multi-sided stone fireplace as the centrepiece. Around the lobby are three stories of interior walkways that lead to guest rooms, meeting facilities and corridors to the outer wings. The resort has amazing facilities: golf, tennis, pools, bikes, boats, hiking trails, skis, snowshoes, curling rink, you name it. It's an ideal place for a Canadian vacation.

This is also the site of major international conferences; in this case they focus on world-wide economic issues.

Continuing on up the river and viewing the villages and countryside, we see that the terrain is relatively flat again, with a mixture of forest and dairy farms. Houses populate the river bank much of the way. There is some industry, such as a paper plant at Thurso.

I can remember a wonderful visit, some years ago, to a maple syrup farm in the forested hill area to the north of here. It was early spring, there was still some snow in the woods, and the sap was running. Metal taps are driven into the trees and the oozing sap is caught in hanging pails. It is then all gathered into central locations on the farms where it is boiled down to syrup or sugar. It is fun to observe and certainly great to taste. This has become a symbol of Canada, with its link to the maple trees and, thus, the maple leaf on our flag. Marketers are quick to lever the linkage, offering syrup and candy in maple-leaf-shaped containers. I know that I often take some as gifts for friends and business contacts when I travel worldwide.

At Masson-Angers we hook up to a multi-lane freeway again and enter Hull-Gatineau. There are nearly 200,000 people in this area, the start of the greater Ottawa region, our national capital. Federal government buildings are numerous; the government divides the physical presence and investments between the two provinces.

We leave Quebec after a fascinating visit, crossing the Ottawa River into Ontario with the sight of the Canadian Parliament buildings before us.

Ontario

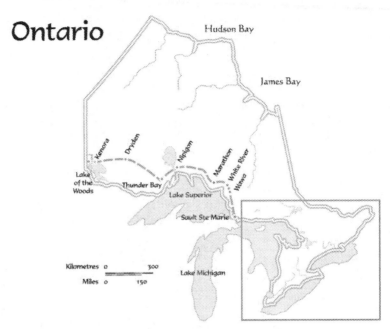

Hudson Bay

James Bay

Kenora
Dryden
Nipigon
Marathon
White River
Wawa

Lake of the Woods
Thunder Bay
Lake Superior
Sault Ste Marie

Kilometres   0   300
Miles   0   150

Lake Michigan

North Bay

Ottawa River

Elliot Lake
Espanola   Sudbury
Lake Nipissing
Huntsville

OTTAWA
Cornwall
Morrisburg

St. Lawrence River

Muskoka Lake
Bracebridge

Brockville
Gananoque
Kingston

Georgian Bay
Gravenhurst

Manitoulin Island

Orillia
Lake Simcoe
Bellville
Trenton
Brighton

Midland
Barrie

Lake Huron

Peterborough

Oshawa
Port Hope

Lake Ontario

TORONTO
Oakville
Mississauga
Burlington
Hamilton
Guelph
Kitchner
Niagara-on-the-Lake
St. Catherines
Grimsby
Niagara Falls

Stratford
Brantford
Port Colbourne

Sarnia
London
Oil Springs
Lake St. Clair   Chatham
Windsor   Leamington
Point Pelee

Lake Erie

N
W   E
S

Kilometres   0   180
Miles   0   100

6. Ontario

Ontario is a bit overwhelming to capture. Every other province has a specific identity, or at least a few key elements to focus on. I can't think of a single defining image for Ontario, other than big.

Big is the true nature of Ontario, whether it is population, economy or political influence. A simple statistic will sum it all up; Ontario has 40% of the people and the economic GDP of the whole country, and its share is growing.

Ontario is about 20% smaller than Quebec and 15% larger than British Columbia in area, but it seems bigger. That is because it is oriented more east-west than north-south and, coupled with its larger population, it has a much larger "reasonably populated" area. Our trip across Ontario will consume about 25% of our total driving distance across the ten provinces.

Even the people of Ontario get confused about their own geography. The area that is called Western Ontario, i.e., the London-Windsor region, is actually all in the eastern half of the province. The extent of Northern Ontario, which we can define as everything from the North Bay-Sudbury-Sault St. Marie level onwards, is mostly forgotten; but it's almost all west of Windsor. Only the curling world seems to notice as they give Northern Ontario their own "provincial" slot in the national championships.

Anyway, let's get started, as we cross over the Ottawa River from Quebec.

Ottawa has two distinct identities. One is as the national capital and the other is as a significant city with its own industries, community identities and recreational attractions.

Even the national capital identity has two dimensions, symbolic and physical. The symbolic identity is captured in political debate or news headlines such as "Ottawa says...," "Ottawa decided...," etc.

The dominant physical images we see are of the government buildings. First and foremost is Parliament. Its three large limestone structures with their green copper roofs surround a central courtyard and are set well back from the busy avenue. The Centre Block, which contains the House of Commons and the Senate Chamber, is distinguished by the high Peace Tower with its many bells. In front is the Eternal Flame. Usually it is also defined by protestors of one type or another who are looking for some attention for a cause. The East and West Blocks contain offices for the parliamentarians and their staff, who can be seen in transit "on the hill," especially as Question Period approaches each afternoon in the Commons. Tours are available and the sights are well worth the time, whether it is the chambers themselves, the corridors with their many statues and paintings, or the ornate library wing.

I will not turn this into a detailed tour directory, but there are so many buildings to visit, or at least pass by and admire. The external architecture is often as impressive as the contents. There is the Supreme Court, the Bank of Canada, the Prime Minister's residence, the Governor General's residence at Rideau Hall with its magnificent gardens, the Mint, and the many museums, galleries and memorials. The Rockcliff district has many spectacular homes and embassies

Such a list of specific sights indicates the many things to see, but it does not capture the beauty of much of the region. Aided, to be sure, by federal funds and the National Capital Commission, the gardens, parks and boulevards are very attractive. They are particularly noticeable where they parallel the Rideau River and the canal system, which creates extensive areas for the residents to enjoy. That is part of the second dimension of Ottawa, its community attributes and attractions.

As we have noted before, Ottawa started as a key location on the early fur trade route from Montreal to the interior of the continent. It grew in significance when it became the capital of Canada in the mid-1800s, partly as a defensive location vis-à-vis the Americans, and partly as a "Solomon-like" decision by Queen Victoria in the face of the rivalries between Montreal, Kingston and York (Toronto).

The Rideau Canal had been built between 1826 and 1832 to provide a military and commercial link with Kingston on Lake Ontario. This contributed to the success of the region, especially as a lumber and paper centre. Today, the canal is a constant source of recreational fun. In the summer, it can be enjoyed by boat, whether it is a small pleasure craft or a medium-sized tour boat with cabins, dining room and entertainment. In the winter, the canal becomes the world's longest skating rink, winding through the neighbourhoods of Ottawa.

The canal was constructed under the leadership of Colonel John By, who became a significant community leader in this area at that time. For this reason, Ottawa was initially referred to as Bytown.

With an area population of about one million people, Ottawa is Canada's fourth largest city. The city centre is nicely developed and used. Just a few blocks from Parliament is the Sparks Street Mall, a traffic-free shopping avenue. There are many interesting shops and eateries. I always take notice of the galleries with quality native art works, and others with old books and maps, always a favourite stop for me.

One sign of interest on the mall says "No Bikes; $53.75 Fine." I don't want to even think about the government bureaucracy that exists to make such decisions.

Past the Chateau Laurier, the stately limestone railway-hotel, and across the canal to the east is the Byward Market, with its restored buildings on narrow streets that are lined with lanterns and treed boulevards. There is everything from a farmers' market to department stores and boutiques. The many restaurants and pubs make it a gathering spot in the evenings, especially in the summers with its outdoor patios.

It may sound strange to some, but I find a lot of similarity between Ottawa and Calgary, where I live. They have about the same population, are affluent and growing, have a relatively young, energetic populace, and have an emerging high-tech industry to supplement their traditional core economies. Of course, there are some obvious differences as well: trees and lakes versus mountains, dairy farms versus cattle ranches, corn versus wheat, government officials versus oilmen, rain versus sunshine, deep snow versus Chinooks, flowing bilingualism versus dominant English, and liberal versus conservative politics. In a recent national survey the citizens of Calgary and Ottawa ranked highest in their sense of pride about their cities.

Leaving Ottawa, we head back south to join up with the St. Lawrence River again. The countryside in eastern Ontario is a mixture of farmland and marshy forest in a gently rolling landscape. It is more populated in the extreme east and along the river, phasing into less populated lake country to the north and west.

Along the St. Lawrence there are a number of medium-sized cities, interspersed with a steady stream of villages and developed acreages. Periodically, there are large bridges with high spans to connect with New York State on the other side. We can often spot one of the distinctive Seaway cargo ships steaming along the river. The St. Lawrence Seaway headquarters are located in Cornwall, the largest of the cities along the St. Lawrence River west of Montreal.

We also notice that most of the highway signs in eastern Ontario are bilingual, reflecting the regional population. Ontario is more pragmatic about these issues than Quebec. Ontario also provides detailed roadside signs for local shops such as cafes and lodges, very similar to what we saw on Prince Edward Island.

Near the town of Morrisburg is one of the most popular tourist attractions in Ontario, Upper Canada Village. It is a large reconstructed village from the 1860s. The pioneer lifestyle is portrayed in the many homes and shops by the costumed staff who play out the roles of the various trades. The whole area is surrounded by large parks.

Brockville is a particularly attractive city of some 20,000 people, located at the point where the St. Lawrence begins to widen again and becomes filled with a "Thousand Islands." It has a number of large stone buildings around a central square, including the courthouse and jail that date from the 1840s. There are also many impressive stone churches and large brick and stone homes situated along the river and on tree-lined streets. Along the riverfront are parks and a large marina where we can charter a boat, go on a cruise through the islands, or rent diving gear to explore the waters. Everything is clean and neat, which was very noticeable even on a blustery fall day when I last drove through. You get the sense of a town with a lot of civic pride.

As we continue west, the terrain becomes more rugged and there are many rocky outcrops along the highway. The town of Gananoque is in the heart of the Thousand Islands recreation country. Cottages, hotels and resorts abound. Water activities such as boating, fishing and island touring compete for our attention with hiking, camping or golfing on land.

As the St. Lawrence connects with Lake Ontario, or rather the other way around since the water flows eastward, we come to Kingston, a city full of national and personal history.

Kingston, with a regional population of almost 150,000, is a dynamic, multidimensional centre located almost equidistant from the large cities of Toronto, Ottawa and Montreal. It has two major universities, five prisons, a number of industrial plants, an Armed Forces base, a historical fort and a vigorous tourist industry created by the confluence of the lake, the river, and the inland cottage country. When I think about it, the population is probably larger than stated since I don't think they count students and prisoners as permanent residents.

Kingston is often referred to as the *Limestone City*, due to the local outcrops and quarries of that rock type and the use of it in the construction of the many impressive buildings at all of the institutions located here.

This is the image of Queen's University, with its many castle-like buildings, often with towers and turrets, spread across a spacious campus. It is surrounded by parks and boulevards filled with grand old trees. Founded in 1841, Queen's is one of the highest rated major universities in Canada. It is a great place to be a student. I'll stop here and admit that I am a Queen's graduate, and so might be suspect as an impartial commentator. I graduated in Engineering Physics in 1964, as did my two sons in the late 1980s. Things did change a lot over those two decades, both in terms of the understanding of the fundamentals of physics and in the dynamics of student life at university. I am not sure which one was the greatest advancement, quarks or student pubs.

We want to visit historic Fort Henry, high on a hill looking over the city and the entrances to the St. Lawrence River and the Cataraqui River, which leads to the Rideau Canal. The fort was built in the 1830s, when Kingston was becoming a key crossroads for the new colonies. Today, staffed by costumed students during the summer, it depicts military life in the 1800s in a colourful and educational way.

Kingston started as a fur-trading fort, established in 1673 by Count Frontenac. It was captured by the British in 1758, the same year as Louisbourg and a year before Quebec City. With the arrival of the Loyalists and other British settlers into the region over the next fifty years, it became more significant in size and a centre for trade and industry, including ship building.

After the War of 1812-14 with the United States, in a drive to improve defenses against further attacks, a number of projects were undertaken — first the Rideau Canal, and then Fort Henry. It is worth noting that, because of this timing, Fort Henry was never involved in any actual military action, unlike the fortresses we visited earlier on this trip.

Reflecting its central location and growing significance, Kingston became the first capital of the United Provinces of Upper and Lower Canada in 1841. Remember, at that time Canada was a single colony with two provinces spread along the St. Lawrence River and the north shores of Lake Ontario and Lake Erie. The choice was short-lived as the capital moved to Montreal in 1844, and then, finally, to Ottawa in1857.

Kingston was also the home of John A. Macdonald, the first Prime Minister of Canada when it became an independent colony — pardon me, Dominion — in 1867. There is a statue of Sir John A. in a park, and his gravesite can be visited, but, in typical Canadian fashion, it is all very low key.

Down below Fort Henry is the Royal Military College, the military university that trains the officers for Canada's Armed Forces. Again, it is an impressive campus with many substantial limestone buildings and open areas, this time with surrounding arches and stone walls with gun-slotted turrets. Planes, tanks and armoured vehicles are on display around the RMC grounds. We can observe uniformed cadets in the central parade square.

The downtown area of Kingston is modest, but it has been renewed over the years with trees, street decorations and distinctive shops, boutiques and eating establishments. A busy marina area and new condominiums line the nearby lakeshore. The growing suburbs are full of new housing developments and modern shopping malls.

Traveling west from Kingston along Highway 401, we remain somewhat inland from Lake Ontario for the first 100 kilometers. The terrain is a mixture of forest, rock outcrops, marshes and some farms that look tough to work.

Side excursions show us that the shoreline in this area consists of many bays and channels with strings of offshore islands. The area is attractive with small villages, cottage developments and marinas.

The largest city along here is Belleville, which is the regional commercial and shopping centre. With the emergence of dairy farms in the area now, this is also a centre for cheese production, much of which is shipped internationally as good examples of Canadian cheddar.

Nearby is Trenton, site of a major air base for the Armed Services. It has many large hangers and big grey planes on the tarmac. One area open to the public is the Air Force museum, which includes a field full of vintage planes that are always interesting to see.

Once we pass Brighton, a pleasant town in an apple-growing region, we get our first sight of the open waters of Lake Ontario and, thus, the first sense of the huge expanse of the Great Lakes. It's not just that we cannot see across the water, but it is also our general awareness of just how distant the far shores are, and this is the smallest of the Great Lakes. Even on a calm day the waves are noticeable. On a stormy winter night it can be frightening.

The cities along the lake all have a similar appearance. They have old, established city centres, lots of brick buildings, solid churches, and substantial old homes in treed neighbourhoods. Usually there is a local river and signs of old mills or factories. Some modest new developments appear on the outskirts.

These cities were all founded with the influx of the British Empire Loyalists fleeing from the American Revolution, soon to be followed by new British and European settlers. Belleville was founded in 1784, Toronto (York) in 1787, Port Hope in 1792 and, Cobourg in 1798. Sometimes we forget how long it took settlers to move inland, even just as far as Lake Ontario. This is 300 years after Columbus and Cabot, 250 years after Cartier, and 175 years after Champlain. It's even 25 years after the British defeated the French on the Plains of Abraham.

The Loyalists, who created all of these new towns, obviously became the core influence-holders in those local communities. We can read all sorts of tales about the social and political leadership of these original families and their descendants. General rebellions that took place in the 1830s were driven by the desire to make the government processes more democratic and less dominated by the "establishment" of the wealthy landowners, clergy and British appointed officials. This became a contributing factor in the drive for "independence" of Canada a few decades later.

From Port Hope we are going to detour north and visit the city of Peterborough. The drive passes through farmland, which will be the norm from here to Windsor at the western end of southern Ontario. The farms and small local communities are quite different in appearance from those of Quebec. The farms tend to be rectangular in shape, extending from road allowances a mile apart and having a basic size of 100 acres. Today, a specific family farm will generally comprise more than one such piece of land in order to be economic. The farm houses and barns are set well back from the road, more near the centre of the farm, as compared to the ones in Quebec that tend to be near the road and the neighbours. In this area the farms have a wide mix of crops, including corn, wheat, oats and barley. There are usually some cattle grazing in small fields and, often, pig and chicken barns in the yards.

Peterborough, with 70,000 people, is typical of many mid-sized cities in Ontario with its historic economic base of manufacturing. Here, a large General Electric heavy machinery plant has been the dominant factor. Other plants have made boats, clocks, cereals, pumps and outboard motors. Some have closed and a few newer technology plants have emerged. There are probably a dozen or more similar cities in Ontario, each with different specific industries.

Peterborough is situated at the northern end of the farm belt. It is the gateway to the recreational region of the Kawartha Lakes, with its many forest-lined lakes and rivers. It is one of the vast areas for cottages, lodges, fishing, boating, hiking and just getting away from it all that spread across central Ontario, from the Ottawa River to Lake Huron. It's gorgeous country.

A focal point of the Kawarthas is the Trent-Severn canal system that connects many of the lakes and rivers. It runs from Trenton on Lake Ontario to Port Severn on Georgian Bay. It was originally conceived as a commercial waterway for industries in the area, and it had some limited use for that purpose in the past, but it was built after the peak of canal commerce and was surpassed by the emergence of the railways. Thus, it became primarily a recreational route. It is now used for local day trips, a few days' journey between various sections, or longer voyages along its full length, either in a personal boat or on one of the commercial cruises, all a beautiful adventure.

A tourist and engineering highlight of the canal system is the Lift Locks at Peterborough. It is basically two large counterbalanced concrete containers of water that can lift or lower boats over twenty meters in elevation. It's the largest lock system of this type in the world, and quite a sight to watch as it operates.

Cities like Peterborough are good places to live. They are large enough to have most amenities, the convenience of big city attractions are only an hour or two away, and they retain the charm of smaller community living and the close proximity of fabulous recreation country.

Peterborough was prominently in the news during the summer of 2004 when it was hit by a series of violent wind and rain storms that caused a great deal of flooding and residential damage.

Peterborough has been considered so "typical of Canada" that many new products and marketing programs are piloted here. It is large enough and affluent enough to represent a good market test area, and it is isolated enough that sales campaigns can be managed and contained.

I finished my high school years here and enjoyed it very much. I should note that Ontario has now finally eliminated its Grade 13 system. I think this was the only jurisdiction in the world that had five years of high school, rather than four. When I moved from Manitoba to Ontario during Grade 11, I essentially added one year to my high school time. Students from Manitoba, or, for that matter, any other province or U.S. state, could enter Ontario universities one year earlier. Classmates I left behind in Winnipeg would get to university one year earlier than me. That was in the late 1950s; the system continued until 2002. It was hard to explain it to people in other places. I don't think the students in Ontario were slower; I think the teachers union had a good thing they didn't want to let go of. Of course, they argued that it was a good system that made the students more mature and, thus, more prepared for university, which was a backhanded slap at Ontario students if you think it through. Anyway, it's now history.

The challenge for cities such as Peterborough is to sustain their economic growth as industries change and populations shift. It is also a challenge to maintain their city centres as a commercial and civic focus, when new subdivisions are built and the outlying malls and big warehouse stores emerge. As we travel to a number of these cities we will observe varying success. For example, so far on this trip across Ontario, we have seen Kingston that seems to be doing very well. Peterborough's success is not as obvious; downtown doesn't look much changed from decades ago. Of course, this is an issue everywhere in Canada, not just Ontario.

Driving west of Peterborough, we see a road sign that confuses me and makes me think of other signs that we have seen driving through Ontario. It says, "Welcome to the City of Kawartha Lakes; Population 70,000." The problem is that there is no significant city anywhere near, and the Kawartha Lakes area is composed of many towns and villages, all spread across the farm-, lake- and forest-filled terrain.

What I was finally able to learn was that, a few years ago, when the provincial government was streamlining local government processes, it consolidated many communities into larger ones with a single council, school board and tax base. These were called cities, even when they encompassed many rural villages and farms. Thus, we have the City of Kawartha Lakes, a somewhat phantom thing. This also explains why we now even see signs welcoming us to large cities, such as Ottawa, placed tens of kilometers or more before the first encounter with any significant residential or commercial developments.

Highway 7 provides a pleasant trip through the farm country and its many small towns and villages. The scenery is comfortable: big barns with gambrel roofs set on solid stone foundations, silos stretching to the sky among large spreading trees in the farmyards, split-rail fences dividing the fields with their serpentine paths, white frame or red brick farmhouses surrounded by hedges and gardens, cattle and horses grazing among the gentle hills, woodlots interspersed with the crop-filled fields, village general stores and modest local churches.

This route is always a nice alternative to the busy, multi-lane route from Ottawa to Toronto. One phenomenon that we notice is that almost every one of the towns has exactly one stop light on the highway. This is obviously designed to slow down the through traffic and, perhaps, make us notice the local shops and stop for a bit. It's worth a periodic stop, whether just for a drink, an ice cream cone, or to browse in the craft and antique shops that are plentiful.

Our next stop is the city of Oshawa. Its general area population is almost 300,000 people and it has one of the higher average family incomes among large cities in Canada. How do you spell G.M.?

When we drive by the automobile manufacturing plants in the city, they are truly a staggering sight. The plants cover huge areas; even the employee parking lots are mind-boggling, with the thousands of vehicles parked there during the major shifts. Convoys of vehicle-carrying trucks leaving the gates and sidings full of dedicated railway cars help to define the scale of these operations. This is big-time economic value and employment.

This is repeated throughout southern Ontario at the other manufacturers' and suppliers' plants. In Oakville it will be Ford, in Windsor it's Chrysler, and so on. The Auto Pact that was signed with the United States in 1965 was very beneficial for Canada as it allowed plants to operate on a large scale, building specific models for the enormous combined markets. The U.S. plants received the same benefits in return, but of course the incremental impact of the Canadian sales was not as dramatic.

Of course, there are the many other manufacturing industries everywhere around here. For visitors from other parts of the country, the economic activity and wealth generation in the 400-kilometer stretch from Oshawa to Windsor is always a bit overwhelming.

Now we are nearing greater Toronto. Just where it actually begins is a matter of time and attitude. I'll explain.

The time dimension refers to the fact that Toronto is growing so much; its reach expands constantly. So, a community that is outside "Toronto" in one decade can be encased in its web by the next one. The 2001 census put the area at 4.6 million people, up 400,000 during the previous five years and 1.2 million in fifteen years! Think about that; in fifteen years Toronto has added the equivalent of today's greater Calgary or Ottawa, both of which have grown significantly themselves.

A contributing factor is immigration. Canada has about 200,000 new immigrants each year, half of whom go to Toronto initially. It is expected that even more later migrate to the area in secondary moves. This has provided Toronto with a rich mix of cultural elements.

The attitude dimension to being part of Toronto is harder to define. With time, as Toronto expands, the peripheral cities become absorbed in its economy and the population becomes more Toronto focused. Their booming new residential subdivisions, in effect, become bedroom communities for commuters.

The people of Oshawa or Hamilton would be appalled if you said they were part of Toronto. The folks of Guelph and Barrie can still deny it with some credibility for a while longer. Oakville, Newmarket and Pickering are fooling themselves if they don't think the tentacles of the big city have arrived.

Attitude is something Toronto has lots of. It's not that they actually say they are "the centre of the universe," as that Montreal radio station mentioned. It is just that they "know" it. They can't understand, and easily dismiss, reports from the United Nations and other groups that place Calgary or Vancouver at the top of their lists of best places to live in the world.

It even shows up in how they talk about themselves. If this was any other city, we would hear radio reports on local news, weather or traffic referring to Greater Toronto or Metro Toronto, or maybe even just Toronto. Not here. It's "The GTA," i.e., The Greater Toronto Area, with emphasis on the word *"The,"* just in case we mix it up with some other Toronto I guess. They love initials for their roads as well, like the *QEW* or the *DVP*.

The pronunciation of Toronto varies greatly. Only visitors and people that speak formally seem to find three "o" sounds, Tor-on-to. Some leave in two of them, Tor-onna. Others have just one, Tran-no, while many often say it as if there is no "o" in it at all, Trana. Whatever!

Such a contraction is not limited to here of course. For example, many New Brunswickers will shorten down Fredericton to sound more like Fred'icton, i.e., without any trace of an "r" sound.

In the aftermath of the major power outage in Ontario and the northeastern U.S. in the summer of 2003, the mayor of Toronto was very serious when he said that the rolling blackouts and rationed service should not apply to Toronto since it was the "economic engine of Canada." This did not impress the folks in the rest of southern Ontario. Of course, this is the same mayor who said his family was afraid to go to Africa because they might get boiled in a soup-pot. He said this shortly before the Olympic committee vote on the site for the 2008 summer Olympics; Toronto lost. There is a new mayor now.

Having said all that, I really like Toronto. I lived here for a while in the 1970s and have visited scores of times. It is a great city. It is full of energy and has tremendous natural and cultural attractions. Although obviously different in detail, it is the one Canadian city that feels like the booming, modern American cities such as Atlanta, Houston and Minneapolis, and is our closest parallel to New York.

Toronto has the same dual personality for Canadians as does Ottawa. There is the city itself, with all of its specific attributes, and then there is its symbolic role as the economic centre of Canada. Ottawa has the Federal Government, Toronto has Bay Street.

Downtown Toronto is a busy place. The tall office structures are full of tens of thousands of people every day. The surge of humanity in the subway stations and at the central railway station during rush hours is amazing. The surface streets are very narrow, so automobile traffic is painfully slow. This is compounded by the electric streetcar system that still exists and which runs right down the middle of many of the key avenues.

We can take all of this in at MINT Corner, so called because of the large bank office complexes that are located at the four corners: Montreal (now BMO), Imperial (now CIBC), Nova Scotia (now Scotia Bank) and Toronto Dominion (now TD). Nearby is the Toronto Stock Exchange, the TSE, which is the dominant security exchange in Canada. It used to be fun to visit and watch all of the action on the trading floor, but that is just a historic memory now with electronic trading taking over.

This concentration of economic power, and the need to travel to "Bay Street" to raise money, is what irritates many business and political leaders in other parts of Canada. They are always concerned that their needs are not understood or that their priorities are not addressed. Economic reality drives it, of course. Plus, I think Toronto serves a key role in keeping Canada together, just by being the common focus of complaints for everyone else.

An international study released in early 2004 showed that Canada was ranked the best in terms of the cost of doing business in the developed world, a reflection on the cost and effectiveness of establishing and operating a commercial enterprise. Toronto and Montreal both rated in the top rung for cities with populations over two million people.

I have been describing the conventional Canadian attitude of "loving to hate Toronto." However, there was one period when everyone was a big fan of the city and was cheering wildly: when the Blue Jays won the World Series. It brought us all together. Even out west you constantly heard, "How about those Blue Jays?" This later became a bit of a standing joke, as something you could say when a social conversation flagged.

As I mentioned when we were visiting Montreal, Toronto has a huge labyrinth of underground passages that connect the downtown buildings. We can travel for many blocks in all directions without surfacing. The passageways are lined with every imaginable shopping opportunity from fast food and convenience stores to fashion boutiques. Since there are also high rise condominiums in downtown, or at least clustered around the subway network, I believe it would be possible to live in Toronto and never go outside.

There are many attractions in the city centre. The Skydome, with its retractable roof, houses the Blue Jays. Maple Leaf Gardens, oops, I mean the Air Canada Centre, has the Toronto Maple Leafs. (By the way, why do the folks in Toronto think the plural form of leaf is leafs?) I noted that by the time of the 2004 World Cup of Hockey announcers were simply calling the facility "The ACC," true to Toronto fashion and I am sure to the consternation of Air Canada. Whatever they call it, it was the scene for the great victory by the undefeated Canadian team. Of course, that was followed by the downer of the NHL labour shut-down.

The NBA Raptors, Thompson Music Hall, live theatres, many upscale and distinctive ethnic restaurants, and grand hotels like the King Edward and Royal York all combine to make a visit here very entertaining. The view from the CN Tower, the highest freestanding structure in the world, is impressive.

There are some upscale lakefront developments near downtown, primarily high-rise condominiums. Historically, the highways and railways have provided a buffer between downtown and Lake Ontario. The lakeshore was occupied by warehouses, factories, wharves and loading docks. That is changing.

Farther away from downtown, there are many parks and attractions along the lake. To the west there are the Canadian National Exhibition Grounds, the sports Hall of Fame and Ontario Place, which is a fun family entertainment attraction. Historic Fort York, which was established in 1793, has restored buildings and costumed students to depict the military life of two centuries ago. We can also take a ferry ride out to Toronto Island in the harbour, where there is an extensive park area.

Going north from the city centre, up University Avenue, there are some of the major institutions of the city. We first pass the major hospitals, including the well-known Toronto Sick Children's. Then there is the Ontario legislature, Queen's Park, in the middle of the avenue, which splits around it. At the corner of Bloor is the ROM, the Royal Ontario Museum, which always has world class exhibits. To the west is the campus of the University of Toronto. U of T is Canada's largest and certainly one of its best universities. Remember, I went to Queen's and still must concede that. Yet, it is very hard to actually get a sense of the campus as a distinct identity, as you do at Queen's, McGill, Western, or UBC, which are also large institutions. U of T sprawls over a large area and encompasses many old residential buildings, blending into the government area around Queen's Park.

One of the natural attributes of the Toronto area is the many ravines that follow the rivers and creeks that drain toward the lake. These provide fantastic settings for homes, whether it is in the large, old, established neighbourhoods, with their mammoth trees and mansions, or in new subdivisions, far from the centre. Often visitors only see the attractions and busy patterns of the downtown areas and don't get an appreciation of how nice the city really is for living, with its many parks and beaches.

Being such a large city, there are many satellite business districts and concentrated high rise condominium developments far from the city centre. Often these are located at major stops on the subway system. For example, when we go many miles north on Yonge Street, we find developments at York Mills, Shepard and Finch, complete with the underground warrens.

Toronto is a true city-state and has a lot to offer.

Escaping the city to enjoy the huge expanse of cottage country we described earlier can be a challenge, especially on Friday evenings as the weekend traffic builds. Toronto does have an elaborate freeway system, but it struggles to keep up with the growth. Still, we get a sense that they plan ahead with new roads and expansions of existing ones. At one point in my travels of 2002 I was in a construction zone on highway 401 near the outskirts of the city, where it was being expanded from eight lanes to something more. The signs simply warned us that there would be periodic construction delays until 2005!

There is also a toll highway, 407, that parallels the 401 to the north across the city. It is taking some time to attract a full traffic load due to the inborn reluctance to pay tolls here in Canada, but it is providing some traffic relief to the area. When I think about it, the only tolls on major roads in Canada, other than ferries, are the PEI bridge, a stretch of the Trans-Canada in Nova Scotia, over what they called a pass, and the mountain-pass route in the Coquihalla region of British Columbia. Our trip bypasses those latter two sections. I guess I am true to my Scottish heritage.

As another aside, why are there tolls for ferries? Aren't they just extensions of the highways where it is not economic or feasible to build bridges?

We notice one other thing when listening to the Toronto radio stations; they still give the temperatures in Fahrenheit as well as Celsius; I did not notice this anywhere else in the country. I guess the British Empire Loyalists do still control the area. It probably also explains why the stores are not open on Boxing Day, that traditional British day off for the servants. Almost everywhere else in Canada it's the biggest shopping day of the year.

Driving west out of Toronto proper on the QEW (that's the Queen Elizabeth Way for traditional old-timers or recent newcomers), we pass the cities of Mississauga, Oakville and Burlington, which together contribute a million people to the GTA census. They have their own industrial and commercial bases, high-rise office buildings and condos, and cultural and entertainment centres, but their tremendous growth reflects their roles as significant upscale residential areas responding to the economic and population boom of Toronto.

We drive by field after field of sprouting new subdivisions, filled with the characteristic, gabled, two-storey, brick-faced, double-attached-garage homes of the region. Individually they look great; clustered as a neighbourhood they give the appearance of a solid brick wall going up and down the streets. In the more costly areas there are lots of big trees and ravines to break the monotony, as well as more extensive architectural variations.

One sight that will be familiar to Canadian golfers, at least from watching television, is the golf course at Glen Abbey, in Oakville. This has been, and will be, the site of Canadian Open Championships, where the best players in the world compete every year. Tiger Woods won the event a couple of years ago, playing a spectacular shot on the final hole: a six iron to the edge of the green from over 200 yards away out of a sand trap and over a lake. Glen Abbey is a public course, so anyone can book a tee time and play here. It is a given that every first-time golfer at Glen Abbey will try to hit *Tiger's shot*. It's a good deal for golf ball manufacturers since a high percentage of those shots end up in the lake.

At the extreme west end of Lake Ontario we cross the long causeway and very high bridge that spans the opening into the large inland Hamilton Harbour. The view of the harbour shoreline is probably the most dramatic heavy industry scene in all of Canada.

There are huge steel plants with their many massive concrete buildings and high smoke stacks, large stockpiles of coal and ore, hills of waste steel for recycling, extensive warehouses, and wharves with sturdy ship-loading arms. Everywhere are the distinctive Great Lakes ships. There is no doubting that Hamilton is a busy, heavy-duty, working area.

Beyond Hamilton, we are now going back east along the south shore of Lake Ontario, towards Niagara. The lake is on our left. A short distance inland is the Niagara escarpment, a cliff some 100 meters high that traverses this whole region between Lake Ontario and Lake Erie. This will lead us to Niagara Falls in a while. Locally the escarpment is referred to as Hamilton Mountain!

As we pass Grimsby, the *Gateway to Niagara*, we can detect a noticeable change in the landscape and the farms. The land is relatively flat and the fields are now full of fruit trees and grapevines.

The city of St. Catherines sits in the transition zone. It is a pleasant city of 130,000 people on the lakeshore. We can observe large industrial plants that tie into the logistics network of the industries back towards Hamilton and Toronto, but you also get the sense that the community living and general ambience is far removed from the big city, back to the sense of Kingston or Peterborough. The Lacrosse Hall of Fame is here — Canada's national sport that very few Canadians have ever seen played.

There is a very high bridge on the highway at St. Catherines that spans the Welland Canal, one of the greatest engineering feats in Canada. The problem to be solved is straightforward: how to move ships from Lake Ontario to Lake Erie over the Niagara Escarpment, i.e., around Niagara Falls.

The original canal system was built in the1820s and consisted of 39 small wooden locks. There have been many improvements and modernizations over the decades. Today, there are 8 large locks, which are part of the St. Lawrence Seaway. This represents half of the locks on the whole Seaway. It is fascinating to watch the large lake freighters move slowly but determinedly through the openings that have essentially no clearance. It is also a good reminder of our priorities and the pace of life when we drive along the local roads in the area and need to wait while the tall lift-bridges are raised to allow the ships to pass. There is an elevated viewpoint and information centre located at Lock Three.

In my travels I have seen the Panama Canal and the Suez Canal, both huge projects. The channels and locks of Panama are amazing, as you watch the huge ocean-going ships maneuver through the system. In fact, the dimensions of the Panama locks determine the maximize size for most of the world's commercial and military ships. Otherwise, it requires long detours around South America to get between the Atlantic and the Pacific oceans.

I must admit to a confusing, and somewhat amusing, mistake I made on a trip to see the Suez Canal. My wife and I were on a vacation in the Middle East with some friends and were spending a few days in Egypt. After visiting the pyramids, the bazaars and the sights along the Nile in Cairo, we set off one day with our driver/guide to see the Suez Canal, some distance to the east. We knew that the canal joined the Red Sea with the Mediterranean, and so set out for the upper end of the Red Sea. When we arrived, we could see some large ships headed north through a narrow channel that traversed between very high sandy banks. There was a small local ferry that could take vehicles across this waterway. After watching this for a while, I asked our guide to take us to the nearest lock on the canal. Now, his English was somewhat limited, but I just could not understand why my request seemed totally confusing to him. After a while, we just gave up trying to explain what we were looking for and went to one of the nice tourist hotels on the edge of the Red Sea to look at that view and get some help with directions. It was only there that I learned that there are no locks on the Suez. The canal was dug across the land area in northern Egypt that separates the Mediterranean from the Red Sea. However, since they are both at sea level and there are no intervening high rivers or lakes to use in a canal system, the whole Suez is one open waterway from one end to the other; in other words, a "big ditch," as I think Lawrence of Arabia called it. They just designate different times of the day for northbound and southbound traffic. No wonder I confused our guide.

Our next stop is Niagara-on-the-Lake, a beautiful little city at the mouth of the Niagara River on Lake Ontario. There are many old frame-and-brick classic homes set back from streets that are lined with huge maple and oak trees. The main street is filled with quaint, old-fashioned store fronts that contain craft shops, galleries, restaurants, ice cream parlours and boutiques of all sorts. The boulevards are full of flower gardens and a colourful clock-tower sits in the middle of the road. Quality hotels and B&Bs abound, all done in the old-fashioned motif. It is a popular tourist destination and one of my favourite places to visit.

A highlight of visiting Niagara-on-the-Lake is the Shaw Festival, a presentation of plays by George Bernard Shaw and many other authors primarily from the first half of the twentieth century, in well-appointed theatres that are reflective of earlier times. They can be the core element of a vacation to the area, or just a weekend getaway if you live close enough.

As I mentioned before, the countryside here is full of fruit orchards and grapevines. There are many wineries in the area, large and small, that all seem to offer tours and tasting rooms, plus sales of their product, of course. There has been a remarkable transformation of the area over the past three or four decades, as the vines have been replaced and the wines have been upgraded, so that there now are some very respectable wines made in Canada.

One unique offering in the area is "ice wine," a very sweet dessert wine that sells for a substantial premium. It is made from grapes that are left on the vines until the first hard frost and then quickly harvested. This results in the freezing-out of some of the water in the natural grape juice, which creates the intense sweetness.

We also learn there is a specific vocabulary to the area and the business. Farms are called Estates, fields are Vineyards, processing facilities are Wineries, stores are Cellars, and small, expensive combinations of all those things are Boutiques. Bring your palate, your wallet and a designated driver.

Driving south along the Niagara River is very pleasant, through tree-filled parks and the serene countryside populated with many beautiful homes.

Across the river we can see the United States, as the river forms the border here. This is the area to learn about the War of 1812, although it is a difficult thing to understand.

Basically, the United States was expanding and wanted to annex Canada. They had become independent from Britain some 30 years earlier and, with the Louisiana Purchase from France in 1801, had expanded westward to the Gulf of Mexico and across the prairies to the Rocky Mountains.

The Napoleonic Wars had been raging in Europe for 20 years, which was consuming British forces and energy. The Americans believed conquering Canada would be easy, since it was lightly populated, the British were distracted, and there was some unrest in Canada about British governance. Thus, they expected the Canadians would put up little resistance. In fact, they expected the Canadians to welcome their liberation. Recall that this American theory had been equally popular, and proved to be totally false, earlier in Quebec in 1775.

In any case, the Americans decided to attack from Detroit and upper New York. To their amazement, they quickly lost the first few battles, losing control of Detroit, Chicago and Mackinac. They did fight back from the south and capture York (Toronto) for a while, but were eventually forced back with defeats in the western area at Beaver Dam (Thorold) and Stoney Creek and to the east at Chateauguay and Crysler's Farm (Cornwall).

We have two Canadian heroes who are famous from all of this: General Brock, who led the troops to the early victories but was killed at Queenston Heights in 1812, and Laura Secord, who walked 19 miles and warned the British troops of American plans, which led to their decisive defeat at Beaver Dam in 1813. There is a very tall monument to Brock along the Niagara Parkway as we reach the escarpment and a testimonial to Laura Secord at her home site nearby.

I have a number of reactions when we visit the Laura Secord site. The first is that she is a real historical hero for Canada and, yet, most of us know little about her or the war. The second is that the recognition for her, even here, is very minimal, and it pales into insignificance when compared to the shrines to the fictional character Anne of Green Gables in PEI. It is also a disappointment to learn that the chocolates which bear her name, and that we all know so well, have no link to her or her family.

The war continued until 1814, during which period the British attacked Boston, Baltimore and burned the White House in Washington. Actually, they burned the presidential residence, which was painted with white-wash only after it was quickly rebuilt, thus creating the name.

The war ended in late 1814 with a treaty that just restored all borders back to where they were before 1812. As I said, the War of 1812 is hard to understand.

Back to the present. After we drive up the escarpment, we continue on high ground and the river is far below in a deep and narrow gorge. There are high bridges over the gorge that carry heavy volumes of traffic between the two countries. Along the river is a major grid of high voltage power lines that carry away the electricity from the large plants in the lower reaches.

As we move forward through this area of parks and flower gardens, we can see a rising mist in the distance and realize we are approaching the falls. They are, in fact, a few miles west of the escarpment edge, due to the erosion of the face of the falls by the water over geological time.

Niagara Falls is truly a spectacular sight. I have seen higher, wider and much larger falls around the world, but Niagara seems to create a special awe. Perhaps it is the fact that the street and broad walkway pass right along the bank of the river. We can stand just a few feet from the top and sense the tremendous energy, as the foaming blue water surges over the edge and falls to the river bed below, with a huge roaring sound and a rising wet mist. I can stand at that edge for long periods, mesmerized by the motion and noise.

There are many ways to experience the falls. Walking along the edge for some distance downstream from the precipice provides a panoramic view of the full breadth of Niagara, the main Horseshoe Falls and the secondary Bridal Veil Falls, often called the Canadian and American Falls, respectively. They are separated by an island in the middle of the upper river. There is a walkway under the upper edge that provides a superb sense of the energy here, as does a boat ride on the lower river into the rapids and churning water below the falls. In all cases, just be prepared to get wet.

The area is a significant tourist destination, of course, and thus there are always lots of people present, especially in the summer. Many hotels and restaurants are located along the cliffs above the falls, providing some spectacular views day and night. There are many other sights to see in the area, some of which I have mentioned earlier. In fact, my favourite way to visit the area is to stay at one of the quaint hotels in Niagara-on-the-Lake and then drive around the whole region to see things, including the falls, on day trips. Niagara Falls is a must-see area for travelers, honeymooners or not.

As we exit Niagara Falls to the south, we come to the east end of Lake Erie, probably the least known, almost forgotten, Great Lake in Canada. Its northern shore runs for more than 300 kilometers to the west from here, and, as we will see, there are many nice towns and beaches along the way, but there is no significant city in the whole stretch. I haven't figured out why this is the case. On the south shore, in the U.S., you can find Buffalo, New York, Erie, Pennsylvania, and Cleveland, Ohio. On the Ontario side all the larger cities are inland, away from the lake.

Port Colborne is a pleasant little city of almost 20,000 people at the Lake Erie entrance to the Welland Canal. It has a very long docking area for the large lake freighters and a significant marina behind a protective rock barrier, where many impressive power and sail boats can be seen.

The countryside here is relatively flat with extensive farms. Lots of grazing cattle are visible, along with accompanying fields of hay and corn.

The beaches along the shore, such as Long Beach, are wide and sandy. They are populated with cottages that range from older and modest to large and new. This is obviously a popular vacation and weekend retreat area.

A couple of names caught my attention around here: the *Horse Play* riding stables and the *Whiskey Run* golf club. The former is cute; the second conveys the exciting images of the illicit whiskey trade that was rampant in southern Ontario, sending liquor into the United States during their period of prohibition and gangsters.

North and inland some 30 kilometers from Lake Erie, we come to the city of Brantford. It is also only 20 kilometers west of Hamilton, as we have gone around a large circular route through the Niagara peninsula.

Brantford is the *Telephone City*. You will recall our discussion, when we were in Baddeck, Nova Scotia, that Alexander Graham Bell lived in Brantford for a year or so with his parents when they migrated from Scotland. He then moved on to Boston, where he created the telephone a couple of years later. The plaque beside the old family home in Brantford carefully states that he conceived of the idea of the telephone when he was here. Thus, we have the reflected glory for the city.

I think the city is more focused now on being the hometown of Wayne Gretzky, a more modern and a true local celebrity. There is a major parkway and the local sports centre named after him.

The town is centred on a local river and the downtown area is full of old stone and brick buildings, including a noticeable stone clock tower on the federal post office building. In general, commerce seems to have moved out to the suburbs and the shopping centres; downtown is pretty quiet.

Farther north again is the city of Guelph, now on the outer fringes of Greater Toronto. It is a thriving city, again centred on a river. The University of Guelph has a spacious, modern campus and is well known as one of the leading agricultural teaching and research centres in the country.

It is always fun to observe the competitiveness between cities and universities. It so happened that when I last drove through Guelph a survey of university students had just been compiled and released by a national newspaper. The first report I heard on the local radio said, "Guelph led the way in a recent survey of students. It was recognized for its food, safety and open access. In comparison, Queen's was ranked low in physical activities." That was all it said!

By the time of the news broadcast an hour later, obviously some feedback had been received. The story now said, "Guelph placed fourth in a national survey of student satisfaction. Its strengths were .... (repeat above). Queen's placed first overall."

To the west are the cities of Cambridge, Kitchener and Waterloo, again, large, modern communities. In fact, in this part of the province the main image we get is not so much of the individual cities, but of the composite impact of their booming economies. Their success is built on heavy and light industry, rich agricultural lands, picturesque settings and quality institutions, such as the many universities. For example, the University of Waterloo is well known for its innovative and high quality co-op engineering programs.

There are a lot of people here; Guelph, Cambridge, Kitchener and Waterloo encompass a population of well over a half million. We get a real sense of the economic power of Ontario outside of Toronto, and this awareness continues to build as we move on westward toward London and Windsor.

On the way let's visit the small city of Stratford and its Shakespeare Festival, which has been a major cultural event since its inauguration in 1953.

There is actually a small village called Shakespeare nearby, but it seems limited to a cluster of antique shops and the fire hall for North and

South East Hope Townships. That name almost makes us feel like we are back in Newfoundland.

Stratford is located on the Avon River; what a surprise. The river is bordered by pleasant parks full of ducks, geese and swans. The centrepieces of the city are the theatres for the very popular summer festival — the large modern Festival Theatre and a few smaller ones around the downtown area. Streets are named Romeo and Falstaff. There are many large frame homes on round-stone foundations in the sedate residential areas; we can imagine ourselves in an old English town. Of course, there are many shops and galleries, and quite a few bookstores, which fit the theme. Stratford has not developed the upscale quaint-and-cute image that Niagara-on-the-Lake has achieved around the Shaw Festival, but it is a pleasant place to visit.

Next, we come to London, the cornerstone of western Ontario with an area population of over 400,000 people. Yes, I realize that I said earlier that western Ontario is not really in the west, but that is the way they describe it and so we will stick with it. The name goes back to the early days of the province when it was limited to a narrow band across the north shores of Lake Ontario and Lake Erie. Thus, Kingston was in the east, London and Windsor in the west, the shores of Georgian Bay in the north, and Toronto in the centre. Heaven forbid that you thought Toronto might have been in the south, rather than the centre! Haven't you been paying attention? By definition, there is no south here.

London appears as an affluent and booming city. It has a well-developed downtown, with some tallish buildings, wider streets, a large shopping mall and a convention centre. The ever-expanding suburbs are full of the usual large modern homes, malls and big-box stores.

London is located on the Thames River. Can there be any doubt that this region was first settled by the British Empire Loyalists? Cities are called London, Stratford, Cambridge and Chatham. Rivers are the Thames and Avon. The townships are Oxford, Perth, Norfolk, Essex and Middlesex. And every town has the familiar King, Queen, George and Charlotte streets.

The campus of the University of Western Ontario is one of the most impressive in Canada. Its large limestone buildings are similar to Queen's, McGill and Saskatchewan, but there seems to be more open space and park-like areas here. I got to know the campus when I attended Western's well known Business School in the 1970s and '80s.

During my career I also had the opportunity to visit Western to recruit new engineering and business-school graduates. This process generally takes place early in the year and, for that reason, I came to experience one of their record snow storms.

In Canada we all learn to cope with winter and cold weather, but the area that stretches from Western Ontario across to Ottawa and on to Quebec gets the largest volumes of snow, being downwind of the Great Lakes. The weather changed quickly that January afternoon and bare streets filled with huge volumes of wet snow in only a few hours. Just getting from campus to a hotel downtown required joining a gang that was pushing a city bus out of a snow bank, me being dressed in a suit and dress shoes for the interview process, and thus slipping and sliding all over the place. By morning, all traffic was stopped, cars were totally buried in snow, and the airport was closed. It took a full day to be able to move on at all, and that was tenuous.

Now we continue to the southwest, still generally following the north side of Lake Erie, but somewhat inland from the shore. The area is relatively flat farmland. As we proceed, we see more vegetable farms and fruit orchards mixed in with the corn and hay fields. As we turn down to the Erie shore near Leamington, we also see many large greenhouse complexes that grow flowers for the markets everywhere.

Following the Erie shore south of Leamington, we see many vacation cottages clustered along the wide sandy beaches. They are relatively small, old and very close together, which indicates that this has been an active retreat area for a long time.

At the end of this road we come to Point Pelee National Park. This is a triangular-shaped peninsula of land that juts out into Lake Erie. It is full of hiking trails and boardwalks that take us through the preserved forest, sand dunes and marshlands. It is a fascinating place to walk, visit, learn about nature, and have a picnic.

Point Pelee, and the near-by Pelee Island that can be reached by ferry, are the southernmost spots in Canada. On our trip we have visited the easternmost point at Cape Spear in Newfoundland, and, now, the southernmost. There are just two more extremities to go. You can guess the north, at least generally, but where do you think the western edge is? We'll see.

You may need to look at a map to realize just how this is the most southern point. Many of us don't realize, without seeing a map, that the trip from the Gaspé, up the St. Lawrence and along Lake Ontario and Lake Erie, is in a definite southwest direction.

If we use the familiar 49th parallel that defines the Canada–USA border in the west as a reference, Point Pelee is below the 42nd parallel, and thus slightly south of the California–Oregon border. It is about 1000 kilometers farther south than the general Winnipeg–Regina–Calgary–Vancouver latitude. Toronto is near the 44th parallel. Ottawa, Montreal and Halifax, all near the 45th, generally line up with Minneapolis; St. John's lines up with Seattle.

So, when you hear people refer to Canada as "north of the 49th parallel," you should now realize that, in fact, more than two-thirds of Canadians actually live south of the 49th. This knowledge might win you a beer in a bar-bet some time.

Our westward travels in southern Ontario will end in Windsor. Again, we find an affluent and steadily growing area, with a population of over 300,000. It has one of the highest per-family average incomes in the country, driven by heavy industry such as automobile manufacturing

The countryside, as we approach the city, is relatively flat and full of large, neat farms and orchards. Driving into the centre of the city along a relatively wide avenue with a slight but steady decline, we can see the skyline ahead with very tall office buildings, some in the classic stepped stone style, and others with a gleaming glass and chrome modern architecture. It is only when we reach the end of the avenue, as it terminates against a wide river, that we realize the tall buildings and city skyline we have been approaching is actually downtown Detroit, across the river and across the border.

Windsor has a more modest, but attractive, downtown itself. Along the riverfront, above a pleasant park and pathway system, there is a string of office buildings and apartment condominiums that take advantage of the view.

The dominant structure along here is the Casino Windsor, a large modern building which includes a tall hotel with a bright, white-stone and blue-glass exterior. It is complemented with fountains and colourful neon signs out front. All of this is focused on the river, or, more specifically, on the people of Detroit it strives to lure across to try their luck. I guess it has been a big success for employment and the local economy since it opened a few years ago.

There are many noticeable signs in the area that advertise Cuban cigars. I presume this is a good business with the American visitors who face an embargo on Cuban goods back home. I am sure they smoke the cigars before they return back across the river.

There is one historic site in Windsor that must be visited. Since 1858 Hiram Walker has been distilling whiskey here. Taking the Canadian Club Distillery Tour is almost a national duty. CC has been an internationally famous brand name of Canadian whiskey for a long time; we find it everywhere we travel. To provide balance, I should acknowledge that, back in Waterloo, there is the Seagram distillery that has been in existence since the mid-1800s as well. Certainly, Crown Royal, with its distinctive purple cloth bag, has been equally identified with Canadian whiskey worldwide. Decisions, decisions! Will that be CC or Crown Royal?

There are two border crossings between Windsor and Detroit, a tunnel and a very high bridge that allows the Great Lakes ships to pass underneath. This is one of the busiest border points between the two countries and it is not unusual to have very long delays, especially with the extra security checks that have developed over the past few years. We do not have to be concerned about that; we are going to head back towards Northern Ontario and take the Canadian route above Lake Huron and Lake Superior.

As we start back east from Windsor, we follow the south shore of Lake St. Clair. Near the city there are some spectacular homes on the lake. This is also true across the lake, where some of the most upscale neighbourhoods of Detroit, such as Grosse Pointe, are located. The lakeshore has many good beaches. To the east, there are cottages and resort villages with marinas and golf courses.

Lake St. Clair is a good-sized lake, almost square in shape with 30 or 40 kilometers of shore along each side. It certainly is large enough that we cannot see across it, and the waves and whitecaps can be significant when the wind blows. There is an apparent inferiority complex associated with the lake, being situated in the midst of the other enormous lakes. Listening to the local radio station one day, I actually heard an extensive dialogue between the program announcers and various listeners about whether or not Lake St. Clair was a Great Lake, or just a Very Good Lake! And they were serious, focusing on the social aspects of the lake, with its proximity, accessibility, developments and water temperatures. It was weird. But all things considered, it may be a great lake, but it is not the sixth Great Lake. Its 1000 square kilometers does not compare with the more than 80,000 square kilometers of Lake Superior, or even the almost 20,000 square kilometers of Lake Ontario. There are at least 20 other lakes in Canada larger than St. Clair.

Just to the east of Lake St. Clair is the city of Chatham. It has done an excellent job of renewing its city centre. Although the streets are narrow and the buildings are old, they have attractive boulevards with trees and flowers, nicely-finished and colourful fronts on the commercial buildings, and a central four-sided clock on a high pedestal. It makes the area very inviting.

Chatham is recognized for its historical role as the destination for many fugitive slaves who left the southern United States in the 1850s via the Underground Railway, a network of sympathizers, organizers and safe-houses over the long distances. These were some of the earliest black settlers in Canada.

To the north of Chatham is the oil-producing region of Ontario. It does not compare in significance to the resources of the western provinces but it does have a rich history.

In the area around Petrolia and Oil Springs, "gum-beds" that yielded an asphaltic material which could be used to waterproof ships had been discovered. By the mid-1800s, processes were developed that could distill crude oils and make useful products, such as kerosene and lamp oil. This led to the desire to find sources of oil that were more substantial than those available from the seepages at the surface.

In 1858 the world's first oil well was dug at Oil Springs. The first well was dug by hand, but they quickly developed spring-pole rigs to penetrate the earth. Within a few years they were going deep enough to find oil under some pressure; it would flow to the surface. They also invented a system of putting small pumps down the wells to lift the oil to the surface more quickly. The pumps were powered by a central engine that activated wooden "jerk lines." These loosely-connected, rough-hewn poles were spread over the surface to a series of wells. This primitive system is still in use today for the hundreds of existing wells that continue to produce small volumes of oil. It's a quaint and historic sight. All of this activity created a boom town in the 1860s.

There is a very informative museum and interpretive centre located in Oil Springs, just off the highway on Gum Bed Road. It has an amazing amount of old equipment on display, and well-done video presentations on the history. There is an 1879 quote on display in the museum from an old book: "To a stranger it is an interesting place, for a time, but it requires a short time to become monotonous. Everything smells and even tastes like oil; everybody is covered with it, thinks of nothing but oil, and talks of nothing but oil. And still they are not happy, but are ever sinking more wells."

I love this quote, both for its imagery and for its uncanny description of what would happen again in various parts of western Canada over the next hundred years.

And, yes, that was the first oil well, here in 1858. The well-publicized and hyped well drilled by Drake in Pennsylvania did not happen until 1859. It's something like watching the "world premier" of some hit movie on an American television network a week after you have seen it on the CBC, CTV or Global.

All of the activity at Oil Springs also led to the creation of an oil processing facility at Sarnia, located nearby where the St. Clair River flows out of Lake Huron. Sarnia has subsequently grown into a world-class refining and petrochemical centre.

I have known quite a few people who have lived in Sarnia and they are always very positive about it. A city of 70,000, with a strong economic base, nearby beaches on the big lakes, and U.S. shopping just across the river, it provides a good lifestyle.

The southeast shore of Lake Huron, which stretches for a couple of hundred kilometers north of Sarnia, is a long series of beaches with scattered small towns and villages. This is one of the many recreation destinations for the people of southern and western Ontario. There are many areas with weekend homes and cottages, waterside resorts, marinas, golf courses and hiking trails. Inland, away from the lake, is different, with a vast expanse of well-developed farm land and many small rural communities.

Our journey cuts across country here, skirting the heavily populated areas between London and Toronto that we have already visited, and joins up with highway 400 as it heads north out of the clutches of the GTA.

Barrie is a modern city on the west side of Lake Simcoe, about 100 kilometers north of downtown Toronto. Lake Simcoe, similar in size to Lake St. Clair, provides an attractive setting for the city and lots of recreational opportunities. We are also approaching the end of the farm country, with the attractions of the northern woods and the wilderness not far away.

The downtown area has the basic three-storey buildings that we have seen many places. There are also many modern, tall condominiums emerging along the waterfront-view avenues. Marinas and fishing wharves dot the shoreline. There is a series of parks along the water with fountains, walkways, play areas and artistic statues. Most impressive is a steel statue of a stylized Indian figure with outstretched arms draped in feather shapes. It stands over 20 meters high and gleams in the sunshine and in the reflections off the lake. It is titled "Spirit Catcher," and appropriately seems to stimulate one's quiet inner thoughts and imagination.

Is it or is it not part of the Toronto bedroom community network? Although I sense there is some denial by many of the residents, the tentacles are reaching in. The fact that the population is now over 100,000 people, having grown 25 percent in the five years up to the latest census, indicates the current reality. I do not envy the commuters who must travel the gridlocked highway to and from work, but this city feels like a great place for family living.

Just 30 kilometers north, at the upper end of Lake Simcoe, is the city of Orillia, about a third the size of Barrie. It is somewhat unique; it's neither a busy, modern, growing bedroom community like Barrie, nor one of the more rustic towns in the cottage and lake country that we will come to soon. It is a quiet residential town in a fabulous setting.

Its lakefront development has a pretty park and marina. In the summer we see medium-sized river cruise boats with overnight accommodations. They work the Trent-Severn canal system from Georgian Bay on Lake Huron to Lake Ontario, via the Kawartha Lakes, Peterborough and Trenton. It is a very scenic and relaxing way to take a vacation.

Some old railway dining cars have been converted into a nice restaurant that looks over the lakeshore park. The downtown has tidy streets with tree-lined sidewalks and quaint store fronts. One group of stores with a distinctive old-fashioned appearance is called the Mariposa Market, a direct reference to the fictional town created by Stephen Leacock in his outstanding humorous tales.

Leacock was a university professor who taught political science and economics at McGill in the early years of the twentieth century. He was a prolific writer of history, economics, famous biographies and literature, but is probably most famous for his home-grown, humourous writings. His *Sunshine Sketches of a Little Town*, written almost a hundred years ago, is typical and a classic. It describes the people, politics and social antics in Mariposa. I re-read this recently and was pleased to note how well the characters and the community dynamics in these tales hold up to all the changes in life since then, and how well his humour still entertains. As the saying goes, "The more things change, the more they stay the same." Everyone should go back and read some of his works; they do add sunshine to the day. The closest parallel today would likely be Stuart McLean's *Vinyl Café* show on the CBC and his books such as the entertaining *Welcome Home*.

The Stephen Leacock museum is located on a quiet bay of Lake Simcoe, in a residential area of Orillia. It is the site of the grand old frame mansion that was his home. The setting is park-like, with walking paths through the tree-filled grounds. It is an interesting place to visit. To be sure, there is a full collection of his works and other memorabilia available in the gift shop.

A few miles east of Orillia is another modern Canadian phenomenon, a huge, modern casino complex on a First Nation reservation. It includes a large entertainment centre and a tall hotel. The parking lot covers acres. There are also many other new hotels and other facilities being built nearby. This is obviously becoming a destination spot for travelers and gamblers. There are "For Sale" signs on many of the farms for long distances around, as people who live in this previously quiet farming area look to cash in on the boom.

I haven't quite figured out all of the dynamics related to the big casinos that have emerged on Indian lands across North America. I know that the First Nations people have control over their lands under various treaties and, thus, can develop such facilities under federal regulations, although they also need provincial and local approvals for much of the infrastructure. I give them full credit for pursuing this economic opportunity.

What I do not understand is why so many non-native jurisdictions have not seen the economic wins and allowed the casinos to flourish, as has happened in Windsor. The communities seem to be hung up on the social and moral issues of gambling and can't seem to allow nice facilities to be constructed. It's not that they turn away from the money; look at the huge number of government-run lotteries. My hometown, Calgary, is a good example. It has four good-sized casinos that run every day of the week and which, by law, benefit various charitable causes in two or three day stints. The charities compete aggressively for the opportunity and provide volunteers to staff many of the roles. All that is fine, but the settings are so poor — low ceilings, smoke-filled noisy rooms, limited service and no entertainment is the norm. The politicians have decided that gambling is OK, as long as it is not too much fun. Now there is a proposal emerging to create a modern complex on the reservation lands just outside Calgary, as in Orillia. Go figure!

Our next destination is the southern shore of Georgian Bay, some 30 kilometers west of Orillia. We first come to Victoria Harbour, a secluded local bay. It is fully developed with many homes and cottages, powerboat and sailboat marinas, wharves for boat launching, fishing docks, and pretty parks along the sandy beach shoreline. Another area for quiet vacation retreats.

Midland is a small city a little farther west. It also has great vacation facilities. The harbourfront here has an extensive town dock, elaborate flower displays and a large, shiny, metal sculpture of a goose in flight. Throughout the city there are many colourful murals on the sides of buildings. They depict natives, settlers, missionaries, trappers, boat builders and tradesmen. They are quite attractive and reflect on the rich history of this area.

This region was populated by the Hurons before the arrival of Europeans. French-Canadian fur trappers and Jesuit missionaries arrived in the early 1600s, being among the earliest adventurers to come inland from the settlements on the St. Lawrence. This became the centre for a Jesuit mission and a significant French farming community. It thrived for ten years, 1639 – 1649.

In the end, it became a casualty of the Iroquois–Huron wars, as the Huron were routed and dispersed. The Jesuits were forced to flee the area, burning down the settlement as they left to keep it out of Iroquois hands. Some of the priests and settlers were killed in the process, often after suffering extreme torture. There is a Martyrs' Shrine to recognize all of these events on a hill just outside Midland. There is also an elaborate reconstruction of the settlement of the 1600s nearby with staff who recreate the villagers' roles.

Here I must confess my confusion about the village and the martyrs. The signs and tourist brochures all encourage us to visit the site of Sainte-Marie Among the Hurons and the Martyrs' Shrine. Somehow, I concluded that someone named Marie was a young woman who was caught up in the turmoil and who became a tortured martyr. I had thoughts of a new heroine to learn about, right up there with Laura Secord and Anne of Green Gables. Well, it was not to be. Sainte-Marie Among the Hurons was the name given to the mission and the settlement by the Jesuits. This is like the hundreds of other communities in Canada named after saints; it was just done with a little more flair here.

Speaking of the names of towns, there are some great ones in this area: Penetanguishene, Waubaushene, Wahnekewaning Beach and Ossossane Beach among them. Your tongue gets a workout here that is reminiscent of Nova Scotia and New Brunswick.

Recall that the area just east of Kingston, at the start of the St. Lawrence River, was called the Thousand Islands. I assume it is an exaggeration, but it conveys an image of an island-filled river. Well, the folks along the eastern shore of Georgian Bay are not going to be outdone on this score. The area there is called Thirty Thousand Islands. There must be a lot of rocks sticking out of the water in all those bays.

Going back inland and north now, we enter the Muskoka cottage country. It is usually just called Muskoka, although there are many lakes in the area, all of them surrounded by forest and lined with vacation homes and lodges. Lake Muskoka itself is a significant lake that connects via narrow channels to Lake Joseph and Rosseau Lake, creating an extensive boating route between the various recreational locations.

When I look at the cottages on these lakes, I cannot help but visualize all of those beer commercials full of young folk having a fun time on the docks and in the water on a hot summer day. I am sure this is where they invented the phrase "two-four weekend," which is an effective play of words related to the first long weekend of the summer around May 24, and the fact that beer in Ontario is usually sold in cases of 24 bottles or cans.

Activities in the region are prolific, as with most retreat areas: boating, fishing, swimming, hiking, biking, fishing, golfing and more. Skiing and snowmobiling fill the winter afternoons.

There are three towns of 10,000 people or more that are the commercial and visitor centres for the area — Gravenhurst, Bracebridge and Huntsville. They are all attractive and geared for support to the vacationing visitors. They have many guest facilities, of course, along with many shops, ranging from the practical for the cottage owners to the arts and crafts galleries and restaurants for everyone. Lake boats, reminiscent of Leacock's era a hundred years ago, can take us for a tour or dinner cruise.

Beside the highway at Gravenhurst we spot a large stone Inukshuk, one of many we will see as we travel through northern Ontario, seeming to both welcome us and to guide the way. There is also a cute sculpture of a life-size black bear on a tree stump, attempting to catch a fish from a pond down below.

Bracebridge is set beside the north and south branches of the Muskoka River, where the fast-tumbling Bracebridge Falls is located. There are a dozen or more falls in the local area that can be the destinations for interesting nature hikes. Among the many shops and red brick buildings in town is an antique and collectibles store called *Worth Repeating* that I thought was appropriate.

There is a sign here declaring that we are at "45⁰ North – Halfway to the North Pole." Of course that presumes we started at the equator, rather than St. John's, Newfoundland, but that is just a detail. We are obviously in berry country as well, as there are signs everywhere advertising blueberries, raspberries, strawberries and cranberries.

Huntsville is a similar, neat, tree-lined, riverside town with welcoming inns and pubs. *Diamond in the Rough* seems like a good name for the golf course carved out of the woods, but wouldn't it be a great name for a baseball park, reminiscent of the corn fields in *Field of Dreams*?

Here we have also reached the end of the four-lane divided highways, except for limited stretches near the larger cities, until we approach Winnipeg, which is still some 2500 kilometers ahead of us. Yes, Northern Ontario is big.

North of Huntsville we are now truly in the Canadian Shield, the vast region of lakes, forest and rock outcrops that occupies almost half of Canada's surface area. We have glimpsed its southern edges as we have traveled across the eastern part of the country, but now we will experience it full time.

Traveling across the country, as a refresher for writing this book, I took a lot of notes along the way. I quickly developed shorthand for describing the terrain that we will see for days as we continue north of Lake Huron and Lake Superior — TRRLPAM, simply meaning Trees, Rocks, Rivers, Lakes, Ponds And Marshes. It saved a lot of repetitive writing. In hindsight, I should have used something like CHDF for the corn, hay and dairy farms we saw so much of back east.

That shorthand notation in no way diminishes the rugged beauty of the northern areas. I never tire of seeing a pristine lake set in the woods, a fast-running river tumbling through the rocks, or a quiet pond with a beaver lodge among wild grasses and lily pads.

North Bay calls itself the *Gateway to the Near North*, which, I guess, distinguishes it from the Far North. Presumably this is designed to attract more visitors from the south by making it seem accessible. Also, there is major highway work being done between here and Muskoka that will result in four-lane access all the way from Toronto in a few years, which will help.

North Bay is a mid-sized city located on the eastern shore of Lake Nipissing, a large lake that stretches for more than 50 kilometers to the west. It has the charm of a relatively old, established town, with brick buildings and roadways, wide sidewalks and flower beds on the main street, and nicely laid-out parkland along the lake.

The area is ideal for fishing, boating, canoeing, and hiking, as you would imagine. I noticed there are many watercraft dealers here, which display some very large, fancy boats for cruising on the big lake.

One claim to fame here is that it is near the birthplace of the Dionne Quintuplets. The farmhouse where they were born in 1934 has been moved to town and it is on display for visitors. It is a bittersweet story, to be sure — attention and fame mixed with loss of privacy and exploitation by the government agencies.

There is a broader historical significance to the area. This was an early settlement on the route of the fur traders and explorers who first ventured into the interior of the country. The upper Ottawa River is only 50 kilometers to the east, accessible across a portage to the Mattawa River that traverses most of the way. Some 100 kilometers to the west, via Lake Nipissing and the French River, you reach the north end of Georgian Bay and, thus, access to Lake Superior. I find it fascinating to sit on the shore and gaze out over the lake, visualizing the early explorers and large fur-laden canoes making their way through the region.

Turning west now, we travel along the north shore of Lake Nipissing and into serious mining country. And what says "mining" more than Sudbury?

Driving into Sudbury, we cannot help but be awed by the huge ore-processing and metal-refining plants in the area, with their many large stacks thrusting into the sky. Long ore trains move on the local rail lines, delivering the feed to the plants from the nearby mines.

At one time the terrain around Sudbury was compared to a moonscape, as the rocky ground was virtually denuded of vegetation by the toxic emissions from the operations. With new technologies and better environmental controls the ground is showing signs of recovery; new grasses, plants and trees are emerging.

The city is the largest one between Toronto and Winnipeg, with a population of about 160,000. No, I do not consider London and Windsor to be between Toronto and Winnipeg, even if it is western Ontario, and you can take the shortcut through there to go west via the U.S. route south of Lake Superior.

It is worth noting that the population of Sudbury has not grown for decades and, in fact, is slowly shrinking. The mining and forestry region does not display the booming economic signs of the south. Sudbury has the normal housing subdivisions with residential malls and warehouse stores, but the downtown is basic and the city centre mall sits partially empty and in some disrepair. Urban renewal needs to wait on better economic times.

The city is centred on a local lake, which is quite scenic in the middle of the heavy industrial surroundings. Parkland, marinas, galleries, theatres and museums line the lake, as does the local university, Laurentian. Its campus sits on the lakeshore and looks back across to the city centre.

In the park on the south side of the lake is the most famous site in Sudbury, the "Big Nickel." Mounted on a stand, it is a replica of a Canadian five-cent piece about six meters across. It shines brightly, like a new coin, in the sunshine. It has the dates 1751-1951, an industrial plant and maple leaves on one face, and the profile of King George VI on the other. This was erected in 1951 to commemorate the bicentennial of Sudbury.

Traveling west from Sudbury, we approach the north shore of Lake Huron, or, more specifically, the North Channel that runs out of the north end of Georgian Bay and leads the way to Lake Superior. The channel is bounded on the south side by Manitoulin Island.

We can approach the island by going south from the main highway at Espanola, a modest town located by a falls on the local river and the site of a large fine-paper plant. It has ample accommodations for visitors and some very nice restaurants. This is typical of the many towns we will encounter across Northern Ontario. Pulp, paper and lumber plants located by local rivers that run into the Great Lakes define the population patterns here.

There are a couple of highway signs to inform tourists here. One acknowledges that the channel we cross to get to the island is on the Route of the Voyageurs, as we have discussed earlier. The other notes that Espanola is the *Home of Ringette*. What can I say?

The road to Manitoulin Island winds its way through rocky outcrops and marshy forest lands. The channel is crossed via a narrow one-way bridge that swings open for a while every hour to let boats pass. We can sense, instinctively, that the pace of life here will be calming and peaceful.

The island itself has rolling hills, farmland, light forest, many lakes and numerous small villages. There are quite a few arts and crafts stores, many linked to the Ojibwe population and culture of the area. Tourist cottages, lodges and campgrounds abound, as do marinas and beaches.

The island can also be reached by ferry from the Bruce Peninsula, which protrudes out of southern Ontario and divides the main body of Lake Huron from Georgian Bay. The ferry is named M.S. Chi-Cheemaun, or "Big Canoe" in Ojibwe.

A bay on the west end of the island is named Misery Bay. It is the site of a large Nature Reserve that is partially supported by donations from individuals and corporations. The brochures that solicit support use the catchy phrase "Misery Loves Company."

Okay, I have a puzzler for you. When we are here, we learn that Manitoulin is the largest island in the world that is located in a freshwater lake. We also then learn that Lake Manitou, which is in the middle of the island, is the world's largest lake in a freshwater island. There are some islands in Lake Manitou. So, is one of them the largest island in a lake in an island in a freshwater lake in the world? It isn't necessarily so; there might be a smaller main island with a smaller lake, but a larger interior island. The islands in Lake Manitou are not very big. No one I asked knew the answer. In fact, I think they thought that I was a little weird to even ask the question.

Anyway, let's return to the mainland and head west again along the North Channel of Lake Huron. There are quite a few scattered towns, again usually at the outlets of rivers that flow into the big lake from the interior highlands, often via a small local bay. The tiny village of Massey, inexplicably, has a traffic light on the highway, probably practicing for the day when it will be the size of Calgary. I'll explain later.

Forestry, mining and tourism sustain the economy. For example, the town of Blind River, which calls itself the *Heart of the North Channel*, is a lumbering and uranium processing centre, as well as a base for visitors.

Some 30 kilometers inland from the North Channel is the small city of Elliot Lake, the site of major uranium mining operations for decades. Although the mines are now closed, there is an extensive museum that describes the industry and its history. The area is quite impressive, with the lakes and forest and all of the recreational activities that are associated with the North Country: camping, canoeing, fishing, hunting, hiking, boating, biking, snowmobiling, and cross-country skiing. I seem to repeat that a lot, but that's the way it is in the north. Just think CCFHHBBSS? I guess not. Of course, there is also today's ever-present golfing. Elliot Lake advertises itself as a place to retire and relocate, with many signs back along the main highway extolling its virtues. It might be a little remote for me on a year-round basis, but I can sure see its appeal on a seasonal or part-time basis.

Also of interest is that the main town building is the Lester B. Pearson Civic Centre. This reflects the fact that Lester Pearson, the former Prime Minister of Canada, was elected to Parliament from this area for years. He was a U. of T. and Oxford educated university professor who became a world-recognized diplomat and winner of the Nobel Prize for Peace before entering politics, a far-away world from Elliot Lake. But this reflects one of those quirks of Canadian election rules and practices. After he lost an election in his home constituency, he was subsequently elected here in a by-election. This is a safe Liberal area that became available when the incumbent MP resigned to make way for Pearson. You can be sure that the government processes rewarded this loyalty.

Sault Ste. Marie is located alongside the fast-churning rapids of the St. Mary's River, which is the link between Lake Huron and Lake Superior. It was first established in the 1600s and has a long history of explorers, fur traders, missionaries, military garrisons and industrial activity.

These rapids represent the last natural barrier to water travel from the St. Lawrence to Lake Superior. The first canal around the rapids was completed in 1895 and serves today as a national historic site. It has been upgraded over time and is still used for small recreational craft. Boat tours are available.

The modern canals here are, in effect, the final section of the St. Lawrence Seaway. There are four parallel locks of various sizes, designed to move the large volume of ship traffic that passes through. The locks of Sault St. Marie compete with the Panama Canal for most tonnage moved in a year, which is amazing when you realize that the system here is shut for many months in the winter.

There is a wide and extensive boardwalk along the river that attracts walkers, joggers and sightseers, with an adjacent path for bikers and roller-bladers. Plaques with historical descriptions, carvings and nearby museums dedicated to early settlers, ships, and bush planes make it a pleasant place for wandering. The local park and tent-covered, open-air pavilion is used for concerts, festivals, art exhibits and the like. It is named for Dr. Roberta Bondar, the medical researcher and environmental scientist who was the first Canadian woman to travel in space.

A large shopping centre, called the Station Mall, is nearby. This is the site of the old railway station for the Algoma Central Railway. This rail line was constructed at the start of the twentieth century to access the lumber and mining resources inland. Although it has limited commercial use now, it provides the opportunity for tourist travel into the rugged interior, both on day trips and overnight excursions that travel 500 kilometers from The Sault. It travels past picturesque lakes and rivers and spectacular deep canyons with cascading waterfalls.

As at Sarnia, Windsor, St. Catherines and along the St. Lawrence River, there is a very high bridge across the river here that allows the lake freighters to pass under without delay. In this case it connects to Michigan and could provide a shorter route west, south of Lake Superior. As before, that's not for us. North of Superior is our route; it's 750 kilometers from here to Thunder Bay.

About 50 kilometers north of The Sault we come to Batchawana Bay and our first sighting of the big lake. It seems overwhelming, and feels special, to look out at the vast expanse. This can only come about because of a prior knowledge of the lake and its legends. We have seen other lakes on our trip that are too wide to see across, have wind-blown whitecaps parading across the surface, and that create a noisy roar from the waves breaking on their rocky shores. Somehow this is different. You want to scan the far horizon, even more so if it's rainy and foggy, staring through the mist and searching for the *Edmund Fitzgerald*. We can sense Gordon Lightfoot peering over our shoulders.

Lake Superior is the largest freshwater lake in the world, covering over 82,000 square kilometers. There are only four lakes in the world, including Lake Huron and Lake Michigan, which are even half as large.

There is one body of water that is classified as a lake which is almost five times larger than Superior, the Caspian Sea. Located in southwest Asia, its water is brackish, not fresh, due to the presence of natural salts. However, being located well inland from the open oceans, it is categorized by geographers as a lake. This contrasts to the Black Sea, which is larger again, but which connects to the ocean via the Bosporus, the Dardanelles, and the Mediterranean Sea. Therefore, the Black Sea is not a lake, but a sea, like the Red Sea, the Caribbean Sea, The Gulf of Mexico and Hudson Bay. In recent years the decision about the classification of the Caspian Sea has become more political than scientific. There are large deposits of oil under the Caspian Sea, which is bordered by five different countries. The rules for dividing resources between bordering countries are different for seas and lakes. Thus, we have the dilemma and the debate. If the "sea goers" rather than the "lakers" have their way, which seems to be happening politically, then it seems to me that Superior becomes the largest lake, period. I don't expect this headline will become the fast-breaking news item on our local TV station's evening report anytime soon. So, with that, let's get back to our trip around Superior.

The road along here varies from hugging the rocky shore to venturing inland through the rugged terrain. There are many high lookouts over spectacular views. At times, there are extensive provincial parks that preserve the natural beauty and provide campgrounds and cleared beaches. In Lake Superior Provincial Park there is a bay called Old Woman Bay and nearby are lakes called Mom, Dad and Baby. I suspect the former has some meaning in history and the latter reflects an explorer or park official with a sense of humour.

Old Woman Bay is also the outlet for the Michipicoten River, which represents the southern end of the canoe route from Lake Superior to James Bay that was first established in the 1700s by the Hudson's Bay Company. Connecting to the Missinaibi and Moose Rivers via portages, it became a major route for the fur traders. Today it appeals to the adventurers who love to canoe and camp in the wilderness. The total trip is not for the faint-hearted, as the total distance is well over 500 kilometers, one way. I wish you well if you decide to try it.

At times along the highway, there are Trading Posts that carry goods made by the local Indian communities. Some of the stores are very elaborate and carry a wide range of quality goods. Usually fur pelts – fox, wolf, and rabbit — are hanging out front, very soft to the feel. I never saw a beaver pelt although that would be interesting, as it represents a huge part of the early history of the country. We can also find carvings, beaded leather goods, stone and glass creations, sweaters and blankets, and homemade candies and baked goods. Somehow, there is a natural justice in the Indians selling pricey beads and blankets to the tourists.

Wawa is an interesting town, set on a small lake slightly inland from Superior. The name means "wild goose" in Ojibwe, which refers to the large flights of migrating geese that pass through the area every year. There are quite a few large replicas of geese throughout the town, which are eye-catching and somewhat attractive. One of the motels in town is called *The Big Bird Inn*. Founded in 1898, Wawa was the site of one of the earliest hematite, i.e., iron ore, mines in the North Country. It has been closed for a few years now, but it was part of the driving force for the Algoma Central Railway that we visited in The Sault.

Next we come to the small village of White River that boasts (?) that it once recorded the lowest temperature in Canada, -57⁰C or -72⁰F. Now that's cold, even for a guy from Winnipeg! (Since then there has been a colder record set in the Yukon.)

Along here we also pass a large mining operation. If the names on the signs — Hemlo, Barrick, Tech — don't clue us in that this is gold country, then perhaps the street called The Yellow Brick Road will. Also, there is the Gold Field Campground to be sure we get the picture.

Marathon is a pleasant surprise on Lake Superior just off the highway via a tree-lined parkway. A large pulp plant and the regional mining industry provide the economic base, as expected everywhere up here. The lakefront is a driftwood-filled beach of round, weathered pebbles, with a view across the lake to the far horizon. As the regional centre, it has a wide range of facilities: arena, library, hospital, shopping mall, industrial suppliers, auto and RV sales, golf course and a small airport.

I stayed at a pleasant motel and had a nice dinner at a local steak house last time I passed through. The restaurant was relatively quiet, and I was alone, so I could not help but overhear an extensive conversation that was taking place at the next table. Four fellows were talking about various jobs and duties at the local plant in some detail. It became obvious that they were preparing themselves for negotiations the next day. There was a lot of to and fro about the relative importance of certain factors, and how to best present the opinions. I was quite fascinated, given my background in industrial operations. What was most interesting to me, however, was that even when I left I could not decide if they were union or management representatives. The setting and byplay suggested that a couple of them were visiting labour advisors, but for which side?

This is a good story to tell people who like to discuss business in public places. You never know who might be listening. During my career in the oil business I was always amazed at how many exploration maps and reports one could easily see on an airplane flight from Calgary to Toronto, as exploration executives were preparing their presentations for eastern bankers. It always pays to keep your ears and eyes open, and your mouth and books shut.

Our drive west continues through very spectacular scenery. There are a number of high cliffs and deep gorges that we pass. At one point we can see some large islands offshore. My maps show that some of the islands have interior lakes, but their scale cannot resolve if there are islands in those lakes; you never know. I will have to check that out someday.

We next encounter a string of elaborate signboards that tell us we are in amethyst country, and that we can stop at a local mine to gather a specimen of our own. We can also obtain them from the trading posts. These semi-precious, coloured crystals are pretty, and they have mystical powers for many people. Amethysts have been used as jewelry since the times of the ancient Greeks and Egyptians and have been the subject of many legends, including ones of the native groups that live around here. They all relate to supernatural phenomena.

As we approach Thunder Bay, there is a special memorial monument to Terry Fox. It is set on a hilltop that looks over the lake and marks the point at which he ended his remarkable journey. I think we all know the story of the brave and determined 23-year-old with cancer who ran more than 5000 kilometers on his artificial leg from Newfoundland to this point in his quest to travel across Canada, raising money and awareness for cancer research. Although he died before he could complete the journey, he became a hero to us all. Terry Fox Runs are held every year in many communities to support his cause. In the spirit of Terry, to "run" can mean everything from a slow walk or a wheelchair push to a marathon race. He left a great legacy. The memorial at this spot is well done, with a statue that effectively captures his distinctive hopping gait.

Thunder Bay has a strong physical presence. It is here that the Great Lakes freighters connect with the inland railways. The harbour is extensive, lined with wharves, warehouses, storage tanks and elevators, all serviced with heavy booms and cranes. There is an amazing network of railway sorting-yards and sidings spread out everywhere. Grain, lumber, minerals and manufactured goods from inland are loaded for the world markets. To the interior come all manner of commodities and equipment. All of this makes Thunder Bay Canada's third largest port.

I know that the image I have always had of this area is of the massive grain elevators at the shoreline, with the golden harvest from the prairies flowing into the holds of the large, low-slung ships. There is storage capacity here for over 100 million bushels of grain.

I grew up with the popular name for the area being "The Lakehead," although, officially, it was two distinct cities of Ft. William and Port Arthur. A few years ago, the decision was made to consolidate the two cities and a vote was held to determine its name. Believe it or not, there were three names on the ballot: Lakehead, The Lakehead and Thunder Bay. Although Thunder Bay received fewer than half the votes, it was the winner, since the other two options split the rest of the votes relatively evenly. It is hard to believe that the inability to resolve the word "The" decided the outcome.

In discussions with locals you often hear the sentiment that the result did not satisfy a lot of the people, but it doesn't matter. They still refer to the different areas as Ft. William and Port Arthur, and people continue to identify with one or the other.

With a population of over 100,000, Thunder Bay has all of the usual malls, shops and services, perhaps more so, since there is no other major centre for hundreds of kilometers. The marina and parkway along the harbour front are attractive and a local hilltop vantage point allows for a great view of the area and the activity. The downtown area itself is fairly modest; I suspect that's a reflection of the fact that this was two separate smaller cities before.

On the outskirts of the city, along the Kaministiquia River, is a full scale reproduction of old Fort William, one of my favourite historical reenactment sites. On this trip so far, we have seen replicas of military forts, such as Louisbourg, and of old settlements, such as Caraquet and Upper Canada Village. Here we have the site of one of the largest fur-trading posts.

The original fort was constructed by the North West Company in the very early 1800s as a keystone location for their fur-trading empire that was competing with the Hudson's Bay Company. This is where the large cargo canoes from Montreal arrived each summer, laden with provisions and trade goods for dealing with the natives. They had made the journey we have been observing on our trip: up the Ottawa River, across the connection to Georgian Bay via the local rivers and Lake Nipissing, and then through the North Channel and up the long expanse of Lake Superior. The fur traders would arrive from the other direction, the interior of the continent, in their smaller river canoes filled with the furs from the past winter's trading activities.

The two disparate groups would rendezvous and make the exchange of goods, all under the control of the company officials at the fort. Both groups could then make their return trips before winter set in. This very efficient logistical arrangement meant that the turnaround of trade goods for furs could happen in one summer season, thus providing a very advantageous benefit compared to their commercial competitors.

The replica fort is impressive. Set beside a long plank dock along the river, the log-walled fort has more than forty buildings that duplicate the functions of the originals. This includes barracks, managers' homes, meeting halls, store rooms, shops, accounting offices and even a gaol (that's "jail" today). During the summer, as is the case at most historical sites, the staff plays out the roles of the various groups that came here — company men, tradesmen, settlers, Indians, voyageurs and fur traders — including their arrival in birch bark canoes.

There is a information centre at the fort, as well as many interpretive displays throughout the area. This includes the explanations of how natural materials were used by the native inhabitants. Ash wood, being strong and supple, became the frames for snowshoes and toboggans. Birch bark sheets were joined with tree saps and gums to form canoes, tents and even utensils. Canoes and snowshoes were Native American creations that became critical to the success of the European explorers and traders. The Ojibwe word for birch bark is *wigwas*, which became interpreted as wigwam for the bark-covered teepees.

From here, we continue west and inland from the big lake, traveling another 500 kilometers of serene TRRLPAM toward Lake of the Woods. There are a few towns and villages along the way, the most significant being Dryden, located on a local lake, right beside the railway mainline and the highway. Large pulp, paper and lumber operations are the core industries of the town. As with most of the towns of the northern woods, the air is filled with that pungent but sweet smell of the process chemicals. There is a long covered walkway over the highway and railway tracks that allows folks to safely travel from the residential areas on the north side to the town centre and large plants on the south side, a unique structure for a small community.

I have already commented on highway designs and driving habits in some of the other provinces. Here in Northern Ontario there is the wildest — I would say most dangerous — phenomenon I have ever seen. The trees tower up along the sides of the highway, such that we do not see long distances forward very often as the road winds through the woods. There are periodic side roads that go off to homes or cottages. As in most jurisdictions, every once in a while there is a third lane of the highway that provides for the passing of slower vehicles. All this is fine, except for those pesky side roads and signs that are posted saying, "Watch out for Stopped, Turning Vehicles in the Passing Lane." And so, can you imagine? You pull out to pass a slow vehicle, probably accelerating as you do so, and you round a corner to see a stopped vehicle in your lane! All I can say is that I use those passing lanes with great caution in the daytime and almost never at night. I guess the locals get used to it, at least those who survive.

The road signs indicate many hunting and fishing lodges in the area. Some advertise fly-in services to remote lakes by float-equipped bush planes. This is a sportsman's paradise.

That label applies to the Lake of the Woods, in spades. Tucked into the corner of the province, this large lake spills over at the edges into Manitoba and the U.S. state of Minnesota. In fact, it is the cause of that anomalous bump in the border between Canada and the United States that protrudes above the 49th parallel.

The border between the countries was debated and disputed over many decades as the countries developed. Following the War of 1812-14, there were a number of treaties between Britain and the United States. In 1817, a treaty defined the U.S.–Canadian border through what is now Ontario by the waterways. Thus, the border cuts down the middle of the St. Lawrence River in eastern Ontario, bisects Lake Ontario, Lake Erie, Lake Huron, Lake Superior and the rivers that connect them, and then follows the chain of rivers and small lakes west from the shore of Lake Superior to Lake of the Woods. That entire border, to the eastern side of Lake of the Woods, is south of the 49th parallel. In 1818, it was agreed that the border from The Lake of the Woods to the Rocky Mountains would be the 49th parallel. The anomaly occurs because the border through the Lake of the Woods, which traverses the lake based on the location of the major islands as was done back east, actually goes north of the 49th parallel before it reaches the west shore. The border then goes south, to join up with the western line at the 49th parallel. Therefore, Minnesota ends up with a small protrusion, about forty kilometers square, which is the farthest-north piece of the U.S. except for Alaska.

The Lake of the Woods is actually misnamed. The lake contains more than 14,000 islands and was called Lake of the Islands by the Ojibwe. A bad translation by an early explorer created the name we use today. And, yes, some of the islands have lakes, but...?

This is definitely vacation country. Cottages, lodges, resorts, hotels, B&Bs and campgrounds are everywhere along the shoreline and on the islands. With all of the islands taken into account, there are over 100,000 kilometers of shoreline. The facilities on the islands can be reached by canoe, boat, ferry, water-taxi or float-plane, depending on the location and your preference. A snowmobile or an ATV is required if you want to visit them in the winter.

Kenora is the main city on the lake. It has 15,000 inhabitants, but it feels like it's twice that in the summer tourist season, when it is a beehive of activity. The area is popular with visitors from everywhere, and it is particularly accessible for people from the midwest United States, as it is not blocked off to them by the Great Lakes.

The surrounding terrain is fairly hilly, so there are many buildings, homes and vantage points that have panoramic views. A close-up view of the area is best seen from one of the lake cruise boats, a particularly nice experience at sunset.

In the downtown area itself, the city hall is a striking building of red brick and white stone with a distinctive clock tower. As with a number of places, there are large murals on the sides of downtown buildings that depict local and historic events. They are always interesting and informative. How else would I know that the Kenora Thistles were the Stanley Cup Champions in 1907? Lord Stanley's silverware was competed for by amateur teams on a challenge basis in those years. The story of their victory is a complex and controversial one, but I will leave the details for visitors to discover on their own. Suffice to say, they held the cup for only two months. It was not until 1926 that the NHL assumed permanent control of the trophy.

In a park on the waterfront is a twelve meter long statue of a fish, "Husky the Muskie." This was designed to recognize the importance and attraction of the recreational fishing business here. The lake has a wide range of fish including the desirable walleye, bass and lake trout, and the skinny-boney northern pike, otherwise known as a *jackfish* to many of us. The king of the lake is the muskellunge, or more colloquially, the *muskie*, which can weigh over 25 kilograms. This is the prize catch for many anglers and, thus, the reason for the monument.

West we go again, winding through rugged rock-cuts in the rolling forested landscape and passing many beaver lodges in marshy wetlands. Ontario has been fascinating in its size and tremendous variety of sights.

Now we have reached the Manitoba border, and it's time to visit the province of my birth.

Manitoba

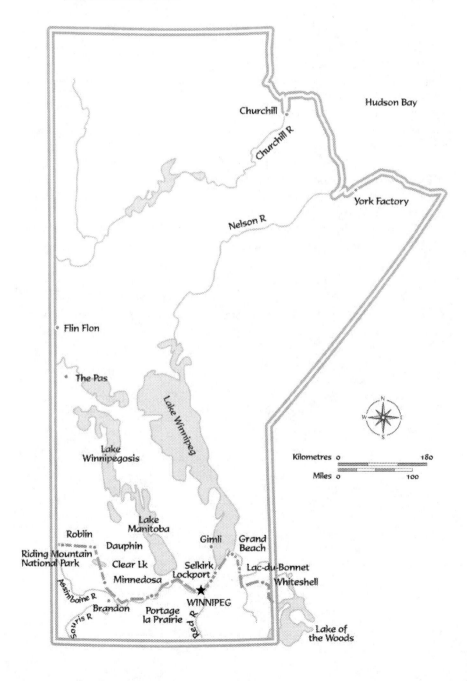

Hudson Bay

Churchill

Churchill R

York Factory

Nelson R

Flin Flon

The Pas

Lake Winnipeg

Lake Winnipegosis

Lake Manitoba

Roblin

Dauphin

Gimli

Grand Beach

Riding Mountain National Park

Clear Lk

Selkirk

Lac-du-Bonnet

Minnedosa

Lockport

Whiteshell

Assiniboine R

WINNIPEG

Brandon

Portage la Prairie

Red R

Souris R

Lake of the Woods

Kilometres 0   180

Miles 0   100

7. Manitoba

The start of Manitoba looks a lot like the end of Ontario; this is no surprise since we are still in the Canadian Shield and TRRLPAM still dominates.

The first attraction we encounter is a series of three lakes, West Hawk, Falcon and Caddy, which are well-established vacation areas with beaches, water facilities, shops, accommodations and cottages for visitors. The vacationers are predominantly from Winnipeg, which is not much more than an hour away on the four-lane, divided highway that has now materialized.

However, we are going to take a bit of a side trip and go north on a narrow, two-lane road that traverses the Whiteshell Provincial Park. This route will pass by quite a few modest-sized lakes that are generally populated with private cottages, tourist cabins, campgrounds and boat launching ramps. A series of the lakes are called the Seven Sisters, having names such as Eleanor, Dorothy and Betula.

The lake that most interests me is Jessica, as I have a personal history with it. I have mentioned that I was born and raised in Winnipeg. When I was a youngster, my parents started to spend time in this area on weekends and holidays. In the early 1950s they bought a lot on Jessica and built a small cabin.

It was quite an adventure. With the help of my brother and me, aged about six and nine at the time, they carved a path some distance through the woods from the local gravel road to the lake shore, and erected the cabin on a large granite outcrop that rose more than ten meters above the waterline. It was great fun in the wilderness. At that time there was hardly another cottage on the lake, and certainly none in our line of sight.

Things were simpler and more straightforward in those days. For example, when my father needed to eliminate some large boulders in the way of the road that he was building, he just obtained some dynamite and blew them away.

This was also when we started our education about Mother Nature's forces, in particular, the force of ice on docks. We started with a wooden crib in the water that was filled with rocks and covered with a plank top-deck. It did not have a chance when the ice broke free in the spring and tore it to shreds. Then came a series of floating docks. They were removable in the fall but it generally required a small army to do the job, with the heavy frame and awkward metal drums to handle.

In fact, during my father's career, as he moved from Winnipeg to Peterborough, to Calgary, to Ottawa and to Edmonton, he always had a lakeside cottage in the woods somewhere, and he was always experimenting with docks. His final solution was to get a series of telescoping stands that could be set on the lake-bottom. These were coupled with pre-built sections of top deck that could be floated out and set on those stands. It was relatively easy to put out each spring and take in each fall.

When I stopped by Jessica Lake recently, not having seen it in 45 years, I observed that the current system there is to build a dock that is anchored to the rocky shore. They lever it up into the air, away from the ice for the winter, by means of a motor that drives cables and winches. Of course, it helps to have electricity, a luxury we did not have there in the early 1950s.

There was no television reception back in the woods then, but we had battery-powered radios. One morning, all the talk on the radio station seemed to be about something called *Elvis Presley* and the antics that had occurred on Ed Sullivan's show the night before. We did not have any idea what they were talking about. Obviously, that all changed quickly.

The area is less changed from the past than I expected. Yes, there are more cottages, electricity and better roads, but the area is still rustic and remote. It was very relaxing to walk through the woods and smell the pine forest, see the ferns and tiger lilies in the undergrowth, pass ponds with reeds and lily pads, listen to the birds and frogs, and climb up the rocky outcrops to look across the forest-enclosed lake.

I could picture myself in my youth, drifting in a canoe through the reeds and grasses along the lakeshore, trying to catch a fish or attempting to gather some wild rice. Almost all the fish I caught were northern pike or jackfish, which are a bit of a hassle to eat since they tend to be very slender and they have an extra row of bones along each side. The hope was always to catch something tastier, like a pickerel, or something more exotic looking, like a perch. That didn't happen often.

The other characteristic of these lakes, something less pleasant, is that they are full of leeches. When you go swimming it is quite likely that you will end up with one of these bloodsuckers stuck on you somewhere. They are quite harmless, but very ugly to look at; they are slimy and black, sometimes with subtle coloured stripes or spots. I never did learn to swim well or to really like going in the water – all due to my early experiences with them, I am sure. Yet we all know that leaches have been beneficially used over the centuries to draw out blood, and that modern medicine still uses them in certain situations to help heal surgical wounds.

On the river that flows out of the lake are a series of shallow rapids and a waterfall, Rainbow Falls. It is basically a rocky outcrop that the water flows over before dumping into a swirling pool below. Again, I recalled playing there as a child, but I must admit that the scale had grown in my memory. The falls are only two meters high.

I think that standing here in the woods beside a quiet river in eastern Manitoba is probably a good place to talk about the birds and the animals.

Our national symbol is the beaver. This impressive rodent is a decent choice, in that it was the backbone of the country's economy for a long time. It was the driving force that stimulated much of the early exploration; it symbolizes hard work by example; and it can be found in almost every part of the land. Personally, my first instincts would have been to pick something more majestic, such as the moose, the prairie bison, the grizzly bear or the northern polar bear. My preference is probably also influenced by my past battles with a beaver colony in a relatively futile attempt to protect trees around a cottage in the woods from their incessant foraging.

As to birds, there are so many interesting species. The impressive Canada goose is "ours." Mallards and cranes and puffins are so colourful. Blue Jays are our symbol for baseball. Hawks and eagles are awesome as they float in the sky and then dive for prey. But the symbol we have chosen is the loon. It is a great bird, not just for its looks, but also for its sound. There is nothing more distinctive than the long, low call of a loon as it carries across a lake at sunset. It is both the sound of the wild and the sound of nature's peaceful harmony.

Don't you love the look on visitors' faces when they realize that we call our one-dollar coin a *loonie*? Even when you point out the picture of the loon on the face of the coin, they are skeptical. Then they just think we really are loony.

The story of the coin is a bit strange, to be sure. The original plan was for a different design, an image of fur traders in a large voyageur canoe. However, in 1987 one of the original forming dies for the new one-dollar coin was misplaced en-route to the mint in Winnipeg, and so, to avoid any possibility of it resulting in counterfeiting, they reverted to the backup design, the loon. The experts had no idea that this would lead to our money being labeled "loonie." Do you think our money might have been called a "canoe" or a "furry" if the change had not occurred? I doubt it – we probably would have just called it a dollar, although, when its value fell to 60 cents U.S., I often heard it called the Canadian peso.

When the two-dollar coin was issued, there were many attempts to give it a name based on the polar bear figure in its centre insert, but they were all doomed to failure. What could possibly go with *loonie* other than *twonie*? Th..th..th..that's all folks!

Now, if we were to really honour the one creature that is everywhere, impacts everyone, and probably stimulates the most conversations, we would have only one choice: the mosquito.

Mosquitoes are legendary in Manitoba, but I must say that stories of people being carried off by swarms of them have never been verified. In fact, such tales are probably based on people jumping off cliffs on their own volition, just trying to avoid them.

Research into mosquitoes has discovered many things. There are probably 100 trillion of them at any time, and they are truly everywhere. They kill more people than any other animal by transmitting diseases such as malaria, yellow fever, encephalitis, dengue fever and, now, West Nile fever. And, worst of all, malaria has become immune to quinine, and thus drinking gin-and-tonic will not prevent it.

There is no documented figure that I could find for the number of people who have been driven insane by the sound of a mosquito in a tent or bedroom in the middle of the night, but it must be significant.

As we continue our trip past the various lakes, cottages and campgrounds, one cottage stands out along the route; it is painted like a Hudson's Bay Company blanket! It has horizontal bands of colour, each a few feet wide: blue, yellow, red and green. I hope it's more sedate inside.

Farther into the park, we come to the Seven Sisters Falls, site of a hydro-electric power plant and the nearby Whiteshell nuclear research station. From here, the Winnipeg River leads us past the beach and vacation town of Lac Du Bonnet and on to Lake Winnipeg.

Lake Winnipeg is about one-third larger than Lake Ontario, to give it some perspective. It also has maybe one-one-thousandth of the number of people living near it, and that might be an exaggeration.

There are extensive beaches along the lake that are summertime destinations for many vacationers. The largest and best known is Grand Beach, with its wide white-sand shore, nearby dunes and local marshes and lagoons to explore. A wide boardwalk conjures up the days of decades ago when it was a party destination, with dance halls, shops and a large carousel on the beach. Then, it could only be reached by train. I can recall family train trips and cottages by the beach that we visited in the late 1940s. I have images of the trains being so crowded that we sat on our suitcases in the middle of the aisles. Times have changed, of course. Now the area is accessible by paved roads and the activities are similar to every other modern lakeside vacation spot.

Fishing in Lake Winnipeg, and in many of the other lakes and rivers of northern Manitoba, is often targeted on catching a goldeye. These relatively small fish, perhaps a foot in length, with their deep, flat bodies and blunt heads are absolutely delicious, especially when smoked first to a golden tone.

The town of Selkirk, about 10,000 strong, is a commercial centre located on the Red River near where it enters the south end of the lake. It is a typical small western town, with low frame buildings on the main street and perpendicular parking. It identifies itself as the *Gateway to the Interlake Region*, which refers to the interior neck of land between Lake Winnipeg on the east and Lakes Manitoba and Winnipegosis on the west.

The focus of the town is on the river and on fishing. There is a big statue of a catfish, Chuck the Channel Catfish, to make the point. There is also a maritime museum that displays a range of old fishing boats and pleasure craft, including a lake cruise ship built in the late 1800s. Often we can see dozens of small fishing boats out in the river near here, all hoping to land that big catfish, some of which weigh over 10 kilograms.

Here, and at many other places in the Red River valley, there are replicas of that unique transportation creation of the early settlers, the Red River Cart, a two-wheeled flat-bed cart with open-stake side rails and long pole-yokes for connecting up with an ox. Such a big animal was required to haul it along the rutted roads and through the gumbo that can suck your boots off when it rains. Every story about the Red River Cart mentions the noise it made, a high pitched squeal that would continue incessantly and carry for miles across the prairies. This was because the wheels and axels were made of wood, and they did not use any greases or oils for lubrication. Those things would have just gummed up the works when contaminated with the prairie dust.

A side road back north from here would take us to the Interlake country. Up there are additional developed beaches on the west side of Lake Winnipeg and the town of Gimli. The town attracted some headlines in 1983 when an Air Canada Boeing 767 passenger jet had to make an emergency landing; it ran out of fuel. It had a flight plan for Montreal to Edmonton, but it had not taken on enough fuel before departing. This was around the time that Canada switched to the metric system and, somehow, the pilots confused liters with gallons when ordering fuel.

Just south of Selkirk is the stone-walled fur-trading post of Lower Fort Garry. There are many restored buildings, historical displays and costumed staff to re-enact the times of the mid-1800s.

Lockport, just a bit farther south, sits beside a wide dam with a boat lock to allow transit around the natural rapids that exist here. It was built in 1910. There is a family entertainment centre here with waterslides and miniature golf, but I think that it has been built just to give people from the area an excuse to come and buy one of the famous hot dogs.

The hot dog shop has been here for decades, I think since the 1920s. They have created a fad around their foot-long hot dogs; I remember our family driving out from Winnipeg for them on weekend afternoons in the '40s. The store is a throw-back to another time: vinyl booths, Formica tables, a juke box, and walls covered with old sports photos. They are still in business and we will definitely stop for a "foot-long" as we drive through.

Now we are approaching Winnipeg, capital of Manitoba, *Gateway to Western Canada*, and my hometown, although I left here more than 45 years ago and have been back only fleetingly over the years.

I will admit that one of the very pleasant surprises for me on the recent cross-country trip was to tour around Winnipeg and to see how it has developed over the years. I knew that it had not grown much and that the economy had been mixed for decades, and so I anticipated it would be old, and perhaps showing signs of depression. Far from it!

To start with, Winnipeg has a good natural setting at the juncture of the Red and Assiniboine Rivers. The city planners have allowed for significant parkland in the city, highlighted by the vast Assiniboine Park in the west end. The open spaces, large tree-filled meadows, beautiful gardens, a conservatory, sports fields, walks along the river and a fascinating zoo make this one of the best parks in all of Canada.

The rivers provide entertainment opportunities, such as boating and fishing. They also provide attractive sites for residential developments, from the old established inner-city bastions of River Heights and Tuxedo to the modern sprawling homes on acreages along the Red River, north of the city.

The Red and Assiniboine, Portage and Main: those are the identifying labels for Winnipeg. Portage Avenue is the very wide main street that, in effect, runs forever west as it becomes the highway to the prairies. The corner of Portage and Main has been called the windiest and coldest corner in Canada; my recollections from childhood certainly would not dispel that notion. *Winterpeg* is often used by others to describe the city, denied by the locals only with a sort of resigned shrug or a slight grimace.

The commercial stores of Portage Avenue, and downtown in general, are undergoing a renewal. There are covered pedestrian walkways over the street to attract shoppers to the new concourses on the north side, which has always been somewhat the forgotten half.

One sight that generates nostalgia is the renewal of the old Eaton's department store site into an arena. For a long time it seemed that Eaton's was Winnipeg, with its large store and equally large mail-order processing centre. It was claimed, back some fifty years ago, that there was someone in half the families of Winnipeg who worked for Eaton's and that something like seventy-five percent of the city's retail sales occurred there. I know that my mother worked there for a period, as did I in my early high school years. Those figures may have been exaggerated, but not by much. Of course, Eaton's is now history, replaced by specialty shops and big-box stores.

The city has developed a good network of inner-city roads and bypass highways that make getting around the city relatively easy. It is straightforward to search out locations that have meaning for me: the homes we lived in, the schools I attended, the golf club and curling rink where I first learned those games, the dikes that were built at the time of the big flood of 1950, the first A&W Drive-In in the country that seemed to be such a novelty in the '50s, and so on. It is fun to reminisce.

The city has many tree-lined boulevards. The towering oak and elm trees, with their large, spreading branches that overhang the avenues and sidewalks, are impressive. We will not see such a sight again for many miles as we cross the prairies.

A historical marketplace development called The Forks is located at the junction of the Red and Assiniboine Rivers, in behind the tall office buildings and large railway station of the city centre and beneath a labyrinth of bridges. There are many interesting shops, arts and crafts galleries, upscale merchants and an assortment of restaurants. There is a tall observation tower in the centre, as well as many historical markers throughout. The décor of the main building is of an old-fashioned railway station and the courtyard of the area is filled with old railway cars. Tour boats, canoes and paddle boats are available for sightseeing and relaxation. It is a quaint and picturesque corner, tucked away from the busy city streets nearby.

There is even a walkway that follows the river's edge, which can lead us to the impressive stone-block provincial legislature and back into the heart of downtown. The statue of Golden Boy sits atop the legislature. It is over five meters tall and depicts a young man holding a torch and a sheaf of wheat, symbolic of the early commerce and the vision of future for the region. It was cast in France before World War I, but was stranded at sea for years during the war as the cargo ship carrying it was diverted to wartime duty. What makes it stand out so much to the observer is its shiny, reflective, gold colour; it is sheathed in 24-carat gold.

Winnipeg has a strong sense of history. It has been at the crossroads of the exploration and settlement of western Canada ever since the first Europeans ventured into the area.

The first significant presence of Europeans in the west came with the formation of the Hudson's Bay Company in 1670, with its English charter and its claim to all the lands that drain into Hudson Bay. Yes, the spellings are right. The bay was originally called Hudson's Bay, but, in later years, geographers decided that features could not be named after people in the possessive form. The company had started with the original name and has stayed with it.

In reality, the Hudson's Bay Company traders did not venture inland very much over the next century, but, instead, they established trading posts on the northern coast and dealt with the Indian groups that brought the furs to them.

In the late 1730s and early 1740s a French-Canadian trader and adventurer from Montreal, Pierre Gaultier de la Vérendrye, and his sons headed west to establish a series of fur trading posts. They included a post on the Lake of the Woods and Fort Rouge at the juncture of the Red and Assiniboine Rivers. They continued to explore farther west, seeing the Rocky Mountains for the first time, and claiming the whole area for France; this claim never came to mean anything.

Although those early ventures did not lead to permanent settlements, they did blaze the way for later adventurers. In 1779, to compete with the HBC, the North West Company was formed by Scottish and American merchants based in Montreal, utilizing the French traders who had ventured into the west before. Their *voyageurs* soon appeared in the Red River area.

In the early 1800s Lord Selkirk of the HBC received land grants for the Red River area and this led to the first arrival of British, mostly Scottish, settlers in the region.

In the period 1815-16 there were actual battles between the Hudson's Bay and North West traders, but this subsided over time and disappeared when the two companies merged into the "new" Hudson's Bay Company in 1821. After that time, there was a large increase in the numbers of settlers arriving.

This changing dynamic created tension between those who had been here first and the newcomers, who were arriving to settle and to farm.

The first group of hunters, trappers and traders was further divided between those of English heritage and those of French heritage, with their different languages and religions. These groups were called Métis, that is "mixed," as they dominantly consisted of the offspring of European adventurers and their Indian wives.

These groups, the Métis and the newcomers, had an uneasy relationship over the ensuing decades, and, in fact, many of the Métis moved farther west, into what is now Saskatchewan. Even in the late 1860s, however, the French Métis were still the majority. But the settlers continued to come, including many from the United States, and farming was becoming more and more significant. Outside the fur-trading forts, a new village arose, Winnipeg, named from the Indian words *win*, meaning muddy, and *nipee*, meaning water.

By the 1860s there were many different forces at work in the North American scene. In 1867 Canada had been formed out of the four colonies in the east. The United States had emerged from its Civil War and was expanding westward. It had railway and telegraph service to St. Paul, Minnesota, which actually was the primary route for travel from Canada to Winnipeg. The U.S. also purchased Alaska from Russia in 1867 and was interested in luring the British territories of the west, i.e., Winnipeg, the open prairies and the colony of British Columbia to join the Union.

From this situation arose one of the most confusing and emotional series of events in Canadian history: the Red River Revolt and the eventual forming of the province of Manitoba.

The catalyst for all of the problems was the decision in 1869 to have Canada buy the western territories from the Hudson's Bay Company. Actually, the legal process was more complicated, as this was done through the intermediary step of the British government taking control back from the HBC and then ceding it to Canada. That process took more than a year and created a period of uncertainty and turmoil.

The people who lived in the west did not accept that they were owned by the Hudson's Bay Company and could be sold to Canada without their involvement. They were loyal to Britain, but believed any agreement to join Canada should be negotiated, as it was done in all the other colonies. Remember, PEI and Newfoundland had decided not to become part of Canada at that time.

There was also the reality of the different priorities of the various groups: French Métis, English Métis, British settlers and American settlers. These differences all flared into serious confrontations, aided by the lack of any clear controlling authority. The main antagonists were the French Métis and a group of English settlers who supported a "Canadian Party."

Enter now our central hero/villain, Louis Riel. I will not do justice to this complex story; you need to read a good history book. With apologies to history purists, I will cover the highlights.

Riel was born in St. Boniface, across the river from Winnipeg, in 1844. He was the son of a Métis father and a French mother. This was a unique combination in those days, as the Métis were usually the result of relationships between European male traders and Indian women. His early education was in the local church, but, then, he went to college in Montreal and studied law for a period. After that, he worked in Chicago and St. Paul, but he had a strong sense of identity with the French Métis colony and shared their dreams of becoming a separate political identity.

He returned to the Red River Settlement in 1868. This was in the midst of bad economic times, due to a drought, and bad political times.

The confrontation with Canada started when a Dominion Land Survey party arrived to lay out the new territory that Canada was to acquire from the HBC; the deal had not yet closed. The survey ignored any holdings or alignments that the current settlers had established, which, naturally, incensed them. It also became known that Canada intended to appoint a new Governor and governing council without consulting the inhabitants. The settlers appointed Riel to lead their attempts at resolving the issues. Their desire and intent was to negotiate a "union" with Canada that would give them a local legislature and appointed officials, along with recognition of established land rights.

However, the frustrations, anxiety and different perspectives led to serious disagreements and armed confrontations. In late 1869 the French Métis took control of Fort Garry. They also jailed a number of members of the Canada Party, including their leaders and a hot-headed Irish malcontent named Thomas Scott. Some of these prisoners were later released. Others, including Scott, escaped and were recaptured, while others were held for months.

There is an oft-repeated story about Riel and his followers marching through the streets of Winnipeg at this time. The story seems to be true, but the image needs clarifying. Winnipeg was a tiny village with two streets, a few stores, some inns and a limited number of business offices. Most people lived on farms or closer to the trading forts.

Amid all this turmoil, including the arrival of the new Governor, the support of the rebels by the U.S., and continuing battles between the parties, Canada sent a group to negotiate with the colony. They tried to convey the good intentions of Canada, but it took months to discuss the issues; the colony had a long list of rights and guarantees that it wanted recognized.

In any case, by early 1870 they achieved an agreement-in-principle. The colony formed a government, with Riel as President, and they organized a delegation to send to Ottawa to finalize the deal. It seemed that they were going to achieve most of their goals as part of Canada, and Riel would go down in history as a "Father of Confederation." That latter sentiment was not to be.

Thomas Scott had escaped from jail and had organized a group of anti-Catholic, anti-Métis followers to attempt an attack on Fort Garry, in order to overthrow Riel and to kill him and his supporters. That failed and Scott was recaptured. After a trial by the Métis, he was executed by a firing squad. He had, unbelievably, refused to be banished to the U.S., vowing that he would return to fight again. Riel did not become involved in the legal process or intervene in the sentence of death.

This had two profound effects. The first was that it forced the Canadian government to recognize that they were dealing with a serious threat to their vision of western growth. Therefore, they rushed to close the agreement with the colony, even when new terms were added, such as immediate provincial status and ingrained rights for French language and education.

In May 1870 Manitoba became a province, although its original boundaries were limited. It was a small rectangle in what is now the southeast part of the province, giving rise to its early label as the *postage stamp province*. Later, when the boundaries were extended north to Hudson Bay, it was called the *keystone province*, reflecting its new shape and position in the centre of the country.

The second effect of the Thomas Scott execution was to make Riel into a villain for the English community and, through their lobbying, for the rest of Canada. Canada sent a military force to Manitoba later in 1870 to establish and maintain peace and to thwart any incursions by the Americans. Fearing that he was going to be imprisoned or killed, Riel fled to the U.S. The Canadian government was so happy to see him go away at that time that they sent him some money!

He periodically returned to the area after the furor died down, but not in any public way. Then, in the federal election of 1874, he was elected to Parliament by the residents of the Manitoba riding of Provencher. Although he knew he would not be able to take his seat in Parliament, he traveled to Ottawa and secretly registered at the House of Commons, an intrigue-filled visit. Then he left for the U.S. again.

In 1875 he was declared an outlaw and banished from Canada for five years. He settled in Montana, where he married and became a teacher. We will hear the rest of his story later on our trip, when we reach Saskatchewan.

Louis Riel's gravesite can be visited on the grounds of the St. Boniface Museum. His family home is also designated as a historical site. It includes information signs about the Métis and Riel.

As I said earlier, Winnipeg calls itself the *Gateway to the West*. That was true for the early fur traders and, later, for the settlers. Both of the national railways converge here, with their enormous marshalling yards, before they branch off in different paths across the western provinces. As happens at the Lakehead, everything passes this way, going east or west.

Recall that my grandparents arrived here from Scotland, via ship to Montreal and then a train to Winnipeg in 1913. That was only forty or so years after the creation of Manitoba and all of the events I just described. It's hard to imagine the drive and determination of all those early settlers. In my grandparents' case, they even went on to a small town for a few years before settling in Winnipeg. I am glad they did it, but I do not envy them the initial experience.

There is also an interesting journey to the north from here. Sitting in a bar in Winnipeg one evening, I struck up a conversation with a group of travelers who were going north to Churchill, on the shore of Hudson Bay, where there is a large colony of polar bears. Although the bears do wander into town and can become a nuisance, the town does advertise itself as the *Polar Bear Capital of the World*. There are more than 1000 bears in the area. The travelers were looking forward to seeing them and taking lots of photographs. It sounds interesting.

Being in the *Gateway to the West* and the *Keystone Province,* the residents here definitely think of themselves as "Westerners." They become a little upset, certainly frustrated, when folks from Alberta or British Columbia refer to Winnipeg as back east; that's reserved for Ontario and points east of there as far as they are concerned. On the other hand, the differentiation between Central Canada and Atlantic Canada, the true East, is not always made by the folks here in their descriptions either.

In fact, Winnipeg is just about dead-centre in Canada. Canada stretches across approximately 90^0 of latitude, east to west; it extends from about 52^0 W in the east to 142^0 W in the west. Winnipeg is at 97^0 W. It often looks farther west than being the central longitude of the country on many maps, depending on the projection format.

The biggest blow to the self-image of Winnipeggers as being western came when the Canadian Football League placed them in the Eastern Conference. This occurred when the league fell to eight teams, with those in Regina, Calgary, Edmonton and Vancouver being farther west. That was when the Montreal team folded for a while. The next stage was to expand, thus leading to Baltimore winning the Grey Cup. Once they figured out that Baltimore was not in Canada, and that U.S. fans did not want to bother deciphering the different rules, they resurrected the Montreal team and moved Winnipeg back west, to the relief of everyone. They also managed to end up with nine teams with nine different names; don't you kind of miss reading about a game between the Roughriders and the Rough Riders? I hope that the current rumblings about adding a team in Quebec City or Halifax pan out.

I have no tolerance for the debate over the "better" game, Canadian versus American: three versus four downs, eleven versus twelve players, small field versus large field, touchbacks versus single points and free catches versus no-yards penalties. They are both good, but different, games; leave it at that. Shall we debate North American football versus soccer, baseball versus cricket, hockey versus basketball, golf versus tennis, boxing versus wrestling, checkers versus chess, bridge versus poker, or figure skating versus gymnastics? And what would we compare singles synchronized swimming to? Singles ballroom dancing?

Last time I stayed in Winnipeg, I happened to have a hotel room that was relatively high and looked to the west. *Flat*, that's the only word to describe the view. It is hard for people who have not seen the prairies to appreciate just how flat it can be. There is nothing like it east of here. And it will go on for a thousand kilometers, westward to Calgary. It's vast and it's open.

It is also difficult to visualize the big floods that occur here periodically. When there is a fast melt of the winter snow and early spring rains, the rivers swell. The Red River flows north, out of the plains of North Dakota; the Assiniboine drains a region that stretches to Saskatchewan. The river banks are relatively low in many places and the land is flat for miles in every direction. Thus, you can get a flood area that covers thousands of square miles. This happened in 1950 and again in 1997. I can remember my father joining the sand-bag brigades in 1950, as they fought to control the waters. I'm sure most of us will recall the television photos of the huge spread of water across the land in 1997. That time, Winnipeg was an island of relative dryness, due to the canals and levees that had been built after the 1950 flood. The locals call the canal "Duff's Ditch," after Duff Roblin, who was the Premier of Manitoba when it was constructed.

However, even with these floods and with other major weather related events in Canada, winter and summer, we don't have the absolutely devastating events that occur in some other places such as earthquakes or the quadruple hurricane attack of Charley-Frances-Ivan-Jeanne on Florida in the fall of 2004. An extreme event, of course, was the tsunami that spread across the Indian Ocean on Boxing Day 2004, killing over 250,000 people and leaving millions homeless.

Now, let's leave the city and head west, out into the prairies. In these early stages, the flatness of the land is broken by groves of trees here and there.

The highway is straight, and I mean *straight*. We can travel for stretches that are scores of kilometers long without any deviation, and then it is only for a slight jog to cross a river or the railway tracks. The highways around Regina probably have longer straight stretches, but, if you are driving from the east, as we are, this section leaving Winnipeg is very noticeable. In some sections of highway on the prairies they actually build in curves, just to break the monotony for drivers and thus reduce accidents.

The main lines of the Canadian Pacific and Canadian National railways run west of Winnipeg, with the former destined for Regina and Calgary and the latter for Saskatoon and Edmonton, before they converge again in Kamloops, British Columbia. As we drive along the highway, we will frequently see the long trains surging across the prairies. They often have a singular purpose, such as hauling grain or minerals. The hundred-or-more similarly-shaped railway cars create the image of a living being, such as a caterpillar or a snake, moving steadily across the landscape.

The Trans-Canada Highway also branches across the prairies, taking routes parallel to the railways. It often comes as a surprise to some that the Trans-Canada is not a single highway. Back east, it branches into two routes to cover PEI and northern Nova Scotia and it becomes three separate routes in western Quebec and eastern Ontario. Thus, the TCH catches Rouyn, Quebec and Kapuskasing, Ontario, even though it does not divert to Halifax, Toronto or even to the north shore of the St. Lawrence River to catch Quebec City proper.

The first significant town we encounter is Portage La Prairie. It also has a long history. La Vérendrye established a trading post here in the 1730s. It became the overland transfer point for the trip from the Assiniboine River to Lake Manitoba, thus linking travel and commerce between the east and the north.

Today, it is a modest-size regional centre of commerce for the local farming communities. The grain fields run right to the town limits. One thing we immediately notice here is the farm implements dealers, or more specifically, the farm implements themselves. The tractors, combines, wagons, balers, seeders and sprayers all are of a scale we haven't seen back east. With farms and fields that are measured in terms of quarter sections, i.e., square areas that are a half mile on each side, large equipment is a necessity.

We also notice that in the rural areas the gasoline stations have pumps that are labeled "dyed gasoline" and "dyed diesel." This reflects the regulations in a number of provinces that fuel used for farm equipment does not incur the provincial gasoline tax, or road tax, as it is sometimes called. That latter label implies that the provincial government will actually use the money to fix the roads, a somewhat antiquated concept. In any case, the fuel for farm use is dyed purple. This allows the authorities to check the fuel in automobiles, snowmobiles, etc. to be sure the tax has not been avoided for those uses. I can recall as a child that my father would encounter check-stops along the highway, where the Mounties would sample gasoline from some of the vehicles. I haven't seen that in years, but perhaps it still happens on rural roads.

We now continue west towards Brandon. Inexplicably, there is a solitary traffic light on the Trans-Canada Highway ten kilometers west of Portage in the midst of open farmland. Perhaps this is part of the anti-boredom campaign for drivers.

At times, we can see large irrigation systems in the fields, usually very long, spidery, metal-tube constructions mounted on wheeled stands, which slowly creep across the fields spraying water from their many nozzles. Often these are in areas where vegetables are being grown. A sign near the town of Carberry declares this as *King Spud Country*.

There is also a sign that advertises a Bull Test Station. I do not know what that means; it does give our imagination something to contemplate as we motor down the long, straight road.

Brandon is a city of 40,000 people situated in a valley that has been carved into the prairie by the Assiniboine River. The road in and out of the valley is a curving, tree-lined parkway. The whole setting is quite attractive. Its downtown is a blend of old, low buildings, new, higher business structures and a modern mall. Some of the main streets around town are divided with treed boulevards. One significant structure is the Keystone Centre, which is used for concerts and sports events; it has a covered area of nine acres. Along the river, again in a truly park-like setting, are dozens of sports fields, an impressive sight. There are upscale homes along some of the valley ridges that have a panoramic view of the city. Overall, Brandon appears as a bit of an oasis in the flat, open prairie that stretches far to the west.

Now we are going to take a bit of a detour from the prairie and head north to the more remote tree-and-lake country of Riding Mountain National Park. The road climbs through a series of cleared hills and open valleys until we reach the forested plateau of the park.

The village of Wasagaming is on the shores of Clear Lake. This is an attractive recreation area. It has been a favourite destination for Winnipeggers, and all Manitobans, for decades. There is a nice lakeside park with a sandy beach, a long wharf and boat-docking facilities. The area is filled with cottages, lodges and tourist cabins; many of the structures are constructed out of logs. There is a variety of restaurants and craft shops. Boating, fishing, swimming, water skiing and golfing are all readily available. It is a pleasant retreat.

The remainder of the park is more rustic. There are many gravel back-roads, hiking and biking trails, horse paths and camp sites to be explored. We can wander through the woods and along the various creeks, marshes and small lakes. There are some significant hills associated with the escarpment, thus creating the somewhat grandiose name of Riding Mountain, similar to Hamilton Mountain. There is even a downhill skiing development.

This is a national park and so the wildlife is protected. With patience, we will see elk, deer, beaver, maybe a black bear, and possibly the ever-elusive moose. I am always delighted to see a small group of white-tailed deer along the road as I round a curve. They will perk up, stare for a moment and then bound away into the woods in their distinctive hopping gait, with the white splash on their rear ends flashing in the sunshine.

A special attraction in the park is the Bison Range. Taking a 30 kilometer washboard-gravel side road through the woods, we find open, grassy meadows where a large herd of bison, or plains buffalo, can be found. They are a magnificent animal with their huge horned heads, big furry humps and sleek hind quarters. They are the largest mammal in the Western Hemisphere. A second species, the wood buffalo, also exists; it is found in the forested areas north of the prairie grasslands and is somewhat smaller in size.

It is estimated that over 50 million bison roamed the Canadian prairies when the first Europeans arrived. The Indians had used them as a major food source and utilized their hides as key clothing and shelter materials for the harsh winters. This was true for the early explorers and trappers as well. We have all heard of pemmican, the food of sustenance during the prairie winters; it's basically dried bison meat, pounded and blended with berries.

The bison became victims of the advancing European hunters and settlers. They were killed for their hides and delicacy food parts, and driven off their grazing lands by the ever-growing farm developments. They were also slaughtered by the thousands in the drive to overcome and control the natives by eliminating their food source. By 1889 there were only about 100 bison in Canada! Finally, there was a determined effort to save them from extinction. The hunting stopped and protected reserves were created. Now, there are about 40,000 bison in Canada.

The bison is the symbol of Manitoba, a tribute to its historical significance and its majestic look. The province has created a very modern, stylized shape of a bison to use as a logo for government publications, highway signs and markers. I think it is the best logo of all the provinces. I guess I like the stylized approach, because I would also choose the flag of Newfoundland and Labrador, a modernized image that conjures up a sense of the British Union Jack, as my favourite provincial banner.

Leaving the national park via its north exit, we now enter the area called Parkland, which extends to the Saskatchewan border. The major town in this region is Dauphin, located in a farming belt that lies in the river valleys that cut through the more rugged areas to the north and south. There is a fairly large lake by the same name just to the east of the town.

The town itself is another typical regional centre with shopping facilities and equipment dealers. There are a couple of distinctive buildings. One is the three-story stone and brick railway station with large overhanging eaves. In the yard is an old railway caboose. If you have ever wondered what happened to all the cabooses when the railways stopped attaching them to the end of the freight trains, I can tell you that they are all sitting in the old station yards of almost every town across the western prairies. Some have been converted to museums, town information centres or restaurants, but most just sit as mementoes of times past.

The other noticeable structure in Dauphin is the Ukrainian Catholic Church. It is a square, white, limestone and marble building, with a large stained-glass window and towers topped by many domes and crosses. It stands out. It also reminds us that much of the northern prairie from here to Edmonton was settled by Ukrainians and other eastern Europeans. We will be seeing many of their domed churches in the cities and towns we visit.

Carrying on west, we pass through the village of Roblin, the *Jewel of the Parkland*. Outside town, we cross over the Lake of the Prairies, a very narrow body of water, but one that extends some 50 kilometers north-south. Even on a very cold and rainy late-fall afternoon we can see many fishermen out on the lake in their small boats. I guess true fishermen are a hardy bunch, or supper depends on their success. Of course, my wife thinks I am crazy to golf in some of the weather I go out in.

Having crossed the lake, we now leave Manitoba behind and start into Saskatchewan, the rectangle in the middle of the prairies that is Canada's breadbasket, with its extensive expanses of golden wheat fields.

Saskatchewan

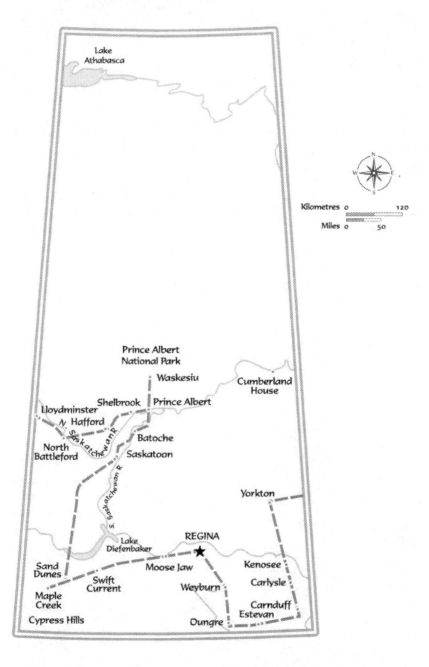

Lake
Athabasca

Kilometres 0   120

Miles 0   50

Prince Albert
National Park

Waskesiu

Cumberland
House

Shelbrook   Prince Albert

Lloydminster
Hafford

N. Saskatchewan R.

Batoche

North
Battleford

Saskatoon

S. Saskatchewan R.

Yorkton

Lake
Diefenbaker   REGINA

Sand
Dunes   Moose Jaw   Kenosee

Swift
Current   Weyburn   Carlyle

Maple
Creek   Carnduff
Estevan

Cypress Hills   Oungre

8. Saskatchewan

Saskatchewan, that unique name for a province, usually conjures up images of flat, wide-open prairies with vast fields of wheat. That is a legitimate image of the southern one-third or so of the province, but, as we will see, there is so much more.

An old joke says that the name came from an Indian word meaning "the place where you cannot jump to your death." It actually comes from the Indian word *ksiskatchewan*, meaning "swift flowing river." This refers to the Saskatchewan River, which flows through the central part of the province and connects, via Lake Winnipeg and the Nelson River, to Hudson Bay. Because of that connection, the Saskatchewan River became one of the earliest routes for the fur traders and explorers to penetrate the west. Its headwaters start in the mountain passes and glaciers of the Rocky Mountains.

The first European to travel into the area that became Saskatchewan was Henry Kelsey of the Hudson's Bay Company, who was sent to explore the interior of the continent in 1690. He was the first to see the vast plains and enormous buffalo herds, but no one followed up on his exploits for a long time. The only benefit of his travels seems to be that more furs were brought by the Indians to the HBC trading posts on the shores of Hudson Bay due to the increased awareness of their presence there.

As I mentioned in our visit to Manitoba, in the 1740s La Vérendrye and his sons developed trading contacts in the region for the French, even venturing far enough west to see the Rocky Mountains in the distance. Again, there was little follow-up.

Finally in the 1770s, one hundred years after its founding and only in response to the growing volume of trading being done with the western Indians by the voyageurs out of Montreal, the HBC's first inland trading post was established at Cumberland House. It is located on a lake that is part of the Saskatchewan River system in today's northeast Saskatchewan. From there, they could navigate their larger, flat-bottom "York" boats via the rivers and lakes all the way back to Hudson Bay, thus expanding the efficiency of the inland trade.

This would be the precursor of an extensive series of Hudson's Bay Company trading posts, called "Forts" or "Houses," across the west.

We are entering Saskatchewan south of there, near the town of Yorkton, a typical prairie centre. Its location reflects a reality of the early west. The town was first settled in 1882. Eight years later, the railway arrived in the region, bypassing the town by some five kilometers. The town moved. It would be no surprise to hear stories that key land ownership, and some speculative benefits, accrued to those who first knew of the railway's actual path.

We are going south from here to the extreme southeast corner of the province. Near the small town of Carlyle is the Moose Mountain Provincial Park, although it is more often just called Kenosee after the local lake and beach by that name. This has been a get-away destination for the prairie folks from Regina and beyond for almost a hundred years. It now has a wide range of recreational facilities. When I was working in Regina and the oilfields of this area in the 1960s, this spot was a welcome relief on hot summer weekends.

The southeast corner of Saskatchewan is rich in natural resources, notably oil and coal. The many extensive oilfields that were discovered here in the 1950s and 1960s are still producing noticeable volumes. The industry is not as large as in Alberta but it is still significant to Saskatchewan. All the local towns such as Carnduff, Steelman, Lampman and Midale are familiar names to oilmen. The open fields are populated with oil wells, distinctively identified by the "nodding" pump jacks that sit on the well head at each location to lift the oil to the surface. Small processing facilities and storage tanks complete the picture. The wells are typically spaced with one every forty or eighty acres, so there is still plenty of land for farming and grazing. The air has that specific odour of crude oil, somewhat peaty and pungent. To the people working in the industry or benefiting from freehold royalties and surface lease rentals it is tolerated as "the smell of money."

Coal is also significant here. Near Estevan, the *Energy Capital of Saskatchewan*, there are extensive open-pit mines with enormous drag-line excavators and power shovels that dig away the overburden soil and extract the coal. It seems that the mine workers like to personalize these large machines; on their structures you can see names such as *Lignite Lady* boldly painted. The area also has wide expanses of large grassy mounds and rolling ridges that reflect the reclaimed and replanted areas that were mined earlier.

I must relate a couple of unique characteristics about names and directions in Saskatchewan. First is the local pronunciation of the names of towns that were obviously French in their origin. You might say they have been Anglicized, but I think it's really "Saskatchewanized." For example, Bienfait is "been-fate" and Oungre is "un-grr."

Second is their method of giving directions or describing locations. I have many friends who come from small towns in Saskatchewan. Often I do not recognize the name of their specific hometown and so I ask them where it is.

Now, I believe that if you were to ask this question of someone in any other province, the conversation might go something like this: "Where is Arbor Vitae, Ontario?" "Well, it's in Northern Ontario, about 400 kilometers west of Thunder Bay, near the Lake-of-the-Woods, not far from the Manitoba and Minnesota borders." I think most people could follow that.

That's not how it happens when you ask the question of someone from Saskatchewan. The conversation that follows is something like this: "Where is Arborfield, Saskatchewan?" "Well, it's about thirty kilometers north of Crooked River. Oh, you don't know that town. Well, Crooked River is on Highway 3, between Mistamim and Tisdale. Still a problem? Well sixty kilometers east on the highway is Melfort. No? Then another 100 kilometers gets you to Prince Albert. Oh, you've heard of that but aren't sure where it is. That's about 150 kilometers north of Saskatoon. Great, you know where that is. So, that's where Arborfield is."

About 60 kilometers west of Estevan (I hope you have kept track of where we are) is the village of Oungre, a border crossing with the United States. I have been there a few times as I visited the oil operations. Without fail, everyone in the office would be sure we went to the local café where the specialty was fried chicken gizzards. And, without exception, we would try them and be surprised at how we liked them. Yes, they are firm and chewy, but very tasty, undoubtedly due to the deep-fried flavour, salt, and spicy dipping-sauce, all complemented with a beer chaser. A large bowl of gizzards will totally disappear by the time a meal is finished. I am sure everyone can remember when chicken wings were an ignored part of the chicken, as opposed to being the premium-priced, sought-after appetizer they are today. Well, gizzards may be the next delicacy; remember, you read it here first.

As an aside, chicken wings are great. Since becoming a fad a couple of decades ago as Hot Buffalo-Style Wings, we now find them everywhere with BBQ, Teriyaki or just plain "hot" choices. Some of the special variations we can find across the country include delicious dry spice wings in Newfoundland and spicy mustard sauces in Nova Scotia.

Sixty kilometers north, we come to another significant town, Weyburn. Like Estevan, it has about 10,000 people. The thing we immediately notice as we pass through Weyburn is a lighthouse sitting on a hill. Now, there is no water body in sight, and so you might wonder,

"Why the lighthouse?" I think it is just to show off the local hill; in southern Saskatchewan a hill is even rarer than a lake. Perhaps it is designed to warn low-flying geese.

For everyone who has read the very popular prairie writer W.O. Mitchell, you should know that his fictional town of Crocus is based on his hometown of Weyburn, as with Stephen Leacock and Mariposa/Orillia.

Weyburn also has a Curling Museum. Where is a more fitting place than rural Saskatchewan, home to the Richardsons, Campbells and so many more? Curling may have been invented in Scotland, but it has become a Canadian institution, not equal to hockey, but above anything else. Who hasn't watched the Brier or the Worlds on TV and cheered on the provincial favourite or the Canadian champion? Perhaps I should say "listened" to curling on TV, with the high decibel screaming of "Hurry, Hard; Hurry, Hard!!" I can even remember being at house parties in the '60s and '70s when people would tune in to catch the curling action of a key match on the radio since it wasn't being televised.

It is also surprising how the curling community has adopted the word Brier as being synonymous with the Canadian Championship. Decades ago, when the event was sponsored by the McDonald's Tobacco Company, the link to a brier pipe was understandable, but why has the label persisted through a number of changes in sponsors? Labatt's first, and then Nokia, stuck with the name. A new sponsor is being sought for the future, but I suspect the Brier name will persist.

I grew up in Winnipeg and learned to curl there in the early 1950s with my father. I came to believe that Manitoba was the centre of the curling universe, which it was in many ways then, with its hometown champion and acknowledged world expert, Ken Watson. Manitoba won 14 of the 22 Canadian championships up to 1953. Those were the days of corn brooms, toe rubbers, cardigan sweaters and little-or-no sliding out of the hack. In recent times there have been outstanding champions from many provinces, but I think the modern era was led from Saskatchewan — the Richardsons won four out of the five years from 1959 to 1963. Statistically, in the last fifty years Alberta has the most wins, 17, Manitoba 12, Saskatchewan 7, Ontario 6 and all the others with a combined total of 8. Their names are all familiar to curlers: Baldwin, Gervais, Northcott, Duguid, Lukowich, Folk, Hackner, Howard, Ryan, Martin, Stoughton, Ferby/Nedohin, etc.

The most amazing record of all is in women's curling where Colleen Jones and her team from Halifax won the Canadian championship, the Scott Tournament of Hearts, for four years straight, 2001 – 2004, as well as in 1999 and 1982.

Now we approach Regina. Did I mention "flat" before? Forget it. Around Winnipeg there were some groves of trees and, perhaps, an undulation on the horizon. Not here! Approaching Regina from the south and looking west, there is nothing to break the line of sight to the far horizon. The land blends into the sky.

People on the prairies often use the term "Big Sky Country." (The U.S. state of Montana has adopted it as a motto.) You might wonder just how much different the sky can look compared to other places. Well, the difference is significant, and very apparent to everyone who looks across the flat plains. The land seems to disappear with the curvature of the earth. There seems to be so much more sky than when there are small hills, or even trees, to limit the sense of space.

Also, it is usually bright and sunny in this part of the country. They average around 2500 hours of sunshine a year, which is an average of 7 hours per day. I expect the folks of Halifax and Vancouver can't even imagine such a thing.

As we drive through this area, we will sometimes see an enormous black streak floating above the land across the far vista. It's just those long prairie railway trains. The illusion is created by the fact that the gravel rail beds are the highest point on the horizon; a meter or so matters here.

In the late summer the scene across the vast prairie is like looking out on an ocean, as golden waves of wheat ripple across the landscape in response to the local breezes.

Regina is the capital of the province with a population of almost 200,000. Population is an issue in Saskatchewan. As with some of the other provinces, such as Manitoba, Quebec and all of Atlantic Canada, the population has been flat or even shrinking over the past decade, while the country as a whole grows. But here it has been a factor for a long time. Saskatchewan's population in the 2001 census was only 5% above the 1931 number! Canada has grown by 300% and every other province by at least 50% in that same time span. In fact, Saskatchewan had the third largest provincial population, after Ontario and Quebec, in the censuses of 1911, 1921, 1931 and 1941. It was not surpassed by British Columbia and Alberta until 1951. There has also been the natural migration of people to the larger cities of Regina and Saskatoon. Putting it all together, it means that rural Saskatchewan has about one-half the population it had during the 1930s. Trends also indicate that a majority of the people in Saskatchewan will have aboriginal ancestry within a few decades.

Regina was originally called Pile-O-Bones, or Wascana, which is the Cree word meaning the same thing. This referred to the piles of buffalo bones that accumulated here when the Indians gathered and dried the buffalo meat and hides. It became a significant centre in the west in the 1880s with the arrival of the railway and with its designation as the capital of the Northwest Territories, which in those days stretched from the Great Lakes to the Rockies and up to the Arctic Ocean, except for the small "postage stamp" area of Manitoba.

Today Regina is a typical modern city. The city's main avenues have treed boulevards; in fact, the city as a whole has a great many trees, again something that stands out from the surrounding prairie. The centrepiece is the impressive, domed provincial legislature building, which can be seen from long distances due to the flatness. It is situated on a little lake and an extensive park that separates it from the downtown area.

It is hard to avoid politics when you think about Saskatchewan and look at that legislature. Saskatchewan has always had an ebb-and-flow of political philosophies and parties, although the label "populist" always comes to mind; just recall the Canadian Prime Minister that came from here, John Diefenbaker.

However, the dominant contribution to Canadian politics from here has come from the left, first the CCF and then the New Democratic Party. Although never close to winning a national election, their presence and their provincial leaders, such as Tommy Douglas and Roy Romanow, have had a profound impact on social programs and constitutional initiatives. Canadian policies such as health care, minimum wages, children's allowances, unemployment insurance and government utilities all started or were institutionalized here.

How times have changed. From the great resistance of many people and special interest groups to government-run health care when it was first introduced, it has now come to dominate national affairs. The federal election of 2004 and the extensive federal-provincial meetings and debates that fall were focused on the challenges of improving the system, with all of the demands for more services offset by the greatly increasing costs. It is all complicated by the competing political jurisdictions and agendas. A new deal was achieved, at least for now, but this will continue as a high profile, emotional issue for a long time.

Another sign of the times is that Tommy Douglas was voted as "The Greatest Canadian" by the viewers of that CBC program series in the fall of 2004, beating out all of the other historical politicians, leaders, scientists, sportspersons, entertainers and celebrities.

Downtown Regina is a blend of modern glass buildings and traditional structures, such as the Saskatchewan Hotel, another railway legacy. The city is neat and compact.

The huge Exhibition Grounds, not far from the city centre, is a clear reminder that we are in the middle of farm country. Nearby is the football stadium, Taylor Field. We talked about the CFL earlier, but I must add here that, undoubtedly, the biggest fans of the game, and of their team, are those who support the "Green-and-White," the Saskatchewan Roughriders. I know the fans everywhere else will cry out in disagreement, but I am sure if you asked every one of them, "Who is number two?" they would say Saskatchewan, which makes the point. What makes it more amazing is that Saskatchewan has only won the Grey Cup twice, 1966 and 1989. Remember, this is a trophy that has been around for almost a hundred years and the modern league has only nine teams. They can relate to the fans of the Chicago Cubs. Perhaps they can be inspired by the Boston Red Sox who won the 2004 World Series in a dramatic come-back performance, thus overcoming the curse that had denied them a championship for 86 years.

The original headquarters of the North West Mounted Police was located here in Regina. The NWMP evolved into the RCMP, as we know it today. Although its headquarters are now in Ottawa, there is a large complex in western Regina that is the central training facility for all of the RCMP. As well as many buildings, there are acres of fields and numerous barns, reminding us that this is still a "mounted" force and it has horses. Of course, they also have cars, trucks, helicopters, bush-planes, boats and radar detectors. One of the most popular spectacles in Canada is the RCMP Musical Ride, the precision riding team in the scarlet tunics that attends many community fairs and special events.

The complex also houses a museum and information centre that captures the history of the force, which, in effect, is the history of western and northern Canada. This is a well-presented display, with lots of historical equipment and artifacts, plus good descriptions of the people and events.

The force was created by Parliament in 1873, and it first appeared in the west after a long and arduous trek across the country in 1874. Due to the political issues involved and the expansionary threats of the Americans, they came across the difficult route north of Superior.

The prairie region was full of renegade fur traders, gun runners, whiskey importers, general bandits and rebellious Indian and Métis factions, all of whom were threatening the peaceful settlement and growth of the western regions. Canada needed to establish its sovereignty and control in this area that it had purchased only recently from the Hudson's Bay Company.

A very significant dimension of this historical initiative is that the NWMP was a police force, not an army. Its job was to create peace and order, not to conquer and occupy. This contrasts with the American decision to send out the U.S. Cavalry to do the job in the American west. We will see more of the RCMP's role in western Canada as we continue our journey.

Continuing west from Regina, we are in the midst of grain country. I think the only way to truly appreciate the scale of the western farm basin is from the air. Anyone who has the opportunity to fly over the west from

Winnipeg to Calgary should certainly secure a window seat and check out the view; it's more spectacular than any in-flight movie viewed in the dark, behind shuttered windows. From on-high, the checkerboard pattern of large fields that continues across hundreds of miles is overwhelming. Driving through Saskatchewan in October, I once heard a local radio news report that the harvest was late and that thirteen percent of the crop was still to be recovered, some 4.5 million acres!

Just west of Regina is a large industrial plant that recovers potash from underground formations using hydraulic mining techniques. This is one of a number of such plants in Saskatchewan. Potash is used in the fertilizer industry and Saskatchewan is one of the leading world suppliers. Driving across the prairies, we can often see the dedicated trains with their specialized hopper cars transporting the mineral toward the seaports of British Columbia.

I learned just how significant Saskatchewan potash is in the world market when I was traveling in the Middle East a few years ago. I was involved with negotiating the feasibility of an oil project in Jordan. As part of our familiarization process regarding industrial project construction and operating practices in the country, we visited a number of existing industrial plants. One of these produced potash. As we walked through the plant site, we noticed that there were two separate truck-loading facilities. The ground and equipment around one of them was covered in a white dust, while, at the second facility, the hue of the area was a definite pink. It was explained that pure potash from here is white. However, Saskatchewan potash is pink, due to some other mineralization. Some customers, such as China, insisted that the potash they bought be like the Canadian supplies they were used to and believed were the best. Thus, the Jordanians colour their product for some markets. It requires a big effort to keep the pink product from contaminating the stockpiles, trucks and loading terminals dedicated to the white product that is desired by other customers. Such is the market reputation of Saskatchewan's potash.

As is the case across all of the Prairie Provinces, many of the very small towns around here have disappeared. Originally, they were situated about every six miles, i.e., one per township, with a grain elevator located on a local railway spur line. Now, the lines are disappearing and grain is trucked longer distances to centres where the old, familiar, wood-sided grain elevators are being replaced by large metal silo-shaped complexes, often painted in bright colours.

Something else that is relatively new around the prairies is the increased presence of grain-oil processing plants. As a means of diversifying their income, and thus reducing the exposure to crop problems and market prices for wheat, many farmers are now growing significant crops of canola, which is a source of "good" low-cholesterol oils. The fields are very distinctive with their bright yellow flowers shining in the sun; there is no mistaking it for the golden wheat crops. The farming community did itself a big service for marketing some years ago when they changed the name of this crop from rape seed to canola.

At the end of an essentially dead-straight drive, some 60 kilometers west of Regina, we come to Moose Jaw, a mid-sized prairie city of 30,000 people. It is situated along the Moose Jaw River valley, which provides some relief from the flat prairie. There is a ten-meter-high statue of a moose near the highway, naturally the "world's largest," as well as a sign proclaiming this to be the *Friendly City*.

I have noted, as we cross the country, that there are quite a few cities and towns that declare themselves to be friendly. I wonder how they decide that, other than wishful thinking. Perhaps there is a self-fulfilling aspect to it; if the town declares itself to be friendly, people might act that way.

I can recall passing through a small town in New Mexico that declared something quite different; their sign said "Home of the Ten Grouches." Apparently, they have an official group called the Grouches who keep the politicians and other civic leaders on their toes. When one of the Grouches dies or moves away, they hold an election for the official replacement. I haven't seen this phenomenon in Canada yet, although I know that many towns have their self-appointed grouches in action.

Downtown is anchored by a wide main street with a number of distinctive buildings, such as the stone city hall, a clock tower, the old railway station and, nearby, a large, domed church of red brick with cream trim. There are some thirty murals painted on the sides of buildings that convey the city's history. A downtown fire during a very cold spell in early 2004 destroyed some of the classic old buildings, which was a real shame.

Moose Jaw was an especially high-flying, rowdy place in the 1920s and 1930s. It had liberal liquor and entertainment laws, compared to the usual, very restrictive practices in most cities at that time. Thus, it became the drinking and red-light centre for Regina and for many miles in every direction. In fact, it became a base for bootleggers and gangsters who were involved with smuggling liquor into the United States during their period of prohibition. They tell stories of Al Capone coming here to avoid American law officers. The story adds a dimension of notoriety and excitement to the area, even if it does challenge credibility. There are a number of fancy old cars and period-decorated speakeasies here now, to take advantage of this historic reputation.

Moose Jaw has another unique dimension; there were tunnels dug between buildings and under streets to store materials, conceal activities and provide secret exits for people during those heydays of the past. Today, there is a major tourist attraction centred on some underground tunnels in the midst of downtown. There are two separate underground tours, one focused on the bright lights and shady lifestyles of the 1920s, and the other focused on the lives and living conditions of the many Chinese inhabitants who came to the west during the construction of the railways in the late-1800s and settled here. In both cases, costumed guides and actors recreate those periods in a very entertaining fashion. You will note that, when we ask the people selling tickets what the tours are all about, they are somewhat abstract and evasive, referring us to brochures and posters that show scenes of the gangster-prone '20s and the subdued life conditions of the Chinese. This is because they position their offering as being the intriguing tunnels of Moose Jaw, leaving us with the initial misconception that the depicted activities and living facilities were originally located underground in the tunnels. Not true. This is just the location for their staged storytelling; nevertheless, it is still a very entertaining experience.

Carrying on west from here, we come to Swift Current, a centre for the agricultural and petroleum industry of southwest Saskatchewan. We quickly realize that the wind can truly blow steadily in this part of the prairies when we observe a significant, wind-driven power-generating project west of town. The large slowly-rotating blades, sitting on their tower-like pedestals, represent the emerging significance of this alternative form of energy. Many believe that this is going to become the most economic form of low-environmental-impact power, depending on your opinion of the visual impact from these whirling behemoths spread across the landscape. Usually, these projects occur in mountain passes or high on prominent ridges, where the wind is focused by Mother Nature. To see this project in a relatively-flat prairie area says a lot about the weather here.

The farthest southwest corner of Saskatchewan provides some dramatic relief from the flat prairie. There is a large expanse of sand dunes and prairie grasses north of Maple Creek, where deer and antelope and prairie grouse can be found. To the south are the unexpected Cypress Hills, an area characterized by high hills and rocky cliffs in a pine-forest setting. In fact, the highest point in Canada between the Rocky Mountains and Labrador is here at over 1350 meters (4500 feet) above sea level, very similar to Banff! It's a good area for sightseeing and camping, and there are a golf course and beaches on Cypress Lake to add to the experience.

Going back north of Swift Current, we come to the South Saskatchewan River and the large Lake Diefenbaker that was formed by the construction of a power dam farther north. The lake, which is, in effect, a widening of the river, stretches for 150 kilometers; it takes a long distance to build up a hydraulic head on the prairies. It has some of the most developed recreational facilities in the province: beaches, marinas, fishing, golf, camping, hiking trails and so on. This area is a treasure for prairie dwellers.

From here we continue north for a couple of hundred kilometers to Saskatoon, the largest city in Saskatchewan. Its setting is very different from Regina's, in that it is located on the South Saskatchewan River, which cuts a deep gorge through the centre of town and becomes the focal point for many facilities.

People of the west are very familiar with the purple Saskatoon berry that grows on large, tree-like bushes on the northern prairies; it makes tasty jams and pies. I had presumed, and I suspect many others have done the same, that the berry was named after the city. It turns out it is just the opposite; the original town was named after the Cree word for the berry, *misaskquatoomina*.

The downtown area is on the west side of the river, set behind a large, tree-filled park that winds along the upper riverbank. Park benches, picnic areas and impressive statues make the area very user-friendly and picturesque.

The most dominant building downtown is the old, stone, railway hotel, the Bessborough, which anchors the area with its ten stories, turrets, towers and jutting windows. Views from its main dining room, conference facilities and many guest rooms are of the parks, the river and the many substantial bridges that span the river from one high bank to the other. In fact, Saskatoon is referred to as the *City of Bridges*.

The downtown streets are fairly wide, lined with a variety of buildings, some old and stately and almost all relatively low. Saskatoon is, undoubtedly, the largest city that still has cars park perpendicular to the curb in the downtown area. You expect to see this in small towns, but not here. Combined with the many interesting shops along the main streets, such as collectibles and book stores, this gives Saskatoon a very comfortable feeling; there is a little bit of a sense of going back in time. This traffic practice also effectively turns the wide streets into narrow ones, since traffic must stop every time someone wants to back out of a parking stall. This happens a lot, as another car inevitably stops to wait for the vacating spot. Driving through downtown is very slow for a city this size.

There is an English tone to many of the shops and names. This is certainly the case at the English Pub, with its long bar, padded booths and dart boards. They have one of the largest selections of beer that I have seen, including Russian beer. It shows that times have changed since Saskatoon was originally established in the 1880s as a temperance colony.

Across the river from downtown, high on the eastern riverbank, is the University of Saskatchewan. It has a sprawling campus, full of impressive limestone buildings connected with lanes and walkways that are complemented with distinctive gates and arches. It is very reminiscent of the eastern universities such as Queen's and Western, more so than most other universities on the prairies. It has a strong reputation in many disciplines, especially engineering and agriculture.

I haven't been to Saskatoon much over the years, and so I will admit it is very pleasant surprise to see it in more detail. It seems to be a very attractive and livable place.

Going north from Saskatoon, the flat farmland gradually transitions into gentle hills and light patches of forest. About an hour out of the city we find the Batoche National Historic Park, where we can pick up the second half of the saga of Louis Riel and all of the tragedies that occurred. There is a well-presented interpretation centre, including restored buildings and facilities, here at Batoche that are well worth visiting, even though it necessitates a bit of a side-trip from the main highway.

You will recall that we last encountered Louis Riel when he led the political and armed activities around Winnipeg that led to the formation of Manitoba in 1870. Following that, he was banned from Canada and he fled to Montana in 1875.

The prairie landscape changed dramatically through the 1870s and early 1880s. The influx of new settlers who sought out land for farming exploded with the encouragement of the Government of Canada, which now owned the area, and with the arrival of the NWMP to preserve order. The CPR crossed the prairies and reached the mountains by 1883; it was voraciously seeking out business – bringing settlers and visitors to the prairies and hauling agricultural and mining production away.

By 1884 there was a lot of discontent in the region. The settlers were upset that they were not getting enough support from the Canadian government and they wanted more local authority, as had happened in Manitoba. The Indians had been subdued but they were confined by treaties to reservations, where their lifestyle was being restricted and where many were near starvation. The Métis had migrated farther north to the areas around the convergence of the North and South Saskatchewan Rivers. They were concerned because their land rights were not being recognized, their language and religion-based education desires were being ignored, and their livelihood was being threatened by the encroaching farming and the resulting disappearance of the buffalo. All in all, it was a difficult situation, and Ottawa was not showing much interest in finding solutions.

The Métis community was particularly upset; they even formed a political "war party" to lead their activities. Their leaders, including Gabriel Dumont, who would become their military leader, were searching for some way to better approach Ottawa. In June 1884 they went to Montana and convinced Louis Riel to return and help them. He came to the Métis village of Batoche.

Over the next six months Riel visited with the various villages and delivered many speeches about what they needed to do — negotiate with Ottawa. In December he sent a proposed Bill of Rights to the federal government. A response in January 1885 totally ignored that request, along with most of the others that had been sent by the various factions in the territory.

At this point, believing the process was hopeless, Riel decided to leave and return to Montana, but the Métis leaders convinced him to stay and try again. This led to the critical action that precipitated so much else — the declaration of an independent "Provisional Government" for the Métis in March 1885.

This was the same action that had been taken in the Red River valley fifteen years earlier, and which got Ottawa's attention and led to the creation of Manitoba. But times had changed. Before, there was no legal presence of Canada, but only the uncertainty of process as Canada negotiated to purchase the region from the Hudson's Bay Company. It was opportune to demand attention then. Now it was different. Canada owned the region, and the institutions of the NWMP and CPR were present. Canada wanted stability and a welcoming environment for the growing population of settlers who would establish Canada's sovereignty over the land and create a source of national economic growth. Riel's declaration of a provisional government was declared treason!

This led to a lot of confusion and misunderstandings. A confrontation between the Métis and the NWMP at Duck Lake, across the river from Batoche, resulted in the deaths of a dozen police officers and supporting volunteers. At the same time, there were uprisings by a few Indian groups farther west that also resulted in deaths. This led Ottawa to form a commission to investigate the situation in the Northwest, a favourite government response then, as now. It went to Regina, far from any of the real problems, and essentially had no impact on events. Ottawa also sent out a militia force to deal with the uprisings and growing threats; this was an army, not a police force.

We won't dwell on all of the details here, but in late April and early May there were a number of battles between the army and the Métis and Indian groups at various locations: Fish Creek, Battleford and Frog Lake. The definitive conflict took place at Batoche.

The battle for Batoche lasted four days, May 9–12, involving about 1000 military personnel and up to 400 Métis and their supporters. Amazingly, although there were many people wounded, only a dozen or so were killed on each side. Nevertheless, the superior forces and firepower of the army eventually prevailed. As a historical note, a Captain Gatling of the U.S. Army had been sent to join the Canadian forces, so as to try out his new invention in battle — a machine-gun that could fire hundreds of bullets a minute.

The stories of the various battles involving the Métis that led up to Batoche, and of Batoche itself, are consistent on two points. First, Dumont was the very effective military leader of the Métis; he used careful planning and guerrilla tactics to offset his significant resource shortage for an extended period. Second, Riel was always trying to restrain the fighting and seek a negotiated political solution.

In any case, both Riel and Dumont managed to escape capture in the battle. Realizing that all was lost, they disbanded their remaining supporters, who returned to their homes or fled to other areas. Dumont decided to flee to the U.S., not trusting his fate to the army and the English Canadian authorities. Riel stayed and surrendered himself to the army General, believing he would be treated reasonably. He was taken to Regina, imprisoned, and charged with treason on June 6.

The trial became a national cause: English versus French, Ontario versus Quebec, East versus West, Conservative versus Liberal, and Macdonald versus Laurier.

On July 28, 1885 the trial began. The judge disallowed any testimony regarding the general situation in the west or any political justification for the actions. He also refused amnesty for any Métis, such as Dumont, to appear and testify as to Riel's actual role. The trial was singularly focused on defined actions deemed treasonable, namely the declaration of an independent government and participation in the armed conflicts.

The only defense left was a plea based on insanity. There were many stories about Riel's wild speeches, religious heresy and erratic behaviour during battle, but they were not persuasive, especially since he spoke rationally and passionately during the trial. On August 1st, the jury found Riel guilty with a recommendation of mercy. The judge sentenced him to hang.

After a few months of appeals all the way to England and back, and a great political and public debate, Macdonald denied any leniency and Riel was hanged on November 16, 1885. After some wrangling, his body was sent to Winnipeg (St. Boniface) and he was buried beside the cathedral after an elaborate procession through the streets and a service conducted by the Archbishop.

It is a bit ironic that Dumont's fate was very different. In the U.S. he joined up with the Buffalo Bill and Annie Oakley Wild West Show. Then, after a general amnesty was declared in 1886, just months after Riel's hanging, he returned to Batoche and quietly lived out his life until 1906.

Thus, we have the saga of Louie Riel: hero and traitor, martyr and lunatic, champion and failure, symbol of western issues with Ottawa and renegade outcast. His legacy lives on in many of today's issues in Canada. As I said on our way in, the side-trip to Batoche is very worthwhile.

Continuing north, we come to the North Saskatchewan River and the city of Prince Albert, self-proclaimed *Gateway to Northern Saskatchewan*. This city of 35,000 people straddles the big river with its high banks. The main bridge over the river is named the Diefenbaker Bridge, after the former Prime Minister who practiced law and was elected to Parliament from here. Although most of his archives and memorabilia, and his burial site, are at the University of Saskatchewan in Saskatoon, his former residence in Prince Albert is nicely maintained and can be visited in the summer. It is a quaint cottage with a stucco-and-batten finish located on a quiet residential street.

As you have gathered by now, I like to listen to the car radio when I travel to pick up some of the local news and a sense of the place. Last time through PA (yes, that's what everyone calls Prince Albert) I heard an advertisement for a boxing extravaganza coming the next weekend. All you had to do was turn up and win three boxing matches in one evening to win $1000. The promotion ended with the booming challenge, "Are YOU tough enough?" I knew I wasn't and just moved on.

The terrain has now changed significantly. We are in the northern woods again and the highways are populated with log trucks, rather than farm vehicles. This is truly the gateway to a world of outstanding wilderness trekking, canoeing, fishing and camping. The Prince Albert National Park, with its lakes and streams and gentle tree-filled hills, provides a wide range of facilities for the visitor. Most people call the area Waskesiu, after the local lake and tourist village.

I have visited this area a number of times in the past, mostly on golf getaway weekends from Regina or Edmonton. I golf a fair amount but have never had a hole-in-one. I did witness one here, however. A friend hit a ball over a pond and off a tree trunk in the rough before it rolled onto the green and into the hole. He naturally received a great deal of ribbing, but he had a hole-in-one. Have you noticed that when golfers hit a ball into a pond, or the trees, or out of bounds, it is bad luck, but when they get a hole-in-one, it is all skill? "That's what I was trying to do," they say. If I ever have the chance, I'll say the same thing.

Seeing a golf course set in the forest brings to mind for me the various animals I have seen on courses in different places, from bears, deer, elk and coyotes in Canada to kangaroos in Australia, alligators in Florida and rattlesnakes in Arizona.

My most amusing story relates to golfing in Indonesia. The golf course was immaculate in its landscaping and care, with the fairways all lined with small, neatly trimmed, but densely packed bushes. Whenever one of us would hit an errant shot into the bush, the caddies would warn us about the snakes that lurked out there; needless to say, we limited our search to a token glance into the bushes and moved on. I hit such a shot on the fifth hole. An hour later, as we made the turn between the ninth and tenth holes, there was a local fellow selling golf balls from a flat display rack. Right there in the middle of the display was the golf ball I had "lost" four holes earlier – there was no mistaking the distinctive logo that was on it. I guess the snakes, or at least the snake stories, only deter visitors.

Now, after returning to Prince Albert, we can continue west, staying in forested land and encountering small villages for a while. Shellbrook is the *Heart of the Parkland*. Parkside is the *Home of the World's Largest Lily*. This latter phenomenon is actually a decorated telephone pole with three large red-metal lily-like flowers attached. I couldn't make that up!

We also pass through an extensive area of marshes and general wetlands. The town of Hartford is *Where Summer Takes Wing*, a reference to the huge flocks of geese and ducks that arrive every spring and leave every fall in migration. It is not unusual to see many "Vs" of geese filling the sky.

We return to farm country as we approach the Battlefords. The main city of North Battleford is, not surprisingly, on the north side of the North Saskatchewan River. The more residential community of Battleford is on the south side, connected by a high multi-lane bridge.

The town of Battleford originally anticipated large growth from the arrival of the CPR in 1883, but the more southerly route via Regina was chosen. Then, in 1905, with the coming of the CNR, the focus of the town was unexpectedly shifted to the north side of the river, as that was where the railway set up its operations and where it controlled the land.

The area is a very picturesque diversion in the middle of the prairie, with parkland and developments along the river banks and down the valley. The town has some old brick and stone buildings, including the library that was built in 1916 under a grant from Andrew Carnegie. It now houses the studio of Allen Sapp, a well-known Cree painter.

This area was very active in the early days of the settlement of the west. It was the original capital of the Northwest Territories, before that designation was moved to Regina to be on the railway. It was also the site of the northern detachment of the NWMP, and its fort was involved in the battles between the Canadian forces and the Indians.

At the same time that the Métis were rebelling against the Canadian authority around Batoche, some of the Indian tribes rebelled against their oppressive reservation conditions. In early 1885 Cree forces attacked the settlements of Frog Lake and Battleford. A handful of settlers were killed. The army responded here as it had at Batoche. The key battle in this case was at Cut Knife Hill near Battleford in early-May 1885, where the Cree surprised the advancing army and drove them back. Like Riel, the Cree leader Poundmaker showed restraint in victory. He then started marshalling his forces to help the Métis at Batoche. When word of their defeat reached him, he disbanded his forces and surrendered to the army, along with some of his key supporters. Although Poundmaker was sent to prison for only a brief period due to the general amnesty of 1886, eight Indians who had been directly involved with the attacks were hanged.

The Fort Battleford National Historic Park contains preserved buildings from that era and, as in many places, costumed staff to provide information about the events of those early days of western Canada settlement. This links to the city's motto of being *The Heart of Canada's Old Northwest.*

Traveling west from Battleford, we again see large, open farm fields. On a fall trip I once saw a field in the distance that looked as if it was covered with snow, only to realize on closer inspection that it was covered with snow geese. These large, white-plumed birds, with black trim on their edges, were obviously gathering for their planned flight south before winter set in. I tried to estimate how many birds were there. By a rough process of counting one small area and extrapolating, I decided there were over a million of them! Even if I was wrong by a lot, the numbers were huge. I saw this phenomenon a number of times across the prairies that fall; it was amazing.

Hay is a big crop everywhere in the country. In years past, we would see stacks of relatively-small rectangular bales sitting in the farm yards. Now, we see huge round bales that have a plastic wrap to keep them dry and to prevent rotting. Sometimes there are very long, white-plastic tubes that contain a number of round bales, creating a closed environment for fermenting the hay into silage. It certainly changes the look of farmyards.

Also, everywhere we travel, we can see many abandoned wooden barns and sheds in the farmyards and in the fields. The folks who use weathered barn boards for decorating or for making rustic furniture and household items need not fear that they will run out of raw materials.

We also pass a small town with a golf course and a sign that reads "Nine Holes, Grass Greens, Visitors Welcome, $20." Now this says a lot about golf in Saskatchewan.

As background, you should know that Canada has the highest per-capita number of golfers in the world, and that Saskatchewan has the highest per-capita rate within Canada. Who would have thought that?

The first thing we learn from the sign is that even a very small town can have a golf course. Next, we learn that the cost is reasonable and outsiders are welcome. Lastly, we learn that to have grass on golf greens is newsworthy!

This latter fact can be a surprise to many people, especially if they have always played golf in big cities, wetter climates, or fancier settings. There are golf courses on the prairies that have dirt greens, although the number has been declining in recent times. The dirt greens are obviously cheaper to build and maintain. They can run true and fast, although golfing in the rain becomes problematic. To increase their resilience, the dirt is often mixed with some oil. Before putting their balls, golfers are allowed to sweep their line of putting with a broom to remove pebbles and such, a major local exception to the regular rules of golf. (No, you cannot sweep while the ball is moving; this isn't curling.) Also, unlike grass greens where a slight bump can develop around the hole during the day due to the footsteps of the golfers, on dirt greens there can be a slight depression develop due to the sweeping. It helps reduce the number of three-putt holes and missed four-footers.

Our last stop in Saskatchewan is the city of Lloydminster, a regional agriculture and oil processing centre and a truly distinctive Canadian creation. It is literally located on the Saskatchewan-Alberta border, which presents a problem and a unique solution.

To set the scene, this general area is blessed with fairly large oil reserves. However, the oil is "heavy," which means that it is more viscous than most crude oils, and, therefore, it is more difficult and expensive to move through pipelines and to process at normal oil refineries into gasoline and other useful products. The solution is to build an "upgrader" which partially processes the heavy oil so that it is more like conventional crude oil. The large facility here in Lloydminster was supported by the industry and the governments of Alberta and Saskatchewan.

So, we find oil production operations in both provinces, a conventional oil refinery in Alberta, and the new multi-billion dollar upgrader in Saskatchewan. All of this surrounds the city of Lloydminster, which is split down the middle by the provincial border.

The situation is complicated by the fact that the Alberta income tax rate is lower than in Saskatchewan, and there is no Alberta sales tax versus the neighbouring six percent. There are other differences. The net result is that almost everyone would want to live on the Alberta side of town.

The solution was to create a single city that spans the border, has one elected city council, one administration and one set of local laws. To do this, Saskatchewan has created a sales-tax-free zone. They have also diverted the defining line between the Central Time and Mountain Time zones to put the whole area on Alberta time.

As an aside, this time zone issue only matters half of the year, since Saskatchewan does not convert to Daylight Saving Time in the summer; apparently it bothers the cows on that side of the border. Of course, at these latitudes the sun stays up late into the evening in the summer anyway. You can easily golf until well after 9:00 p.m. Anyway, it is always amazing and amusing to hear the arguments about not changing the time. In spite of the fact that the daylight hours are naturally varying from six to eighteen hours a day through the year, such a change will apparently reduce the flow of cow's milk and the laying of hen's eggs! I observed the same debate on a visit to Queensland, Australia. There, they were also concerned that their drapes would fade more quickly.

The blending together of Lloydminster is not a perfect solution; in reality there are more residential homes and small businesses on the Alberta side, but it does provide some balance and a sense of one common community.

Just before we leave Saskatchewan, I need to mention the Hollywood movie by that name that was made decades ago. There were scenes of the main characters in a canoe with high mountains all around. I recall thinking that Hollywood had made a big mistake: mountains in Saskatchewan? Well, they were right after all. As the west was being developed, there were a number of different territorial designations that changed with the times, e.g., Assiniboia and Athabasca. At one time Saskatchewan Territory did stretch all the way to the Rocky Mountains. All of those various territories were realigned into the provinces of Saskatchewan and Alberta when they were formed in 1905. My apologies to Hollywood.

Just to note in passing, the three prairie provinces of Manitoba, Saskatchewan and Alberta were the only ones created by Canada out of its territories. All of the other provinces were independent colonies before they agreed to join the confederation.

As we cross the border into Alberta, we are told that this is the longest straight-line border in the world. It is a true north-south line, along a meridian. Nevertheless, the claim is spurious as there are many longer straight-line borders that go east-west; just think of the Canada-U.S. border in the west or the southern border of the Northern Territories. They are straight lines around the globe; they just look curved on many types of map projections.

Anyway, let's cross that border and enter Alberta, now my home province.

Alberta

9. Alberta

Crossing into Alberta from Saskatchewan, we are still in Lloydminster, of course. The larger part of the town is on the Alberta side, especially the small businesses, the newer motels and restaurants, and the modern subdivisions. The differences between the two provinces in terms of growth, taxes, economic prosperity and political philosophy are significant, and as has been said in many other situations, "People do vote with their wallets and their feet."

The route we will take through Alberta will generally follow a circle. We will start down the east side, carry across the south end, follow the mountains and foothills up the west side through Calgary and Banff, continue north to Jasper and then swing back east to Edmonton and on to Ft. McMurray in the northeast before we head for the Northern Territories.

The southeastern portion of Alberta, from Lloydminster south, is much the same as western Saskatchewan. There are farms and oilfield developments interspersed with small towns and modest-sized regional cities that are the centres for business and shopping. That includes Vermillion, Vegreville, Wainwright, Camrose, Stettler, Hanna, Drumheller, Brooks and Taber, all of them with populations ranging from five to fifteen thousand. They are basic communities, generally having wide main streets lined with two-story buildings, farm equipment and car dealerships, Canadian Tire, Wal-Mart or Zellers, Saan or Co-op, and an exhibition grounds for the fall fair.

We can detect the European roots of the early settlers in a specific area from the local names and the architecture, especially of the churches. For example, the area between Lloydminster and Edmonton was settled by many people from Eastern Europe, and we can see many of the "onion-dome" churches of their Orthodox religions in the region. The strong Ukrainian heritage is particularly captured in the eight-meter high, elaborately-decorated, aluminum Easter egg, or "pysanka," in Vegreville.

The largest city in south-central Alberta is Red Deer, halfway between Edmonton and Calgary, with a population of 70,000. Its name reflects the heritage and confusion of early settlers. The Cree name for the elk is *waskasoo* and that is also what they called this area. The early Scottish settlers were confused between native names for the elk and the local deer, which reminded them of the red deer back home, and so they "adopted" the mistranslated name Red Deer for their settlement.

The city is prospering as a major centre for the agriculture and petroleum industries, including the nearby presence of multi-billion dollar petrochemical manufacturing plants. The Red Deer River, which runs through the area, creates some picturesque recreational settings, such as the large Waskasoo Park with hiking trails, canoeing ponds, fishing holes and picnic grounds. In the area there are also some large natural preservation sites — wetland sloughs and ponds where the natural grasses are tall and huge numbers of waterfowl, such as migrating ducks, can be viewed.

In every part of the country there are farms where customers can gather fruit or vegetables right out of the fields. This assures freshness, offers a better price for the consumer, and gives the farmer some added cash income without incurring the cost of harvesting and distribution. Signs that advertise these operations usually say U-Pick, Pick-'em, or something similar. A sign on the highway south of Red Deer has a unique twist on the name: it says *City Slicker Harvest*.

Central Alberta has a large number of good-sized lakes. They are relatively shallow and they warm up nicely in the summertime for boating and swimming, although weed growth can be a nuisance. Cottage developments abound as weekenders come from the entire region, including Edmonton and Calgary.

This region is also the location of some of the wildest summer weather in Alberta. For some reason, the Red Deer River valley generates huge hailstorms in the late afternoon of the hottest summer days, creating havoc for the grain fields, roofs and the finish on automobiles. On top of that, periodically there are tornadoes that always seem to find trailer parks and camp sites to devastate. On those hot summer days everyone is wary, even the golfers who invariably carry one-irons. (Lee Trevino says you should hold up a one-iron in a lightning storm since "Even God can't hit a one-iron.")

Southeast of Red Deer, near the town of Drumheller, are the famous Badlands of Alberta. I am sure most people have seen photos of the rugged cliffs, stratified hills and the hoodoo formations, which are tall pillars of rock carved by Mother Nature's forces of flowing rivers, wind and rain.

What makes this area so dramatic, certainly for a first-time visitor, is that it comes upon us quickly and by surprise. The hills and towers of rock do not rise up above the flat prairie farmland; they are set down in a deep valley that has been carved into the sedimentary-rock layers by the river. This carving-down also opens up opportunities for archaeologists and geologists to study the fossilized remnants of those ancient eras. Most spectacular, at least for us laypersons, are the large dinosaur skeletons that are frequently uncovered here.

All of this is explained at the Tyrrell Museum, which is located right in the middle of the Badlands. This is a world-renowned dinosaur research centre, and an absolutely outstanding interpretation and education centre for visitors. The life-size displays of mockups of the ancient animals and their natural settings, the presence of the actual fossils, and interactive information stations amuse us for hours.

Moving on south, we now head for Medicine Hat. The region is very flat again. I can recall someone saying that the area is as flat as a bed sheet; the only difference from Saskatchewan is that, over there, they iron the sheet. And it's true; this is flat, but there is a hint of a contour here and there on the horizon.

It is also dry, and I am not referring to the liquor laws.

In the 1880s, when the Canadian Pacific Railway was planning its route west, it had many detailed reports about the region. This included the maps and journals of John Palliser, who had made a comprehensive survey of the prairies and mountain passes in the late 1850s. It is important to note that the best route for a railway is not necessarily the easiest one; the success of a railway depends on attracting business. For the CPR, this would require settlers, supplies and tourists coming west, and grain, beef and minerals going back east. (Westerners would say that the other commodity going back east was money.) A route has to meet economic expectations.

Palliser's report on southern Alberta, the area that became labeled "Palliser's Triangle," bluntly stated that the region was very arid and would be relatively worthless in the future, certainly compared to the fertile region farther north along the North Saskatchewan River.

In spite of this, the CPR pushed through the southern prairies, which disappointed Saskatoon, Battleford and Edmonton. Those centres had to wait for the CNR two decades later. It delighted Regina, Swift Current, Medicine Hat and Calgary, and all the land speculators there.

Palliser was not totally off the mark; the vast farmland in Southern Alberta is supported by irrigation. You can see the long, wheeled, spraying systems slowly working their way across the fields during the summer growing season. In periods of extreme drought, such as has been the case for the past few years, even this support does not ensure decent crops. You still need water to put into the irrigation system. This recent drought has affected almost all of the prairie farm regions, with or without irrigation.

One of the great Canadian displays of national togetherness was the shipment of hay from eastern farms to their western counterparts in order to help sustain the cattle herds through the severe feed shortage in 2002. Driving across the country that fall, we would see the steady presence of the large tractor-trailers hauling the hay west. Typically, a load would consist of 34 huge round bales, stacked high and long on the trailer beds; it was a truly awesome sight that created a good feeling of pride for our country.

Medicine Hat, a city of 50,000, sits in the southeast corner of Alberta. As with a number of prairie cities, it is centred on a valley cut into the prairie by a major river, in this case the South Saskatchewan. The valley here is quite rugged, with high ridges rising above the city centre. The downtown is presented as a "historic" place. It is quite attractive, with old, brick buildings, tree-lined sidewalks and the central railway station beside the river. There is a contrasting, glass-and-brick, modern city hall. Many of the newer residential areas and developments are spreading across the upper prairie lands.

The city's name comes from an Indian legend about a historic battle between the Cree and the Blackfoot tribes. The battle was balanced until the Cree medicine man fled, losing his headdress in the process. This perceived bad omen caused the Cree to stop fighting and to be overcome by the Blackfoot warriors. The resulting Indian name for the area meant "medicine man's hat," which again became muddled in the translation.

Today, Medicine Hat calls itself the *Gas City*, which refers to the huge reservoir of natural gas that underlies the area that is owned by the city. This will provide an assured supply of the fuel to the city for a long time into the future, and it generates real value, especially as natural gas prices have risen significantly in response to the more general supply-demand situation in North America. Medicine Hat also sits on a huge underground water aquifer that is so critical in this region. It is a city blessed with natural resources.

It was near here, at Bow Island, that significant natural gas was first discovered in Alberta in 1909. It was being supplied to Calgary by 1912, making Calgary one of the first Canadian cities to have such service, along with Moncton, New Brunswick.

Medicine Hat also calls itself the *Greenhouse Capital of Alberta*, which recognizes the many large glass-covered structures that can be seen on the outskirts of the city. This reflects the fact that the southern prairies are the sunniest region in the country. Medicine Hat averages over 2500 hours of sunshine a year, the most for any city in Canada.

The town of Taber, 100 kilometers west of Medicine Hat, has a special meaning for Albertans; this is where the best corn in the province is grown. Unfortunately, much of the table corn in the west does not compare with the large, sweet varieties that you can find back east. Here at Taber they have the right soil and weather conditions to produce a great product. Albertans all anticipate its arrival in the stores and at the roadside stands each summer.

Continuing west, we come to Lethbridge, a city similar in size to Medicine Hat, also located near a deep river valley. This time, most of the city, including the downtown, is located on the flat upper-plain. One of the most impressive sights here is the very long and high railway trestle that crosses the valley.

Just to the west of Lethbridge is the town of Fort Macleod, the original destination and first fort of the North West Mounted Police when they were formed and sent west in 1874. Their prime purpose was to restore order and to stake out Canada's claim to the region, since the area was being disrupted by American fur traders and the gun and whiskey dealers who had established a trading post called Fort Whoop-Up!

There are replicas of both forts in the area. A replica of Fort Whoop-Up is located in a riverside park in Lethbridge, with period houses and shops, wagon rides and an interactive interpretive centre. The replica of Fort Macleod, in the centre of that town, is surrounded by a weathered, wooden-pole stockade. It presents the history of the local Indians and the NWMP. A special attraction is the Mounted Patrol Musical Ride, a mini-version of the RCMP Musical Ride; it's done here with eight horses and riders in replica 1878 NWMP uniforms.

Outside of Fort Macleod is the Head-Smashed-In Buffalo Jump, along with its accompanying interpretive centre. The Indians depended on the buffalo for their survival: food, clothing and shelter. A favoured hunting technique was to stampede a herd of buffalo over a cliff to their death, or at least causing crippling injuries. They would then process the meat and hides at the base of the cliffs. This site is such a place, its name coming from the tale of an Indian brave who stood too close to the falling buffalo herd one day. This is a well-preserved site, and the tall educational centre that is built into the cliff has informative displays about the culture, lifestyle and history of the Plains Indians.

A short distance to the south of Lethbridge and Fort Macleod is the Milk River and its valley. The main significance of this is that these waters drain south to the Missouri-Mississippi River system and, thus, end up in the Gulf of Mexico. The area was also briefly visited by the Lewis and Clark Expedition, which the United States government sent west to find a route to the Pacific Ocean in 1804. With the bicentennial of that journey now upon us, we are hearing a lot about it in the U.S. press and on television. We will examine the equivalent Canadian journeys when we are a little farther west, in British Columbia.

There are a number of continental divides across Alberta. This southern river system goes to the Gulf of Mexico. The central river systems, e.g., the Bow, the Red Deer and the Saskatchewan Rivers, end up in Hudson

Bay. The northern rivers, e.g., the Peace and the Athabasca, eventually flow to the Arctic Ocean. No Alberta waters end up in the Pacific Ocean since the southern portion of its border with British Columbia is that continental divide and the northern section is well east of the mountains.

Going west from Fort Macleod, we leave the prairie flatland and enter the foothills of the Rocky Mountains. The long, rolling hills, covered in flowing grasslands, are a notable sight in their own right. They become even more attractive as the high, sharp ridges of the Rockies form a backdrop.

Ahead of us is the Crowsnest Pass. The front ranges of the Rockies are a spectacular sight. We won't go on deep into the mountains just yet, but a quick side trip to the town of Frank is in order. This is one of the many coal mining towns that dot the pass. What distinguishes it is that during the night of April 29, 1903 the whole face of the mountain above the valley broke loose and one hundred million tons of rock swept down on the town, killing about 70 people and permanently covering over many of the homes and mining facilities. The local interpretive centre describes the history of the area and the geology involved with the slide. One effect of all this is that you always look at the mountains with a sense of caution, if not apprehension, when you drive through the narrow passes.

This area was also the setting for some of the major forest fires that ravaged the mountain areas of Alberta and British Columbia in the summer of 2003, threatening many of the area's cities and towns. Many people had to evacuate their homes as the fires approached. Due to the valiant efforts of the many firefighters not many homes were lost here.

Our journey turns north from here, staying in Alberta and passing along the leading edge of the foothills. As noted before, this is hilly grassland country, which means we are traveling along the transition zone from prairie farming to ranching. It is quite common to see open ranges with hundreds, if not thousands, of grazing cattle, a sight that's even more eye-catching in the spring when there are all the small calves huddled around their mothers, walking on unsteady legs. If you really want to see the rugged beauty of the western range, *Marlboro Country*, this is the route to take.

The ranches here are very large; some are grazing co-operatives, where a number of ranchers share an area; others are colonies, where religious groups, such as Hutterites, jointly own and manage the area. At the gateway of one large spread there is a sign that says, "Welcome, Enter at your own risk." I interpret the first thought as representing the folks who live here, the second as a dictum by their lawyers in these times of excessive litigation.

The ranching industry was seriously impacted by the discovery of the mad-cow infected animal in northern Alberta in early 2003. Then, just when the international markets seem to be opening up, there was the discovery of the infected cow in Washington State that had Alberta roots. Even with all the assurances that there is little real threat to people and that controls are going to be even tighter, the industry will be reeling for some time. It is all caught up in international politics and trade – never an easily resolved combination.

The impact can be captured with some numbers. Export of cattle from Canada fell off 70 percent in 2003 versus 2002. By early 2004 the total number of cattle in Canada had increased by over one million head versus the year earlier. Forty percent of the more than 15 million animals in the country are in Alberta.

On top of one rugged ridge in the foothills we can see another wind farm for generating power. It is easy to see the suitability of this location, as the wind funnels through the mountain passes, down the valleys and over the ridges.

Along the way, we pass a string of long, narrow lakes, set among the low, bald, rolling hills, which are called the Chain Lakes. A sign informs us that a side road would take us to the town of Nanton, best known these days as the source of the bottled water by that name; it's available far and wide. Isn't it amazing how bottled water has emerged in our society, given that most of us have access to very good community supplies? People pay $2.00 per liter, or more, for something that does not involve any processing or technology. Maybe I was in the wrong business.

Before we actually come to any town back along our foothills route, we do pass a road sign that says, "786 Ave." The folks here are obviously keenly anticipating the future growth of Calgary; at ten blocks per mile they are 78 miles (125 kilometers) from downtown! My only advice is that you be very careful if someone tries to sell you some land on the "outskirts" of Calgary; it's growing quickly, but...

A local rancher has a sense of humour, or else an uncontrollable urge to collect something. We pass a section of strung-wire fence along the highway where there is a baseball cap on each fence post; there are hundreds of them.

The first small village we come to is Longview, known for its saloon with a long bar and as the home of Ian Tyson, the legendary western singer. He is still a key fixture at many entertainment venues during the Calgary Stampede, always singing his classic *Four Strong Winds*.

The most famous of the local towns is Turner Valley. This is where the first real "booms" of the western oil and gas industry occurred. First, with the discovery of light oil condensates, so-called natural gasoline, in 1914, then natural gas in 1924, and finally, crude oil in 1936, the area was a frenzy of activity and speculation. Storefront operations selling mineral rights in exploration drilling programs abounded. The town flourished.

Fortunes were made and lost, based both on the petroleum activities and on the financial maneuvering that accompanied it. Although it was a simple precursor to the big-time oil discoveries that would occur decades later, this area symbolizes the beginnings of the industry. In the "oil patch," when someone talks about the times "back in the Valley," there is no confusion about what they mean: Turner Valley.

There is a fascinating local phenomenon here, the Burning Hill, or *Hell's Half Acre*. Along a local creek there is a steep bank where low-pressure natural gas slowly seeps to the surface from a shallow underground accumulation. It started to flow decades ago, as the result of leakage around one of the early oil wells. For safety reasons, it was set on fire in 1977. It now burns quietly, but steadily, presenting quite a sight, especially at night in the winter when the surrounding area is snow-covered. This will go on for many more decades into the future, as there is no effective way to extinguish it and, in any case, the open flow of raw natural gas would be a significant safety hazard.

The other thing we notice as we travel through the foothills is the number of horses out in the fields. Although in no way comparable to cattle in numbers, there are a lot of them. Horses are used by the cowboys on the range to check the herds and to round up the cattle for branding or shipment to market. These are working animals. There are also the horses that are used for riding and jumping. As well, they breed horses so as to collect PMU, pregnant mare urine, which is used in the pharmaceutical business; this alone has required tens of thousands of horses, but the demand is now threatened by recent research findings on the health impact of hormone replacement therapies.

As we approach Calgary, we pass Spruce Meadows, a rambling facility for show jumping at the world-championship level. There are a number of jumping fields, training rings and barn facilities for the horses. Three times a year horses and riders come from all around the world to compete for millions of dollars. The jumping events and all of the display areas and entertainment activities make it a full day of fun, all priced at a level to attract families. Even for a person who knows little about top-level horse competitions, it is a great experience. We can quickly find ourselves in the rhythm of the horses as they approach the difficult jumps, and personally feel the joy or disappointment as each gate is mastered, or not.

Now we are entering Calgary, the boomtown of the west and the place I call home. We can see the downtown skyline of Calgary from far off when approaching from almost any direction; it sits at the juncture of the flat prairie to the east and the foothills to the west.

I am surprised to see Calgary called the *Heart of the New West* on signs as we enter the city. As I have noted before, there are a lot of cities and towns that call themselves the Heart of something; I had forgotten that Calgary had done the same. In fact, I don't think many people in Calgary actually know this. If I recall, it was done in the aftermath of a huge public rejection of a proposal by the city administration to change the name of the *City of Calgary* to *Calgary City*. They didn't try "The GCA," but did slip in that "Heart" thing. (With all the "Heart of ..." labels around, I am surprised I haven't noticed any "Soul of ..." claims.)

This is a large and modern city. It has grown quickly; today it has essentially one million inhabitants, having doubled in the past twenty-five years, quadrupled in forty, and increased tenfold in sixty. The growth shows in the new residential subdivisions that are sprouting out of the prairie land and rolling hills in every direction. Homes are added by the hundreds at a time. The edges of the city are sharply defined at any point in time as the new neighbourhoods move steadily into the open countryside

The downtown office-tower boom of two decades ago has now been replaced by the growth of high-rise condominiums along the river. The numbers may be down a bit, but you can still say that the city's official bird is the construction crane. Calgary's downtown profile of modern high-rise office and residential buildings is more significant than most cities its size, or even much larger ones, because of the nature of its economic base.

Calgary is the home for most of the hundreds of petroleum companies in the country, large and small. Because this industry is driven by "office work," that is, by geology, engineering and financing, and is characterized by joint-venture projects that involve almost every combination of participants, it is concentrated downtown. That is how work gets done and deals get made. Other cities, which have a wider range of industries that are not as interactive, or which have more of a manufacturing base, tend to be less concentrated in the city centre.

The other phenomenon that is immediately noticeable downtown is the "Plus 15" system of glass-enclosed walkways, which connect the various buildings at the second-story level, fifteen feet above the street. There are many other cities that have a few such connectors, but nowhere else is the system so extensive. We can travel around thirty or more square blocks using this system without going outside. This is especially convenient and comfortable in the winter, meaning we can leave our coats in the car or the office. It also means we can see the sunshine while we are walking to our destination, a dramatic contrast to the underground tunnels of Toronto and Montreal.

In spite of the economic growth and focus on the petroleum business, Calgary can still relate to its label as *Cow Town*. Ranching is a big part of the heritage and the ongoing activity around here. This is captured for the world by the annual Calgary Stampede, the *Greatest Outdoor Show on Earth,* which started as a simple rodeo in 1912.

And what a party it is! The centre of it all is the rodeo and chuck wagon races, backed up by the farm and craft exhibitions and the midway carnival that take place on the Stampede Grounds, close to downtown. They attract over one million attendees during the ten-day run in early July. The final day of the competition is one of the biggest days in rodeo, with the winners in each of the major events receiving over $50,000.

But the Stampede is so much more. The whole city is in a party mode. Everyone, right down to bankers and lawyers, dresses in jeans and bright cowboy shirts all the time. Entertainment fills every venue. Free breakfasts of pancakes, bacon, juice and coffee can be found everyday on the downtown streets and at the shopping malls. Even free hamburger lunches can be located. Western music fills the streets. It's hard to imagine a band or singer that does not get work during this period. This tradition of the Stampede started decades ago when Calgary was truly a small western town. What is amazing is how Calgarians have kept it going, even as the city has grown to be one million strong.

The *Cow Town* theme was emphasized in a fun charity event during the millennium year, 2000. Life-size, fiberglass cows were sold to organizations that had them decorated in some theme, and then turned back to be auctioned off for charity. This was based on similar events that had been held in Zurich and Chicago. Toronto later tried it with moose figures.

Calgary's *Udderly Art* event was a big success. One hundred and twenty-five cows were decorated and auctioned for hundreds of thousands of dollars in total. They are still on display in many locations around the city and they always generate a smile from observers. I'll just let you imagine what some of them look like: *Cowabunga, Oil Moover, Moo West, Udder Shuttle* and so on.

The other special event associated with Calgary is the 1988 Winter Olympics. Again, it was a great party and a great success. The legacy facilities, such as the Olympic Saddledome (the hockey and skating arena), Canada Olympic Park (the ski jump and bobsleigh/luge facility), the Speed Skating Oval (where world records are still established) and the downhill skiing facilities in the Rockies at Nakiska, continue to contribute so much to the city.

The Olympic Saddledome is the home of the Calgary Flames, the site of the amazing "C of Red," during the 2004 Stanley Cup as the fans all dressed in the team colour and energetically cheered the team on – a great spectacle seen by hockey fans everywhere via the TV coverage. 17th Avenue, outside the Saddledome, became the Red Mile as the overflow crowds cheered on the team from the outside party site. That overwhelming experience made the silence of the lost next season, due to the impasse between the owners and players about salary structures, all the more frustrating for the fans.

Two of the memorable sidebars of the Olympics were Eddie-the-Eagle, the British ski jumper who definitely could not "fly," and the Jamaican Bobsleigh Team, which didn't have a sleigh or appropriate winter clothing, but managed to attract a huge following and even have a Hollywood movie made about them. Both of these phenomena competed at Canada Olympic Park on the outskirts of Calgary; they received adulating coverage by the local and international television networks

Calgarians were amused when the American announcers continued to say that the events were taking place on Paskapoo Mountain. Paskapoo was the name of the ski hill that was located on this site before the Olympic developments took place. But the hill is just the steep-sided south bank of the Bow River. The terrain at the top of the Olympic ski jump, when you look back, is open, relatively-flat farm land. You can easily drive to the top of the ski hill on local roads. I guess television reporters just couldn't bring themselves to say that the events were taking place below a farm field and that the Rockies were one hundred kilometers away.

There are a couple of places where the history of the region can be experienced. One of them is Heritage Park, a restored frontier village that includes a steam-locomotive-driven train, a functioning blacksmith shop, an aroma-filled bakery, a wooden-floored saloon and a gun-fight that breaks out periodically between the sheriff and the "bad guys" to amuse everyone.

The other major centre is the Glenbow Museum, a facility with world-class collections of many things, but with an especially impressive collection of items from the frontier days and from the Indian cultures in the area before the settlers arrived.

Calgary is a dynamic city, always full of energy and optimism. It has an extensive system of parks, including many miles of walking and biking trails along the rivers and creeks and in the hills which are used extensively. There are also many gathering areas downtown and in the nearby neighbourhoods that are full of interesting shops and restaurants – the Mall, Eau Claire, Kensington and 4th Street.

One strange thing about Calgary is its smoking laws. As in most cities, there are growing limits to smoking in public places, a welcome trend for non-smokers and those concerned about the health impacts. Calgary has strong rules about smoking in restaurants; in effect, the space must be contained, ventilated and not allow minors in. This all makes sense until we see how it is applied to restaurants with outside patios – there patrons must step outside the defining fence, usually going only a meter or so away, or else *go inside to smoke!*

Speaking of bars and restaurants, Calgary is where the great Canadian cocktail *The Bloody Caesar* was invented. The Calgary Inn bartender improvised on a U.S. Gulf Coast drink involving tomato juice and clam juice called a *clam digger* by spicing it up and garnishing it with a celery stalk – a Canadian favourite was born. You can spot a Canadian traveler world-wide as they ask a confused bartender for a Caesar.

I have mentioned statues and art pieces in different cities. On the downtown mall here there is a realistic life-size bronze statue of two businessmen having a conversation. It has been there for years and, yet, I always do a double-take when I see it.

Of course, rapid growth does bring some challenges, which brings us back to traffic. I know that every city has this problem, but Calgary has turned it into an art form. There is even a significant column in the city's major newspaper every day about traffic debates and developments.

Calgary's traffic issues probably started over a hundred years ago when the city was first laid out. Unlike almost every city in the west, even those that stayed small, Calgary does not have wide streets, not even its main thoroughfare. There is no Portage Avenue (Winnipeg), Victoria Avenue (Regina), or Jasper Avenue (Edmonton). As well, it is located at the junction of two rivers, as are many other cities, but there are only a few narrow bridges.

Modern roads have not kept up. There is a so-called north-south bypass, the Deerfoot Trail, but since the spread of new residential districts outpaces the road construction, it always has some traffic lights and stoppages. There is no east-west bypass. The Trans-Canada Highway through Calgary uses a narrow commercial street that has twenty-five traffic lights.

Traffic was a big issue in the municipal elections of 2001, debated by every candidate and opined upon by every citizen. The first thing the new city council decided was to slow down one of the main arteries into downtown and to eliminate some of the one-way streets that aided traffic flow. Their solution to traffic congestion seems to be to prevent traffic from getting anywhere in the first place. When we do make it downtown, we are faced with limited parking capacity and the highest parking fees in all of Canada; all this in a city that has a downtown-driven economy.

Back to that issue of an east-west bypass; the proposed routing is complicated by some sensitive environmental lands and First Nation control of other areas on the southwest side of the city. This has been known and debated for decades, since the 1960s. So, the new city council took action. First, they deferred any debate for a year, so that input could be received. Then, a year later, they decided to commission a major consultant study that would, wait for it, examine what should be studied in order to make a decision! I know you will think I made that up; I wish!

I will note there are some areas of progress, such as the Light Rail Transit, which is sort of a modern version of the street car. The current mayor is pushing hard to make up for decades of inadequate road building. Perhaps the only large city in the country with less traffic infrastructure is Vancouver, but, true to their west coast frame of mind, they seem to accept it, at least when talking to outsiders.

Notwithstanding the traffic (I just had to get that word in somewhere), Calgary is a great place to live. I would not trade it for anywhere else, especially with the proximity of the Rocky Mountains, just an hour's drive away.

The mountains also contribute to the weather phenomenon called chinooks. These are strong warm winds that can blow in quickly; the temperature can rise by tens of degrees in a just a few hours. This breaks up the winter, and keeps everyone optimistic about the arrival of the next chinook when it is cold.

There is another weather-related reputation for the province. When a cold winter blast arrives in the U.S. Midwest, they refer to it as an "Alberta Clipper." I haven't been able to convince friends and family down there to call them Manitoba Monsoons.

Calgary's higher altitude, and resulting cool evenings in the summer, also makes it relatively mosquito-free, which is a blessing for picnics and barbecuing. But remember, I did say "relatively free"; mosquitoes don't really concede any territory.

I can still remember the first time I saw the Rockies in the summer of 1961, rising up in front of us as our family drove west from Calgary. My parents had recently moved to Calgary and we were visiting. The rugged, steep-faced, sharp-peaked mountains with the white snowcaps overwhelmed me. On that trip I became determined to come west when I graduated, which I did three years later.

The first area we come to in the mountains is called Kananaskis Country, located in a valley behind the first range of mountains. This is recreation territory: campgrounds, hiking trails and developed facilities such as the Olympic ski hills of Nakiska. There are two spectacular golf courses, which are named after the mountains that loom above the forest-lined fairways, Mt. Kidd and Mt. Lorette. This is probably the best golf deal in the country: spectacular mountain courses at relatively low prices, held low because the area was developed with the support of the Alberta provincial government.

Next, we come to the town of Canmore, located just before the entrance to Banff National Park. Its history is as a coal mining town that developed in the 1880s to supply the newly-built CPR. That was its role until the 1970s, when the coal resources became uneconomic and the mines closed. At that time the fate of the town seemed pretty bleak; it could have ended up like Springhill. However, a new phenomenon was emerging – upscale, weekend get-away homes in the mountains for people from Calgary and points beyond.

The emergence of Canmore was created by two factors. First, there are severe restrictions on ownership of properties in the national park. Canmore, with its own superb mountain views, but located just outside the park, was ideal for development. Second, the alternative was to go to the mountain passes in British Columbia, but they are at least two or three hours farther away from Calgary, which inhibits frequent weekend use.

The transition to becoming a recreation destination started slowly in the late 1970s and early 1980s, but it has grown rapidly since, especially after the Olympic Nordic events were held here, which increased the awareness of the place.

I became enamored with Canmore in the early 1980s, just after returning from South America, and built a vacation home here in 1987. Canmore is a super place, with its superb vistas, small town ambience, lots of attractions such as extensive hiking trails, cross-country skiing, outstanding golf courses and the nearby attractions of Banff and Kananaskis. As with many towns and cities in the country, Canmore has a tremendous variety of community events throughout the year; I am just more aware of them here. They include a family-focused New Year's Eve celebration, winter skiing and hiking festivals, dog-sled competitions, Canada Day parades and carnivals, Miners' Day parades and picnics, highland games, a folk festival, art walks, a Calgary philharmonic *Mozart on the Mountain* concert, and numerous charity-based marathons-bikeathons-telethons-skiathons-whateverathons.

One thing that we do become aware of in the mountains is the wildlife. (I need to be careful with the spelling here; I think the members of the younger generation who hike, bike and ski all day, and party all night, probably call it the wild life.)

A recent headline in the local newspaper read, "Grizzly Bear Death Toll Reaches Eight – Residents Up in Arms." The point of the story was that eight grizzly bears had been killed over the summer because they were becoming pests and aggressive around people in various towns. People were upset that the bears had to be destroyed, blaming the problem on careless homeowners and campers who left food and garbage accessible to the animals, which leads to their becoming attracted to the scenes. Most people in the mountains believe that the animals were here first and we should not unnecessarily disturb or destroy them. But, once they become dangerous, grizzlies can't be tolerated.

The best way to avoid problems with bears when walking or biking in the woods is to make enough noise so that they hear you coming. They don't want to mess with people either, but they can become aggressive when surprised. You can obtain "bear-bells," which attach to your clothing and warn the bears that you are coming. This leads to everyone's favourite joke on the subject: "How can you tell the difference between the scat of a black bear and that of a grizzly bear?" "It's easy; the grizzly bear scat has bear-bells in it."

The perceived risk of a bear attack seems to increase with distance, presumably due to a lack of familiarity with the actual situation. For example, during my visits to Australia, people would inevitably be amazed that Canadians would hike in the wilderness with all of the bears around, and skeptical when I tried to explain that the actual risk was very small. They were equally surprised that I thought they were crazy to wander into their wilderness regions, with all of the poisonous snakes and spiders, let alone the crocodiles. It's all what you get used to, I guess.

We have seen many animals around Canmore: deer, elk, beaver, mountain goats, woolly sheep, coyotes and black bears. Once, there was a grizzly bear at the entrance to our small cul-de-sac. Of course, there are also numerous small animals and a wide variety of birds. The town is directly in the pathway of migrating golden eagles; this stimulates a town festival each year. As a result, the town's junior hockey team is quite naturally called the Golden Eagles.

Fishing is a favourite pastime for many people here as well. The Bow River, both above and below Calgary is considered one of the world's leading trout fishing locations; fishermen come from far and wide to try their luck. Of course, even with all of their specialized gear, they put their success down to skill, just as with a golfer and a hole-in-one.

Banff is a Canadian treasure. The town site and original national park boundaries were established around a set of hot springs on the slopes of Sulphur Mountain in 1885, just as the railway to the Pacific Ocean was being completed. The railway wanted to stimulate tourist traffic by building luxurious hotels along its route. Banff was chosen as the site of one of the first. Construction of the Banff Springs Hotel – the *Castle in the Rockies* — began in 1886; it opened in 1888. It was a great success and became the forerunner of the many railway hotels across the country, which often came to define those specific cities.

The Banff Springs Hotel was expanded and rebuilt over the years. It continues to be extraordinary; it's my favourite hotel, anywhere. Its turrets and staircases, stone facing and expansive grounds, spectacular views and facilities, golf course and spa, all make the *Castle* feel like it's your special home. We can spend hours exploring all of its nooks and crannies.

A multi-million dollar renovation recently fixed a flaw that was inherent in the hotel from inception. The original hotel was built backwards! The plans that had been sent from back east had been turned;

the large face of rooms that were to look out at the spectacular view down the valley actually faced into the mountain behind. The entrance was placed out in front of the main view, blocking the scenery and creating a serious bottleneck for traffic, coming and going. They made a number of adjustments to the building as it was being completed, so it was quite functional, if somewhat awkward, for about a century. Now, a new entrance and reception area has been created on the appropriate back side; the front has been modified to have more luxurious lounging and view opportunities.

A ride up the gondola to the top of Sulphur Mountain, where we can get a tremendous panoramic view of the Rockies "from the top," is a must. The fit and adventurous can walk up and/or down, but I choose to ride. This can be followed by a relaxing dip in the hot, sulphurous waters at the Upper Springs. Then it's on to one of the pubs or fine restaurants in town for dinner.

Across the valley, on the slopes of Tunnel Mountain, is the Banff Centre, an outstanding educational institution for the fine arts and management. It has a fabulous natural setting in the pine and spruce forest. The smell of the woods is amazing in the fresh mountain air.

Just don't go looking for the tunnel in Tunnel Mountain; there isn't one, and never has been one. There are stories that the railway was considering a tunnel through this small mountain when it first surveyed its route, having followed the Bow River from Calgary and found a narrow gorge and surging waterfall beside it. It's hard to believe that this was a serious idea for long, since there is an easy, flat route around the other side of the mountain that feeds right into the Banff townsite.

Away from the town are many attractions, such as mountain hikes or river-raft rides in summer or skiing in winter, and fantastic photography opportunities. Among the most photographed and painted sights in Canada have to be the views of Cascade Mountain and Mount Rundle that frame Banff.

West of Banff, we continue to follow the Bow River upstream, as it churns and tumbles across its rocky bed. One of the outstanding images is of Castle Mountain, with its very steep slopes and a massive fortress-like upper structure. This is also a good example of how the naming of geographic features can be very tricky and controversial. This mountain had been called Castle Mountain since the time of the early railway activities of the late 1800s. After World War II the Canadian government changed the name to Mt. Eisenhower, to honour the American General and, later, President. This did not please the local residents and historians. Finally, after decades of lobbying, the name was changed back to Castle Mountain, but the peak was called Eisenhower Peak. This seems to have satisfied everyone.

Back in Canmore, there was another controversy about the name of a mountain. For over one hundred years a distinctive peak above the town was called Chinaman's Peak, which was named by the railroad construction gang in recognition of a Chinese worker who climbed the peak twice in one day. Recent sensitivities made the name unacceptable and so a name change was required. They canvassed the local population. Well, there was no consensus. The traditionalists wanted it named after the Chinese worker, Ha-Ling; many townsfolk wanted it named Miners Mountain (no apostrophe, of course), to recognize the town's heritage. The regional First Nation groups wanted it called The Last Lakota, after an ancient legend. So, we now have Ha-Ling Peak and Miners Peak on the Last Lakota, although the only name that actually seems to be remembered and used is Ha-Ling Peak.

We can all remember the furor, a couple of years ago, when Prime Minister Chrétien wanted to change the name of Canada's highest mountain from Mt. Logan to Mt. Trudeau. Again, traditionalists and historians protested and the idea was dropped. Instead, Montreal's Dorval Airport was renamed Pierre Elliott Trudeau Airport.

Twenty-five kilometers west of Castle Mountain, we come to Lake Louise, perhaps the most beautiful single sight in the mountains. Its bright turquoise colour almost seems artificial, but it is natural, and actually quite a common sight in the mountain lakes that are fed by melting glaciers. The melting glacial waters carry fine particles of rock powder, which have been created by the slow grinding action of the glaciers over centuries, and which cause this colourful refraction.

Lake Louise sits at the base of Victoria Glacier, and, although it is relatively small, being about two kilometers long and half a kilometer wide, it is a spectacular sight with the high mountain peaks and bright white glacier to frame the picture. The water is too cold for swimming; remember, it was in ice form just a short while ago, but the wind-protected lake is ideal for canoeing in summer and ice skating in winter. There is a hiking trail around the lake and a slightly more adventuresome trek up to a tea house on the Plain of Six Glaciers, set amid the rising mountain peaks. The Chateau Lake Louise, a sister hotel to the Banff Springs, has its main lobby, dining room and a large number of guest rooms facing the prime view of the Lake. This is a special place to visit.

Skiing is big-time in the Rockies, of course. We mentioned the Nakiska area earlier. World-class ski facilities also exist at Sunshine, near Banff, and here at Lake Louise. Lake Louise is probably the most famous, as it was developed the earliest and it is the site of World Cup events. Both Sunshine and Lake Louise attract local and international vacationers. The only downside is that most accommodations tend to be a bit of a distance from the hills themselves, in the towns of Banff and Lake Louise. This contrasts to the situation at many of the British Columbia resorts, where it's possible to ski in and out of your hotel. The significant restrictions on developments in the national park create the difference. They have not carved out open-development zones here, as they have in the Parks of Terra Nova and Gros Morne in Newfoundland.

Along the Banff-Lake Louise Highway we observe another indicator that the animals are well protected here. As one of the conditions for the approval to twin part of this road to four lanes, wildlife right-of-ways needed to be built so that the animals could safely cross. In most instances these are built as tunnels under the road. Here, they built elaborate overpasses, faced and fenced with decorator stone and covered with trees, bushes and grasses, to make it seem natural for them. Surveys show that, once in a while, an animal actually crosses over. To me, they conjure up the image of a *Far Side* cartoon, where the predatory animals would be huddled behind the trees and rocks as the deer approach. The caption would be, "It is sure great that they built this herding funnel and hunting blind for us."

From Lake Louise, we head north on the Icefields Parkway, a 200 kilometer trip to Jasper. I have used a lot of superlatives about the sights we have seen as we have crossed Canada, and so I will just say that this is the most spectacular stretch of scenery in the whole country, bar none.

The journey is lined with outstanding mountain sights on both sides. We pass numerous bright turquoise lakes, often set beneath a huge overhanging glacier face, such as the Crow Foot Glacier above Bow Lake. We see deep crevasses in the rocky faces of the mountains, often with enormously high waterfalls cascading to the valleys below. We see the vast Columbia Icefields, where we can climb the front edge or can take tracked-vehicle tours far into the white wilderness. We see the headwaters of the Saskatchewan and Athabasca Rivers, as they separate at the continental divide and flow towards the far-away oceans. We see the tumbling Athabasca Falls and can take a river-raft ride through churning rapids. We might see bighorn sheep and the shaggy, white-haired mountain goats. Maybe a bear or a moose will appear. Deer and coyotes are abundant. This special experience will terminate in the resort town of Jasper, set on the Athabasca River below the tall rocky peak of Mount Edith Cavell.

Jasper is a quieter and more modest town than Banff, primarily due to its greater distance from a major city. Edmonton is closest, but it is almost 400 kilometers away, which means Jasper is not much closer to Edmonton than Banff is. Nevertheless, it has some fine facilities and beautiful mountain scenery and attractions. Fishing, hiking, skiing and camping opportunities abound.

Jasper was created by the Grand Trunk Pacific Railway, a forerunner of the CNR, in the early 1900s. They competed for tourist business with the CPR and its Banff offerings. Here, they built the Jasper Park Lodge, a unique concept in the chains of hotels built by the railways. Its main building and many outlying guest cottages are all built of logs; it's rustic in concept, but decorated and serviced in style. It is set on the shores of the relatively small Lake Beauvert, backed by high mountain peaks. This is a special place to spend time, somewhat akin to Chateau Montebello in Quebec, but much more spread out and blessed with the mountain scenery. One of my favourite experiences is to sit beside Lake Beauvert on a calm summer evening and listen to the long call of a loon coming across the water.

A local hazard to be aware of is the roaming herd of elk that populate the area. Elk are majestic animals, with their significant size and impressive racks of antlers. But, whether it is a male or female that you encounter on the paths, they always believe they have the right of way. I know a number of people who have been forced into the lake by a determined elk, sometimes even while dressed in fancy evening clothes, on the walk from their cottage to the dining room in the main lodge. At least the experience makes a great story for the folks back home.

The golf course at Jasper is one of my favourites. It wanders through the woods at the base of a mountain, with views back across the valley to numerous other peaks. Pyramid Mountain, with its distinctive shape and red-hued colour, always radiates in the sunlight, especially in the long rays of an evening sunset.

As part of the growing competition between the railways for tourist business, the CNR and the Jasper Park Lodge hired the world-famous golf architect Stanley Thompson to build their course in 1925. It was a total success, so much so, that in 1927 the CPR and the Banff Springs Hotel hired him to rebuild their course. There he built perhaps his most famous layout, but it involved moving huge amounts of rock at the base of the mountains and damming rivers. It cost them a then-world-record million dollars, an enormous sum in those days. His explanation was simply, "It costs money to move mountains."

From here, we can now turn back eastward, toward Edmonton. We are on the Yellowhead Route, the northern leg of the Trans-Canada Highway. Over the 400 kilometer stretch ahead of us the terrain progresses from forest to grassy hills to open prairie again. The northwest part of Alberta is relatively sparsely populated, but it contains a number of towns with 5,000 to 10,000 people that are the regional centres for the forestry, petroleum, coal mining, ranching and farming activities. They include Rocky Mountain House and Drayton Valley in the south, Hinton and Edson along our route, and Whitecourt and Peace River to the north. They are basic towns that have a pulp and paper mill, a natural gas processing plant, or a mine nearby. This may be rugged country, but it is rich in resources.

The most significant city in northwest Alberta is Grand Prairie, somewhat north of our travel path. It is in the centre of the farm country that opens up again as you move in that direction, as well as being in the midst of an active oil and gas exploration region. This city of over 35,000 people has been growing rapidly.

As we travel through the ranching country west of Edmonton, we notice some unusual signs from time to time. In addition to the expected cattle and horse ranches, there are ranches that specialize in bison, llamas, alpacas, elk, and even a crossbreed called beefalo. This represents diversification on the farm, and, I guess, reflects a consuming public that is looking for variety on their barbecues. I wonder what the pioneer settlers would think of it all.

Lake Wabamun, some 50 kilometers west of Edmonton, is 20 kilometers in length and provides cottage opportunities for Edmontonians, as do a number of similar lakes in central Alberta. My parents had a cottage here in the 1970s, and our family always enjoyed visiting. Boating, fishing, swimming and hiking filled the days. Evenings always brought a campfire on the lakefront beach, complete with roasted (read *burned*) marshmallows.

From here, we can swing down to approach Edmonton from the south, via the town of Devon, where there is an informative museum and the Oilmen's Hall of Fame. This is the location of the famous Leduc oil field that was discovered in 1947. After years of extensive exploration programs and modest success across the west by many companies, Leduc was a major find. Imperial Leduc #1 was the signal that major resources did exist here. It spawned the large and prosperous industry that we know today. Canada has become a world-scale producer of oil and natural gas and a significant user of those feedstocks to manufacture petrochemical products.

Now we arrive in Edmonton, the capital of Alberta. Like Calgary, it has almost a million people as the result of continuous and significant growth for more than sixty years. However, it is very different from Calgary.

To start with, it has a different geography and climate. Edmonton is located on the North Saskatchewan River, where the banks are high and the valley is strongly defined with many deep ravines running inland, as opposed to the relatively modest Bow River valley in Calgary. Edmonton is lower in elevation and much farther from the mountains, which means that it has hotter summers, colder winters and lots of mosquitoes. During one of the periods that I lived in Edmonton, the temperature for the day did not get above 0°F (-17°C) for more than 30 days in a row! At the other extreme, it can get over 100⁰F (37⁰C) in the summer, which has never happened in Calgary.

The city profile is different. It has a more modest downtown skyline, but it does have a wide main street, Jasper Avenue. The view up to the city centre from back down the river valley is quite impressive, with the provincial legislature, a large convention centre and the Macdonald Hotel perched along the upper bank. Across the valley, on the other bank, is the University of Alberta.

The lesser downtown profile of Edmonton is offset by the many heavy-industry manufacturing facilities for the petroleum and mining industries, and by the many large oil refineries and chemical plants on the east side. This is why Edmonton's growth has kept pace with Calgary's.

We lived here a couple of times, when the children were young, and found it to be a very good city for raising a family. There are many parks and recreational attractions.

Perhaps the most famous attraction in Edmonton is the West Edmonton Mall, a shopping centre. But what a shopping centre! It is an enclosed space with over 800 stores, 26 movie theatres, 110 eating places, an amusement park with a high rollercoaster, a marine display with live dolphins, a water park with a mammoth wave pool, a full-size hockey rink, a theme-roomed hotel, a 40,000 square foot arcade, and a partridge in a pear tree. It is almost too much, but it is a "must-destination" for anyone in the vicinity, which means anyone within 500 kilometers.

Edmonton is also home to the CFR, the Canadian Finals Rodeo. Sure, the Calgary Stampede has the high-profile, big-money event every July, but the Canadian finals, which play a big part in qualifying for the World Finals in Las Vegas, occur here.

Rodeo is a tough life. Jumping off horses, wrestling steers, being thrown in the air by bucking broncos and stomped on by mad bulls; it's all in a day's work. In reality, the rodeo world is mostly one of small towns. The same cowboys and animals appear steadily in towns like Ponoka, High River and Strathmore. In fact, sometimes the cowboys appear at two or three different rodeos in one day, using planes and shared cars to sprint across Alberta, Saskatchewan, Montana, Wyoming and other "near-by" places.

The summer festival here is called *Klondike Days*, which recognizes Edmonton as the *Gateway to the North*, even back in the gold-rush days of the 1890s. It is a fun-filled time with an agricultural exhibition, a midway and lots of parties. Decades ago almost everyone dressed in the costumes of the 1890s for the week: fancy full-skirted dresses and parasols, striped pants with colourful vests and top hats. I can remember our whole family dressing in the fancy clothes, even the small children. However, that has lost most of its support as the city has grown so quickly and become so much larger. It's a lot simpler in Calgary, where the official dress code of the Stampede is jeans.

Edmonton has problems with its identity; it has too many of them. It has been the *Gateway to the North*, the *Home of Klondike Days* and, for a while, *Canada's Festival City*. For the past couple of decades they have been the *City of Champions*. This is a source of great civic pride, as Edmonton won five Grey Cups in a row, from 1978 to 1982, and five Stanley Cups, from 1984 to 1990. But that was some time ago now, and the motto does not do much to attract visitors. Recently, they tried to promote some new slogans that included images of energy, or dreams, or parklands, but the populace said no. They like being *The City of Champions*, even if Wayne Gretzky is long-gone, now living in L.A. and involved with Phoenix hockey.

Edmonton has one other hockey championship of distinction; in 1952 the Edmonton Mercurys won the gold medal at the Winter Olympics in Oslo. Canada did not do this again for another fifty years, not until the pro team, managed by Gretzky, won gold at the 2002 Olympics in Salt Lake City.

In November 2003 they held an outdoor NHL game between the Edmonton Oilers and the Montreal Canadians at the football stadium. Over 50,000 people attended the event, which also included a pre-game contest between the old-timers such as Wayne Gretzky, Mark Messier and Guy Lafleur. In spite of very cold weather, near 0^0C, it was a big success. I expect they will do it again.

There is another phenomenon happening with the Edmonton hockey team; they are promoting the team as the Oil, rather than the Oilers. This picks up on recent trends in sports to use singular names, e.g., Minnesota Wild, Utah Jazz, and Orlando Magic. The name Oil hasn't caught on in the reporting anywhere else as far as I can tell. Maybe Toronto should change their name to the grammatically correct Maple Leaf.

Have I mentioned the Edmonton airport? I think I alluded to it when we passed Mirabel in Montreal. The Edmonton airport makes Mirabel seem like it is downtown. It was built in the early 1960s, far to the south, near the town of Leduc, to allow for growth. Well, forty years later, the city has tripled in size and the airport is still many kilometers from the city's outer limits. For years this was an inconvenience for the long-distance traveler, but there was a smaller downtown airport that supported shorter commuter trips to Calgary, Vancouver and points in the northern part of the province. That has been shut down now and everyone goes to Leduc. In reality, many people just travel to Edmonton less often, or, if coming from Calgary, they drive; it's almost as fast and you can set your own schedule.

This is the capital of Alberta and, so, we should talk some politics. Alberta politics are different, but in many ways more straightforward, than in other parts of Canada.

First of all, Albertans do not change their minds as often as others. In the almost 100 years since Alberta became a province, there have been only three changes of the governing party! The Liberals ruled from 1905 to 1921; the United Farmers from 1921 to 1935; Social Credit from 1935 to 1971; and the Progressive Conservatives ever since. That's 16, 14, 36 and 33+ years between changes. This reflects that Alberta is relatively homogeneous in its political thinking at any point in time.

Also, in Alberta there is always a sense of independence from Ottawa and the national parties. For example, until the recent merger the provincial PCs were more likely to support the Reform/Alliance group in federal elections than the federal PC Party.

The conservatism of Albertans in politics, economics, social attitudes and religious groups is always a strong influence. It is just not as overwhelming as many people in other parts of Canada think. The successful leaders here are able to create a reasonable balance of fiscal conservatism and social conscience. Peter Lougheed and Ralph Klein, the longest-serving current political leader in Canada, who was re-elected for a fourth term in November, 2004, have been able to keep their supporters and the general electorate satisfied over long periods.

Of course, the royalties from the crude oil and natural gas production helps the government fund its costs and stimulate the economy. As a result, Alberta became debt-free in the spring of 2005, a great centennial present for its citizens and taxpayers.

So, Alberta politics are simple. The downside to all of this is that Alberta often has little presence inside the federal government, especially when the Liberals are in power. This has been the case for thirty of the last forty years, and for most of the quarter-century before that.

When Paul Martin became Prime Minister in late 2003 there was an expectation that he would make some inroads with Alberta voters, based on his performance as Finance Minister and the presumption he would easily win the next federal general election. With all the issues that arose in early 2004 over political sponsorship payments and internal party disputes, plus the emergence of the new Conservative party with a broader national appeal, that didn't happen. Edmonton voters have given some modest support to the Liberals, most notably the 2004 re-election of Anne "Landslide Annie" McLellan, the Deputy Prime Minister, who won for the fourth time by a margin of a few hundred votes out of 50,000 votes cast. Only time will tell if Albertans become more pragmatic in their future voting patterns. However, the revelations of the political financial scandals that emerged from the Gomery inquiry in 2005 make any likelihood of them voting more Liberal in the near term very remote.

At least our electoral process is a short one, with campaigns lasting only a few weeks. This contrasts with the U.S. where they seem to be campaigning all the time, certainly for at least two years in the case of their presidential election. Also, our losing leaders have a continuing presence as they lead the opposition forces in parliament and often lead their party again in the next election. Stephen Harper, Gilles Duceppe and Jack Layton play a real role in our parliament, especially with the minority status of Paul Martin's Liberals after the 2004 election. In the U.S. losing candidates just seem to disappear from the scene. Where did Al Gore go, even though he won the popular vote in 2000? Will we hear from John Kerry again, even though he came so close in 2004?

Albertans generally believe in less government, everywhere, all the time. This shows up in debates between the provincial and federal governments, in debates with other provinces, and debates within the province on issues such as privatization. Albertans don't understand why this is not the basic philosophy everywhere, when, in reality, it is not the priority anywhere else at all, not even in prosperous Ontario. This difference of perspective causes frustration and confrontation, especially on issues such as Medicare. Albertans support the principles of accessibility, universality and affordability; they just do not believe that governments can deliver efficient or effective services. Elsewhere, people do not trust the private sector nearly as much. This explains why Alberta is seen as the "most-American" province. The debates will continue.

Let's move on into the north woods to visit one of the most significant new energy sources in the world, the Athabasca oil sands.

Some people might wonder why I call this a new energy source, when there has been production from the area for over thirty-five years. The difference is the emerging scale of the operations and the ability to compete economically with other worldwide projects.

Governments have created the necessary general business environment for companies to come and invest. They have not been as hung up on project-specific details as other jurisdictions, although they always ensure resource conservation, safety, and environmental care. In the oil sands of Alberta there are a number of multibillion dollar investments being made. This is in an area that was once considered to have the highest-cost oil in the world. The positive fiscal environment and the creative technology of the attracted enterprises have made all the difference.

New, much larger mining equipment has reduced the operating costs for the enormous surface-mines that access the relatively shallow resources. Developments in horizontal well-drilling technology now allow economic access to the deeper deposits. Steam can be injected into the ground, reducing the viscosity of the tar-like oil and allowing it to flow up to surface processing facilities. New processing methods have reduced emissions to the environment and made the plants more acceptable. This has led to huge investments, and in Canada becoming a significant supplier of oil to the world marketplace.

In fact, Canada is the eighth largest oil producing country in the world, ahead of all the OPEC countries except Saudi Arabia and Iran. The other leading producers are Russia, the United States, Mexico, China and Norway. Canada is the largest supplier of oil imported into the U.S., ahead of Venezuela. There is always a great deal of political controversy about the riches that accrue to Alberta from its world-scale oil industry; Albertans well remember the punitive National Oil Policy of the Trudeau government. Can you imagine a National Automobile Policy that would require the auto industry in Ontario and Quebec to supply vehicles to the rest of Canada at less than market value?

The centre of all this activity is the city of Ft. McMurray, 50,000 strong, some 400 kilometers north of Edmonton. It has seen a series of booms and busts over the past four decades, as oil prices fluctuated up and down and major projects stopped and started. Before the improvement in the technologies that I mentioned, this was a high-cost source of oil. Its development depended on a view of needy oil markets and high oil prices in the future, a viewpoint that came and went over the years. Now, with the improved economics, there has been a boom for ten years, and it shows no sign of abating.

This creates many pressures on the community infrastructure, of course. There is always the need for more facilities. Workers are scarce for lower-paying jobs, as there always seems to be jobs at the major construction sites. New restaurants can open in response to the real market growth, but then struggle to find people to staff their positions. For a while, the drive-through windows at the highway coffee and doughnut shops were closed due to staffing problems, a blow to the early-morning travelers headed to the plants about an hour north of the city.

It is a good city to live in, full of energy and optimism about the future. For nature lovers, hikers, hunters and fishermen, this is a great region. Sure it may be a little isolated from the big city, and services may lag a bit, but for many of the people here it is much better than most mining towns and oil centres. It has size, growth and a sense of permanence, something not always found in the resource industries.

Well we have about run out of Alberta. Since we are this far north, let's carry on and visit the Northern Territories: Nunavut, the Northwest Territories and the Yukon, Canada's final frontiers.

Nunavut,
Northwest Territories
and Yukon,

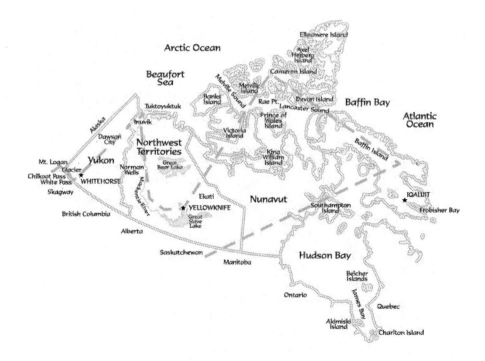

North Pole

Arctic Ocean

Ellesmere Island

Axel
Heiberg
Island

Cameron Island

Beaufort
Sea

Melville
Island

Banks
Island

Devon Island

Baffin Bay

Tuktoyuktuk

Rae Pt.

Lancaster Sound

Atlantic
Ocean

Inuvik

Prince of
Wales
Island

Alaska

Victoria
Island

Baffin Island

Dawson
City

Northwest
Territories

Mt. Logan

Yukon

King
William
Island

Glacier

Norman
Wells

Great
Bear Lake

Chilkoot Pass
White Pass

WHITEHORSE

IQALUIT

Skagway

Ekati

YELLOWKNIFE

Nunavut

Southampton
Island

Frobisher Bay

British Columbia

Great
Slave
Lake

Alberta

Hudson Bay

Saskatchewan

Manitoba

Belcher
Islands

Ontario

Quebec

Akimiski
Island

Charlton Island

Kilometres 0   1000

Miles 0   600

10. The Northern Territories

The Northern Territories of Canada are immense in size but sparse in population. This does not take away from their key role in the definition of Canada, nor from the many adventures that have taken place up here, heroic and otherwise.

We are going to travel by plane for this part of our journey. The distances are great and there are few roads.

We will start with the newest territory, Nunavut. This encompasses the Eastern Arctic region of Canada, generally the area north of Manitoba, Ontario and Quebec, including all of the Arctic Islands. It also includes the islands in Hudson Bay and James Bay. The southernmost of those islands, Charlton and Akimiski, are farther south than Saskatoon and Edmonton.

This territory is the main home of the Inuit, the northern people who were called Eskimos by the early explorers. Nunavut was created in 1999; it means "our land" in the local dialect. The total population is about 30,000, with 5,000 in the capital city of Iqaluit, located on Frobisher Bay at the south end of Baffin Island.

The territorial flag features a stylized Inukshuk, a message of welcome for everyone. You will recall that these are human-like figures constructed of piled rocks that were used for many purposes by the Inuit, but they always signify support and a welcome.

My experience in Nunavut is limited. In common with many people from western Canada, my main observations have been from the air. Direct flights from Calgary or Vancouver to Europe fly over the territory, as they follow the shortest great-circle route. The views from above are amazing.

The first observation we make, flying over the southern portion of the territory in the summertime, is that it is mostly water-covered. This is also true of the northern sections of the Prairie Provinces and of the Northwest Territories. The specifics may vary, from a few very large lakes to hundreds of modest-sized lakes to thousands of ponds and wetland marshes, but it is wet. You can almost "see" the mosquitoes waiting for a rare visitor to arrive. The trees and bushes are short, and they steadily thin out as we move north from Alberta. Nunavut itself is mostly barren of trees. The sense of isolation and inaccessibility is strong.

There are very few people living in mainland Nunavut and those are almost all gathered in villages along the coastlines or at remote mining sites. Mining operations across the frozen hinterland have extracted copper, nickel, iron, gold, silver and platinum for a long time but many of the mines are now depleted and general access to the interior is difficult. There is a developing proposal to build a road inland from Bathurst Inlet, which is on the north shore just south of Victoria Island, and to serve it by summer shipping through the ice-packed northern channels. That will be a tremendous challenge.

There are also a few military sites in the Far North as part of the DEW-line system, the Defense Early Warning network that monitors the northern approaches to North America. Their significance has reduced over the years as satellite surveillance techniques have become more sophisticated.

Moving farther northeast, as we leave the flat mainland terrain, we come to the mountainous profile of Baffin Island. There are steep cliffs that plunge into the sea along the Baffin coastline. Inland, we see sharp mountain peaks that poke up through the extensive white glaciers, one of the most spectacular scenes on the planet. This region is permanently snow-covered.

The large island of Greenland is off to the east, but we will stay over Canada and swing up to the northwest, to the archipelago of the High Arctic. The snow-blanketed and wind-swept islands are connected by ice-covered channels. I try to imagine the difficulties of the early explorers who determinedly traversed these "waters," looking for that elusive, and inevitably impossible, Northwest Passage from Europe to Asia.

The first attempts to go north around the newly discovered American continent were by Martin Frobisher in the 1570s. Since other nations, such as Spain and Portugal, controlled the southern routes, Britain decided to try the northern one. These early voyages did not get far beyond the first ice-packed channels around Baffin Island, but they did establish the first European presence in the area of Iqaluit, which they named Frobisher Bay. There was quite a flurry of activity there for a few years as a result of the stories that gold had been discovered by Frobisher. It was America's first gold rush, but it was all for naught; the mineral was iron pyrite, "fool's gold."

Some three decades later, Henry Hudson sailed as far as the Bay that now bears his name. His exploration of Hudson Bay and James Bay, looking for a passage west, just led to frustration. In fact, the crew became so upset with Hudson's lack of planning and leadership, along with his refusal to head back home after being stranded in the area over a winter with inadequate provisions, that they mutinied and set him adrift in a small boat. He was never seen again. Nevertheless, his discoveries inspired the creation of the Hudson's Bay Company in 1670, which led to the establishment of the trading posts and all of the subsequent influences on the settlement of Western Canada.

The search for the Northwest Passage then went dormant for over a century. Only in the 1800s did the British Navy renew the attempt. Amazingly, one of the earliest attempts made the most progress for a long time. William Parry, in 1819-20, got as far as Melville Island on the western edge of the Arctic Archipelago.

The names Parry, Ross, Franklin, Rae, M'Clintock, McClure, Belcher, Kane, Hall, Cook, Peary, Bartlett and others became legendary. They doggedly persisted throughout the nineteenth century in their wooden, high-mast sailing ships. The crews sawed through the ice and hauled the ships with ropes as much as they sailed them. Journeys took years and death was frequent, if not from the cold and exposure, then, from debilitating scurvy.

The most famous expedition was that by John Franklin in 1845. It was famous, not because of any success, but because he was famous himself and he failed. Franklin had made some notable progress exploring the North a quarter century earlier, but, on this trip, he disappeared.

The search for Franklin over the ensuing many years by many other expeditions significantly enhanced the knowledge of the North, especially the most northerly island groups. These ventures also proved that there was no commercial passage to be found.

When remnants of the Franklin expedition were finally located around King William Island by M'Clintock, far from where most people had gone looking for him but where he had said he would go, it became apparent that the explorers had become seriously disoriented and had lost their sense of survival. They had abandoned much of their food and warm clothes but had carried formal dinner settings with them as they abandoned their marooned ship and trekked overland to their deaths in the harsh Arctic environment

A superb description of all the Arctic expeditions can be found in Pierre Berton's book, *The Arctic Grail*. There are many books about the individual journeys, and more are being written all the time. A fascinating account of all the expeditions, and their failure to find Franklin, is presented by Blair Latta in his recent book, *The Franklin Conspiracy: Cover-Up, Betrayal, and the Astonishing Secret behind the Lost Franklin Expedition*. He analyzes all of the trips and people in detail, and then postulates that the British Admiralty conspired to prevent Franklin from being found. The story is quite compelling; the problem is in trying to determine a motive. I'll leave it to you to judge Latta's creative concept.

One very significant consequence of all these expeditions was that Britain laid claim to the Arctic Islands. They then transferred that claim to Canada in 1880, ten years after Canadian purchase of the mainland territories from the Hudson's Bay Company.

There have been some disputes about this claim of Canadian sovereignty over all of the northern area. In 1944 the RCMP ship *St. Roch* traveled from Halifax to Vancouver across the north in a journey that took 86 days; it was a determined show of control, not commercial feasibility.

The Americans, in particular, have tried to assert that the main channels are international waters. This was a more pressing issue when they were considering the possibility of shipping Alaskan oil to the Atlantic markets by tanker. The ice-strengthened tanker *Manhattan* managed to navigate across in 1969, but the costs and economics were shown to be prohibitive. Therefore, a pipeline across Alaska to terminals on the Pacific coast at Valdez was built instead. The U.S. later sent an icebreaker, the *Polar Sea*, across in 1985, but, after some political confrontations and posturing, the whole issue faded away and has remained dormant ever since.

Now our journey will take us to a couple of the farthest north islands. When you see the High Arctic it is hard to appreciate that the area is technically a desert region, in that it has a very low annual amount of precipitation. It's just that it comes in the form of snow, and it does not go away.

In talking to northern residents we learn that the Inuit have many different words for the various types of snow and ice, and for the corresponding shades of white. Most of us from the south have not developed an appreciation for the nuances that can be discerned on close inspection. I wonder how they translate the fairy tale Snow White.

During the 1970s and 1980s, when the projections for energy prices were astronomical, and unrealistic in hindsight, there was an active exploration program in the High Arctic. Most of the major discoveries were of natural gas, which is difficult to economically move to markets from such remote locations. However, there was an oil discovery on Cameron Island, just north of Melville Island. It is located on a side channel from the Viscount Melville and Lancaster Sounds, which offer a route for shipping the oil out, at least in the summertime if you have enough horsepower.

I was up here in late August 1985, when the first shipment of oil was loaded. August is the best time because, being the end of the summer season, the ice is the thinnest. But make no mistake, the land was snow-covered and the water was frozen over. Everything was flat and white. Parkas, not golf shirts, were the dress code.

Our group stayed at an exploration base at Rae Point on Melville Island, basically a complex built of portable industrial trailers. The runway was made of packed snow. What I remember most vividly was the sign posted on the inside of the camp doors that led outside: "Check for Polar Bears <u>BEFORE</u> Exiting." People had been surprised, injured and even killed by polar bears that were naturally attracted to the camp by the smell of food, be it cooked or walking around on two legs. Needless to say, we were all very diligent and wary of wandering off for a personal view of the area.

At Cameron Island it was quite a sight to see the large tanker ship, with its reinforced-steel double hull, moving slowly but steadily through the channel ice. The ice was being broken by a world-class icebreaker that preceded it. As I said, it's all a matter of brute strength and horsepower. The whole operation of loading the oil and taking it to a Montreal refinery proceeded successfully and it was repeated for many years.

This is the farthest north we will get on our trip, 77^0 North latitude. We are still almost 1500 kilometers (1000 miles) from the North Pole. We are north of the Magnetic North Pole, however, which is far south of the geographic pole and actually moves around over the centuries. This makes compasses very difficult to use for direction finding and navigation when the north-seeking needle points to the south. Elaborate correction tables and charts are required. That was a problem for the early explorers; thank goodness for GPS systems now.

Flying back south from that earlier trip, we saw a polar bear ambling across the ice. It was majestic and certainly left us with the undeniable awareness of who was "king" in this barren land.

Next we visit the Northwest Territories, which generally lies to the west of Nunavut. This has been the name for a vast part of Canada over the years. When Canada first acquired the northern and western lands from the Hudson's Bay Company in 1870, the Northwest Territories encompassed everything from southern Ontario to the Rockies and up to the Arctic Ocean, except for southern Manitoba. Over time, parts were carved away, as the additional Prairie Provinces were created, other provinces were expanded, and the Yukon Territory was made independent.

The latest change was the separation of Nunavut in 1999. At that time the people of the Northwest Territories were given the opportunity to choose a new name, but they stuck with the historic one. Although some alternative names were proposed, the issue never seemed to be in doubt. As a result, there were some whimsical debates suggesting that the name should be changed to Restuvit, Whatsleftuvit, or just simply Bob! Unlike the folks of the Lakehead, oops, Thunder Bay, they got it right here.

The Northwest Territories is generally the treed part of the North. It is home to the Dene, or Indian groups, rather than the Inuit. In the western Arctic the trees, albeit short ones, continue all the way to the northern ocean, due to the climatic influence of the mountains to the west and the Mackenzie River.

Yellowknife is the capital of the Northwest Territories; almost half of the 40,000 people of the territory live here. It is situated on the north shore of Great Slave Lake, one of the two very large lakes in the North, the other one being the somewhat larger Great Bear Lake. They are larger than Lake Ontario and Lake Erie.

The city is probably best known for the gold mines that led to its founding in 1934, and which have been operating ever since. The tall draw-work structures on top of the mine shafts that penetrate deep underground are very visible focal points for the city. However, the city's name does not refer to gold; the name Yellowknife was derived from the colour of the copper knives that the local Indians carried.

Environment Canada has determined that Yellowknife is the coldest city in Canada. Its annual average temperature is -4.6⁰C (24⁰F).

The surrounding territory is full of lakes and fast-flowing rivers which lure fishermen from all over the world. Pristine wilderness and trophy fish that can be caught in the untouched waters are the big attractions. Lodges, local guides and outfitters are waiting for the adventuresome.

And there is golf, sort of. The nine-hole rugged course has artificial-turf greens. Small pieces of the green carpet are also used for positioning the ball in the dirt fairway for each shot. They have a weekend Midnight Madness Tournament at the time of the summer solstice each June that goes non-stop, 24-hours a day, since it does not get dark. You may have a tee-time at 3:00pm and at 3:00am. It sounds like it is more a test of endurance and partying; next time I go north I must make it a point to come here on the right days, for golf and for fun.

There is a new glitter in the air; gold is being replaced by diamonds as the source of wealth and excitement. There are now commercial diamond mining operations just a few hundred kilometers to the northeast of Yellowknife. The Ekati diamond deposit was discovered in 1991 and the mine opened in 1998. The Diavik mine followed five years later. It is not just the fact that there are diamonds here that is exciting; it's the scale and potential. In 2003 Canada was the third largest producer of diamonds in the world, trailing Botswana and Russia and surpassing South Africa. There are more mines on the way, and further potential in the Northwest Territories, Nunavut, Saskatchewan, Ontario and Quebec. Some industry people predict that Canada could be supplying one-quarter to one-half of the world's diamonds within a decade. That is amazing for such a new industry, and a relatively unknown one for most Canadians. It has been said that diamonds are a perfect wealth-transfer medium, since many people can make a good living in the process of producing and selling something to the rich that has no inherent use or value.

The other things that glow here in the North are the Northern Lights, the Aurora Borealis. These natural shows of spectacular light images streak across the dark, night sky. The waves of light seem to pulse across the heavens, often white, but sometimes in pinks, greens, reds and purples. They are the result of the Earth's electromagnetic fields; they do occur around both the North and South Poles.

I can marvel at the Northern Lights for hours. They also create a strange sensation in my mind; I find myself waiting with great anticipation to hear a loud noise. There is none. There is only total silence. I am so accustomed to hearing thunder after seeing a bolt of lightning that I cannot help but expect to hear some noise here too.

The Northern Lights can be seen from many places. I have occasionally seen them as far south as Calgary, but they are so much more intense up here, and they seem to be directly overhead. They are also more frequent here, being visible in Yellowknife over 240 days per year.

We head north again, down the historic Mackenzie River. (Yes, down the river, since it flows north to the Arctic.) This huge river drains most of the western Arctic and northern Saskatchewan, Alberta and British Columbia; its farthest headwaters are back in the Columbia Icefields and the cold beginnings of the Athabasca River.

The river was first navigated to the Arctic Ocean by Alexander Mackenzie and his band of explorers in 1789. He called it the *River of Disappointment* since he was actually searching for a cross-continent route to the Pacific Ocean. Instead, he ended up on the shores of the Arctic Ocean. However, he was an explorer. I love to study old maps and books, and what always comes through in reading the published journals of the early explorers such as Mackenzie is the dedication to discovery that they all possessed. They were not just trying to get from Point A to Point B. They were observing and documenting the geography, the plants and trees, the birds and animals, and the people and cultures they encountered. These journals make fascinating reading, as they are true first impressions of the new lands.

Since the Mackenzie River flows north, in the spring its headwater regions thaw before the downstream areas. This causes some heavy forces to be exerted on the river ice, which can pile up into huge jams at critical locations. One place where this happens is at the town of Norman Wells, not far from Great Bear Lake and just south of the Arctic Circle. I have been here a number of times.

There are islands in the middle of the very wide river here, which tend to hold back the ice and cause large piles to form. A local custom is for people to have betting pools to predict when the ice will move. The pressure beforehand causes all sorts of creaking and cracking noises as the ice compresses and breaks. When the ice jam does give, it is with a huge roar as mega-tons of ice are set free.

Norman Wells basically exists because of the oil field that was discovered here decades ago. Its remoteness would normally have precluded its development, but during the Second World War, after Japan had attacked Pearl Harbour, there was a serious concern about an attack on Alaska. Therefore, with the resources of the American Army to assist, two major projects happened. The first was the construction of an all-season Alaska Highway from northern British Columbia through the Yukon and on to Alaska. The second was the construction of an oil pipeline from Norman Wells to Whitehorse in the Yukon, where an oil refinery was assembled beside the highway. All of this was a major undertaking, through the rugged northern muskeg of the Northwest Territories and over the mountains of the Yukon. There are many stories and photographs of bulldozers and trucks being totally lost in the swampy muskeg, which becomes a real quagmire when it melts in the summer sun.

This so-called Canol Project (Canadian Oil Line) never did ship oil; the threat of a Japanese invasion subsided. The route is now called the Canol Heritage Trail, a challenging trek for the adventuresome.

The Norman Wells oilfield was developed, however, and for the next forty years it supplied oil products to the local northern communities. In the 1980s, a pipeline was built south to join up with the network in Alberta and production has been more significant ever since.

That expansion project of the 1980s had an interesting side issue. Much of the oilfield is situated deep under the river bed, making it necessary to drill wells from the natural islands in the river. As I mentioned, there are big problems with ice-flows as the river breaks up in the spring. As a result, the wells were drilled from sunken pits. This allows the surging ice to move over the well-heads without damaging them.

The pipeline project to Alberta also demonstrated that a pipeline could be safely installed and operated through zones of permafrost. This had been a major concern of some environmentalists during the 1970s, when a natural gas pipeline from the Beaufort Sea was being considered. The concept is being proposed again, as the demand for natural gas in the south continues to grow and the environmental and native rights issues are being resolved.

Permafrost is an amazing phenomenon. As its name implies, it is a permanently frozen area. It lies below the surface, since the shallow, upper surface areas do melt in the summer "heat." However, the summer is not long enough, or warm enough, to melt the frozen soil underneath. The problem comes when a source of heat is steadily present on the surface, such as a building or a pipeline. Then the heat penetrates deeper into the ground, the ice melts, and the structure on the surface sinks into the mud. The solution is to insulate the underside of the structure and, in many instances, to also build it on piles that keep it suspended above the ground. Thus, the cold air can circulate under the structure and keep the permafrost frozen. This is now a standard construction technique in the North.

Carrying on north along the river, we can look across the vast expanse of the landscape, covered in scrub trees, and we can hope to spot herds of caribou or muskoxen roaming in the wild. The caribou have that distinctive protruding horn coming out of their foreheads, as depicted on our 25-cent pieces. The muskoxen have the long shaggy hair on their front quarters.

We next come to the Mackenzie River delta, where the river spreads out across a wide plain as it flows into the Arctic Ocean. The main town in the delta region is Inuvik, with about 3000 people. It was constructed in the 1950s on the edge of the delta as the new regional government and commercial centre. It replaced the town of Aklavik, which was the historic trading post in the middle of the delta. Due to the shifting channels and sand bars, Aklavik could not be adequately developed as the population and activity grew; roads and airports were only temporary things as Mother Nature constantly changed the landscape.

Inuvik is the centre for oil and gas exploration in the North, although it had been relatively inactive through the '80s and '90s. There is now a resurgence of activity linked to the proposed natural gas pipeline to the south.

One of the distinctive sights in Inuvik is the Igloo Church. No, it's not made of ice, but it is shaped like a round dome, reflecting the traditional homes of the Inuit.

Most of the buildings in town are built on stilts, due to the permafrost. Utilities, including steam heat, are delivered through insulated metal tunnels, called utilidors, which are built above ground.

The arts and crafts creations of the people of the North have become world famous. Communities in Nunavut and the Northwest Territories have become identified with the works of their local artists, such as Holman and Cape Dorset. The soapstone carvings, stone cut paintings and leather and bone creations can be found in upscale galleries and shops everywhere, but it seems special to get something from a shop in the North itself.

Being above the Arctic Circle, there are extremes in the daylight hours here. In the summer, the sun never goes down; you need to look at your watch to have any idea what time of day it is, especially if you are planning to phone someone down south. The upside is that you can fish at midnight.

Then there is winter, when the sun does not appear at all. It is not as dark as you might expect however. The skies are usually clear; the moon and stars can provide light, especially when reflected off the white snow and icy surfaces. Still, it is quite an experience to see only a hint of light from over the far southern horizon at noon. We also know it is cold when we hear the loud crunching noise that is created as we walk along the snow-packed streets; the sound does distinctively change with the temperature of the snow.

The trip to Inuvik that I recall with the fondest memories happened in the early winter of 1988. I had the good fortune to be associated with the Olympic Torch Relay that crossed Canada in anticipation of the Winter Olympics in Calgary. I was directly involved with the section of the relay across western and northern Canada; I participated in the ceremonies at each of the capital cities, plus many stops in smaller towns and villages. The smaller centres actually created some of the most memorable experiences. People would have gathered from miles around, often waiting for hours into the late evening by the side of the road, just to get a quick glimpse of the torch as it paused and to be able to light their hand-held candles from person to person as they "Shared the Flame." It was an exciting adventure for the whole country. I have even heard stories about people who turned off their home furnaces, relighting them from their Olympic Torch flame, truly keeping it "forever" for them.

Our group did come to Inuvik and we conducted a fun-filled ceremony in town after bringing the flaming torch in from the airport by dogsled. That was a unique happening. The flame was carried around the North by plane, in specially designed containers that were safe; that's how it got from Greece to Canada in the first place.

You may recall that Petro-Canada, the sponsor of the Olympic Torch Relay, had a promotion involving the sale of glasses with the OTR logo – tumblers, water goblets, wine glasses, shot glasses, brandy snifters, liqueur glasses, you name it. That was one of the most successful gasoline promotions ever. There seemed to be no limit to the number of glasses that Canadians wanted to buy.

Of course, the real emotion of the Olympics relates to the athletes that participate. Every four years we are impressed by the young people that represent our country and we are caught up in the elation of their successes and the agony of their losses.

There have been so many heroes of the games. Our hockey teams, and now our curling teams, are always favourites. We recall the winners of an earlier era such as Percy Williams and Barbara Ann Scott. As television coverage emerged, we saw the victories of figure skaters Robert Paul and Barbara Wagner, skier Anne Heggtveit, and rowers George Hungerford and Roger Jackson, albeit in black-and-white.

In later summers, who can forget the excitement created by the swimmers such as Victor Davis, Alex Baumann, Mark Tewksbury, Michelle Cameron and Carolyn Waldo, the diver Sylvie Bernier, the boxer Lennox

Lewis, the runner Donovan Bailey and so many other rowers, shooters, jumpers, runners …

In those winters we cheered on the skiers Nancy Greene, Kathy Kreiner, Kerrin Lee Gartner and the Crazy Canucks, the speed skaters Gaetan Boucher and Annie Perreault, freestyle skiers Jean-Luc Brassard and Ross Rebagliati, biathlon champion Myriam Bedard and the many other skiers, skaters, bobsleighers …

More recently, in 2002 we were pumped up by the men's and women's hockey victories, the speed skaters Mark Gagnon and Catriona LeMay Doan, figure skaters David Pelletier and Jamie Sale and all their winter teammates.

In 2004 we were excited by gymnast Kyle Shewfelt, cyclist Lori-Ann Muenzer, kayaker Adam van Koeverden and all the summer athletes. The Olympics create great memories.

Inuvik can be accessed by road from the south, via the all-weather (read gravel) Dempster Highway that goes to Dawson City in the Yukon. From Dawson there are roads that connect with the Alaska Highway at Whitehorse or in the interior of Alaska.

A side trip north from Inuvik, by ice-road in winter or by air in the summer, takes us to the small village of Tuktoyaktuk. "Tuk" sits on the shore of the Arctic Ocean, which makes it an attraction for visitors who can take a dip in the freezing water, or at least stick in a toe.

Looking north from here there is no more land all the way to the North Pole; the Arctic island groups are all farther east. This awareness can make you feel that you really are at the end of the world.

This area is very flat in general, but it also has a large number of pingos, which are natural ice-domes that protrude a few meters above the landscape. They are used by the Inuit as refrigerators. Digging a tunnel into the centre and carving out a room-sized cave creates a walk-in cold storage area for their food.

Leaving the Arctic Ocean, we can head southwest across the Richardson Mountains and the continental divide that defines the NWT-Yukon border and arrive at the Yukon Territory capital of Whitehorse. About two-thirds of the Yukon's 30,000 people live here. For reference, that means that the largest city in Canada's North is essentially the same size as Shawinigan, Quebec; Huntsville, Ontario; or Yorkton, Saskatchewan.

Whitehorse is set on a river flat beside the Yukon River. The river flows north between sandy cliffs, with high, snow-capped mountains in the background. This city became the capital of the Yukon in the late 1950s, having become the main centre of commerce and government after the Alaska Highway was constructed through here during WWII. Before then, Dawson City was the capital.

We also need to recognize that before the war the total population of the Yukon was less than 5000 people. This contrasts with a population of nearly 100,000 at the start of the twentieth century; Whitehorse didn't even exist then. All of that was caused by the Klondike Gold Rush.

In the fall of 1896 a group of prospectors, with the names of George Cormack, Skookum Jim and Dawson Charlie, discovered gold in streams that fed into the Yukon River near the town of Dawson City. The gold was described as "thick between the flaky slabs of rock, like cheese sandwiches." The next summer a ship arrived in San Francisco with a "million dollars" worth of gold; the rush was on! Over 40,000 prospectors and promoters headed north that winter alone.

In those days, the border between Alaska and Canada was not well defined. To assure Canadian sovereignty and control, Canada carved out the Yukon Territory from the greater Northwest Territory and sent in the NWMP to preserve order. Their effectiveness became legendary, as did their reputation "to always get their man."

The prospectors arrived from two directions. Some came overland from Edmonton, thus creating Edmonton's linkage to the Klondike and the theme of its midsummer exhibition. Most people came up the west coast by ship and climbed across the mountains to the interior.

One of the most famous images in Canadian history is of the steady line of prospectors, laden down with heavy packs, climbing up the steep Chilkoot Pass. The route they took to the Klondike involved sailing to Skagway, a town on the rough Alaskan coast, climbing up either the Chilkoot or White Pass through the mountains of northern British Columbia, and then working their way some 1000 kilometers north along the treacherous Yukon River, which was full of rapids and eddies.

The NWMP insisted that every new arrival bring enough supplies to last at least one year. This meant that each individual had to climb up and down the high mountain pass a number of times before a sufficient cache was assembled.

Within a couple of years there was a railway built up the White Pass. It traversed steep cliffs and crossed wide gorges on high trestles. There was also a stern-wheeler paddleboat service down the Yukon River to the goldfields. These facilities obviously reduced the hard work required to get there and undoubtedly saved a lot of lives

The gold rush lasted for only five years, but it did find 100 million dollars worth of gold and it did leave behind the legacy of the gay '90s in the Yukon. This attracts many tourists today, most of whom arrive in Skagway by cruise ship and then take the restored White Pass and Yukon Railway line up the treacherous pass to Whitehorse. Costumed bartenders and dance hall girls welcome the visitors, as do the many souvenir shops;

you must get a gold miner's pan to take home, if not an actual gold nugget.

One evening in Whitehorse a small group of us went to a local bar for a few drinks. Along with our drinks we were served carving knives. The tables were made of heavy wood, and it was expected that we would carve our names, or whatever, into the table top. Apparently, after a year or two, when all the carving space is gone, they sand down the surfaces and start over again. I could not imagine it — handing out knives to the patrons in a bar! This just has to lead to trouble sometime. Talk about the "wild north."

I also had a nerve-wracking helicopter experience on that trip. We were going down the White Pass, from Whitehorse to the coastal town of Skagway, on the way to inspect some terminal facilities at Haines, Alaska. Suddenly, the pass filled with clouds and fog, severely limiting our visibility in an area where the mountain slopes were close to our path. Helicopters can hover, and can proceed slowly, but they do need a point of reference in swirling fog. Eventually, we were able to spot a large ore-carrying truck on the road below, winding down the narrow pass; we carefully followed it to the bottom. This event felt more disturbing than the icing episode I mentioned in Newfoundland; I think that was because we were acutely aware of the situation as it was happening.

Needless to say, we did not go back to Whitehorse via the White Pass. Instead, we swung up north, via Haines Junction, and saw tremendous views of high mountain peaks separated by large expanses of glaciers and snow-filled valleys.

From here, looking to the west, we can see Mt. Logan (no it's not Mt. Trudeau), the highest point in Canada at an elevation of 5950 meters (19,500 feet).

A little farther north is the village of Snag, which has recorded the coldest temperature in Canada, -64°C (-83°F). Brrr!

This also represents the farthest point west on our journey together, about 140° West longitude. Our final destination of this trip, the west coast of Vancouver Island, will be at only 125° W. The Northern Territories do stretch a long way across the globe.

With that, we leave the awe-inspiring wilderness of the North and return south to our final province, British Columbia. But don't get off the plane yet; we still have a way to go before we will be driving along the highways again.

British Columbia

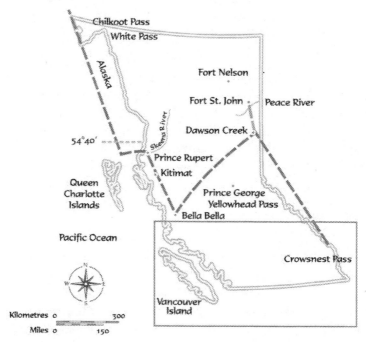

11. British Columbia

Coming south from the Yukon, down the Pacific coast, we skirt the Alaskan panhandle as we approach British Columbia. The coastline of northwest North America is very different from the rest of the continent. Here, the high Coastal Mountains plunge steeply into the ocean and deep, narrow fjords penetrate far inland.

Our first stop in British Columbia is at Prince Rupert, Canada's farthest-north Pacific port at a latitude near 54^0 $40'$ N., a politically significant reference that we will discuss later. All of the coastal areas north of here are part of Alaska.

As we fly into the city, the ruggedly spectacular nature of the area is apparent. Prince Rupert is located on a couple of islands that hug the mountainous shoreline in an extensive bay-like area called Chatham Sound. Just to the north is the Portland Inlet, a fiord that penetrates some 150 kilometers through the mountains. Just to the south is the mouth of the large Skeena River, which flows from the interior highlands.

Prince Rupert is a major industrial centre and port city. It started out in the mid-1800s as a fur trading post and later became a stopover point for gold seekers journeying into the interior. Salmon fishing and forestry became its economic backbone. With the construction of the railway across the mountains in the early 1900s and the creation of large storage and ship-loading facilities, it became a major export point for coal, minerals and prairie agricultural products. It is much closer to the markets of the Far East than Vancouver, which we can see if we check out the great circle routes on a globe. It is always surprising to people who fly from Vancouver to Japan or Hong Kong that their route goes east of Vancouver Island and essentially over Prince Rupert.

The view from a restaurant or hotel room located on the steep hillsides provides a panoramic image of the busy harbour. However, if we decide to take in the view from an uncovered vantage point, we should be sure to have an umbrella; Prince Rupert is the rainiest city in Canada with over 2.5 meters of precipitation annually.

Tourism is becoming more significant, whether it be by driving overland from the interior, by ferry from Vancouver Island, or on an

Alaska-bound cruise ship. Attractions include all of the wilderness activities of hiking, camping, sea kayaking, fishing and tours to see whales and wildlife. The Queen Charlotte Islands are directly offshore here.

The northwest coast has also been the home to a number of Indian tribes, such as the Haida, for thousands of years. Their cultural art work has become very recognizable and valued. The distinctive totem poles and stylized images of animals such as whales, bears, eagles and salmon are unique, as are their ceremonial masks. Modern artisans continue to produce outstanding art works; they can be found in galleries worldwide. We have collected a few masks and a small totem pole to welcome visitors to our home.

As we leave Prince Rupert, still going south for a short distance, the coastal scenery continues to be spectacular. Looking down, we can see the mouth of the Dean Channel and the old native settlement of Bella Bella. This is where Alexander Mackenzie reached the Pacific by an overland route in 1793, becoming the first person to cross the North American continent north of the narrow Mexican region. Recall that he had inadvertently diverted to the Arctic on a previous trip. This time, he entered the Rocky Mountains via the Peace River and, after much paddling and portaging through the mountain passes, he reached Bella Bella. He was very concerned about the hostile Indians of the region and so he stayed for only one day, but he did inscribe his name and the date on a boulder that survives. This is sometimes called Canada's most famous graffiti.

Our next destination is in northeast British Columbia — the Peace River region. The Peace River flows out of the Rockies, crosses northeast B.C. into Alberta, and then continues north, with its waters eventually reaching the Mackenzie River. The Peace is a significant river, as are most of the main rivers across the west, but somehow it has become legendary as the *Mighty Peace*. That name is so ingrained in common language that I find myself almost unable to say "Peace" without the attached "Mighty."

The Peace River Block of British Columbia is a very productive agricultural area. The forest has been cleared for farming and some of the largest vegetables are grown here. This often surprises visitors, since the growing season is obviously relatively short this far north; at best, there are three frost-free months. The reason for the enormous produce is that the summer days are so long. The sun goes down for only a few hours each day, so the growing cycle does not pause overnight as it does farther south. This is hard on the drive-in movie business.

Dawson Creek is the official start of the Alaska Highway, marked by Milepost Zero in the middle of town. The drive from here, through northern British Columbia, across the Yukon and on to Fairbanks, Alaska, is a formidable 2500 kilometer trek.

My family lived in Dawson Creek in the late 1960s. It was a good experience. In a city of 10,000 you get to know many people and everyone participates in local events. We moved here from Houston, Texas, when my youngest son was just one month old. The doctor in Houston had the disturbing image of us taking this newborn to Dawson City in the Yukon, as depicted in the old Sergeant Preston movies.

In those days, the Alaska Highway was not paved all the way. Travelers were faced with hundreds of miles of constant dust caused by their fellow travelers, often slow-moving campers or house trailers. Many a group returned to Dawson Creek with broken windshields and dented, dirty vehicles, not having gone any farther than Fort Nelson, still in northern British Columbia, before they surrendered and turned around. Today, it is paved all the way and is a much more pleasant experience.

Fort St. John is a basic rural city located near the Peace River. It is the centre for the oil and gas industry in British Columbia, and thus is full of activity these days as natural gas exploration programs expand into the northern B.C. wilderness.

When I lived in Dawson Creek, much of the oilfield activity was north of the Peace River and east of Ft. St. John. It was a relatively long, inconvenient drive there from Dawson Creek via the bridge in Ft. St. John. In the summer there was a ferry across the river that shortened the trip considerably; in the winter, there was an ice bridge. The tricky season was in the spring, when the ice was melting. We had to decide how long we could continue to use the bridge. I can recall us driving over the ice when there were a few inches of water on the surface; we kept the truck doors ajar in case we had to "abandon ship" quickly. We were crazy; somehow people did those things then.

This is another region of Canada that does not switch to Daylight Saving Time in the summer. It does seem unnecessary when the sun stays up until 10:00 or 11:00 p.m. anyway. Also, I think it allows the area to be on the same time as Alberta for half of the year. Due to the mountains to the west, the farming and petroleum base of the local economy, and the main highway system going east to Edmonton, the folks in this area can often relate more to Alberta than British Columbia. They often feel they are a forgotten corner of the province by the government in Victoria.

Now, let's finish our air trip by going back to southeast British Columbia. Recall that when we were driving across southern Alberta we took a peek into the Crowsnest Pass through the Rocky Mountains. We'll start back there, on the B.C. side of the pass this time.

Our route across southern British Columbia is going to be snake-like as we move up and down the various valley systems that are created by the mountain ranges that run in a general north-south direction. This will enable us to see as much of B.C. as possible.

Sparwood is in the first valley we come to in the midst of the Rockies. As on the Alberta side, this region of the mountains contains many large coal mining operations. A very large coal mining truck, with wheels that are much taller that we are, and which can carry a few hundred tons of ore, sits in a shopping mall beside the highway. It tells us that this is "Coal Country" and gives us some sense of the scale of the operations. An old local mine on Coal Mountain is available for touring.

Farther down the valley, we come to Fernie, again an old mining and railway town, which celebrates its centenary in 2004. Its downtown area features wide streets and a few old brick buildings, including the court house, school and church. There is also a lot of new development here. New subdivisions of homes and townhouse condominiums are sprouting at the base of the surrounding mountains and in the developing local ski resorts.

Fernie is emerging as one of the new ski and vacation areas in the interior of eastern British Columbia that are competing for the attention of Calgarians and others who have traditionally gone to Banff and Lake Louise. Although it is a longer drive from Calgary, about three hours, Fernie has all of the attractions of golf, fishing, rafting and hiking, and the advantage of better prices than Canmore, at least for now. The other big advantage here, and in many of the other towns throughout the B.C. interior, is that vacation homes can be built adjacent to the ski hills. The famous ski slopes of Banff, Lake Louise and Nakiska are all in national or provincial parks and, thus, such private homes cannot be built close by.

Going west from Fernie, we follow the winding road through a narrow pass in the next range of the Rockies. The land is mostly covered in evergreen forest, with the presence of some open meadows from time to time and the odd small cattle ranching operation. As is the case in most towns and cities we will see throughout southern British Columbia, there is a lumber mill in the town of Jaffray. Past there, we enter a wide valley and approach the city of Cranbrook, the regional commercial centre with a population of about 18,000.

What is so strikingly noticeable here is that the high, rugged, snow-capped peaks of the Rocky Mountains dramatically define the view back eastward, but to the west the mountains are lower, rounded and tree-covered.

It is often surprising to visitors to find that the Rocky Mountains themselves occupy a narrow band along the Alberta-British Columbia border; the rest of the interior of B.C. consists of a number of lower mountain ranges and areas of high, wide, but relatively flat, plateaus. These various mountain ranges create long north-south valleys, which usually have long, narrow lakes stretched along their lower elevations. We will be working our way up and down a number of these valley systems as we drift westward. Once we leave the western slopes of the Rockies, we will not see an abundance of snow-peaked sharp ridges again until we reach the Coastal Range.

Cranbrook has been a railway centre for over a century. It has preserved some old railway equipment and facilities that are interesting to visit, notably the restored set of railway cars from the 1920s, when travel could be first-class with fancy cars for sleeping, dining, lounging and even having business conferences.

Just outside town is a new resort complex at the site of an old mission on First Nation property. The mission building has been renovated and integrated into a stylish hotel with an elaborate casino. A golf course runs along the picturesque local river valley beneath steep sandstone cliffs.

A short distance farther up the valley is the town of Kimberly, another old mining town that is keen to attract visitors to its ski hills and mountain setting. Here they have created a theme for their downtown area, the *Bavarian City of the Rockies*. A three-block "Platzl" features a walking mall on cobblestone streets lined with buildings which display wood-battened stucco sides, steeply sloped roofs, and balconies encased in carved wooden pickets. Restaurants have names such as the Gasthaus and feature bratwurst, schnitzel and strudel. It is a touch of Bavaria in the midst of an old mining community. New developments are rising around the base of the mountain and the ski hill, as everywhere in the interior.

The mines in this region have been very prosperous in the past, representing some of the world's largest silver, lead and zinc operations. There is a local tour on a narrow-gauge mining railway which describes much of the area's history.

Continuing north along this valley system, we come to the Invermere area, straddled by the hot springs developments at Fairmont and Radium and centred on Lake Windermere. The Panorama ski village sits above the lake on the western mountain slopes. This is a well-developed vacation and recreation area, being less than three hours from Calgary, coming from the north on good highways. Compared to the Alberta side of the Rockies, the summer season is a couple of months longer and the lake is warm enough for swimming as well as boating and sailing. There are a number of obvious signs that this area is economically linked to Alberta vacationers, such as the high percentage of Alberta license plates on the cars, or, more precisely, the SUVs, and the fact that this valley uses Mountain Time, not the Pacific Time of the rest of British Columbia.

The hot springs are very popular. The naturally-hot mineral waters flow out of the mountainsides and are captured in the spas and swimming pools. Here, they do not have the smell of sulphur that is usually associated with the hot springs in the mountains.

I particularly enjoy playing golf on the various courses in this valley, some of the most attractive ones in the country, but always difficult because of the many local ravines that golf course architects just cannot resist.

This valley also contains the headwaters of the Columbia River, starting with Columbia Lake just south of the Fairmont Hot Springs. The route and source of this river confused explorers around the start of the nineteenth century, as the northwest regions of North America were being defined and claimed by various countries. We'll pursue that later, but, for now, just note that here the Columbia River is flowing north.

We could continue down the Columbia River to the town of Golden, but in doing so we would miss the Kicking Horse Pass, the historic route of the CPR through the Rockies and the route most people would take driving from the east to B.C. So, let's head northeast from Radium, up a long mountain valley that follows the Kootenay River. This river, like the dozens we will be seeing through the interior of the mountain ranges, has crystal-clear water that runs quickly over boulder-filled stream beds in an almost continuous series of rapids. This route takes us back into Alberta for a short distance and leads us into the Kicking Horse Pass on the B.C. border.

As I noted, the Kicking Horse is famous as the location of the first railway route through the Canadian Rocky Mountains. As we learned on the prairies, originally the CPR was thought to be going across the northern areas of Saskatoon, Battleford and Edmonton, which meant that it would cross the Rockies via the Yellowhead Pass, a known and not extremely difficult way. With the decision to stay south through Regina and Calgary — a shorter route and one that better offset the encroaching American presence — a new route through the Rockies was needed. This was the Kicking Horse, a picturesque name derived from a simple incident where a horse reared up and kicked one of the early surveyors.

The only problem with this pass is that it was too steep for the railway, obviously a significant issue. The original rail line through here had a section called "the Big Hill" that was twice as steep as the CPR specifications allowed. They handled the problem by building spur lines, or *runaway lanes* as we would call them on highways today. The switches were primarily set to divert the trains onto the spurs, with the positioned switchman allowing the train to continue on the main line only when he heard a whistle signal from the engineer that signified the train was under control. This was not a great solution. Therefore, the construction of the Spiral Tunnels into and out of the mountain faces was undertaken. There are two complete loops that effectively reduce the grade of the rail bed to a tolerable amount. It is fun, even today, to stop along the highway and wait for a train to come by, entering and exiting the mountain at the different levels.

The Kicking Horse Pass is the highest point on The Trans-Canada Highway at an elevation of 1629 meters (5340 feet).

Down the western slope of the pass we go, following the churning Kicking Horse River to the town of Field at the bottom. This is a railway town where the trains are reconfigured with the addition or removal of engines, depending on the direction they are going.

There was a strange event that occurred in Field recently. The national parks officials (we are now in Yoho National Park) insisted that the townsfolk make their ice rink less white! The town had been painting the concrete base white, as do many towns, to better reflect the sun and thus preserve the ice coat for use longer into the spring. However, the officials felt that the whiteness distracted from the natural beauty "when seen from above." Presumably they meant when seen by mountain climbers, not airplane passengers. Remember, this is a small town on a busy highway, with a large railway marshalling yard and brightly-lit traveler facilities like restaurants, gas stations and an information centre. You can see how a white skating rink would distract climbers. To make this bureaucratic decree seem worse, they issued it at the time of the major forest fires in B.C., when many fellow parks employees and thousands of others were engaged in those critical firefighting activities.

On many of the routes in the mountains there are signs that indicate remote lakes that can be reached by hiking in from the highway, often a trek of many kilometers. One of the more accessible is Emerald Lake

Here, we can park in a remote lot and be shuttled into the lakeside resort. There is a main lodge and numerous multi-unit cabins in a rustic, yet upscale, style. A large stone fireplace graces the sitting area of the lodge and the cabins have their own smaller versions. Walkways lead along the lake and into the woods. Canoes are available to paddle out into the calm, bright-blue waters, surrounded by the towering peaks. What makes these retreats so special is the lack of civilization's intrusions of noise and light. Everything is so peaceful; the sounds of nature, such as the birds and the squirrels, are easily audible. At dusk the sound of a loon can make it perfect. At night the clear dark skies allow the stars to shine brightly; you sometimes forget how many thousands of stars are visible when there is no competition from the glow of a city.

Back to the Trans-Canada, we now travel towards Golden along one of the most winding, narrow, steep and, therefore, dangerous sections of highway in Canada, especially in winter. The vertical rock faces of the road-cuts are sheathed in steel netting which restrains the boulders that can slough off the sides and fall onto the highway.

The Kicking Horse River that surges through the deep and narrow valley offers impressive sites for white-water rafting, a popular attraction on many of the rivers throughout the mountains. We can don a wet suit, grab a paddle and join a group of fellow tourists for a wild ride. The wet suits remind us that these waters were recently mountain ice. We finish the trip wet and tired, but enthused about the next time we can try it.

Golden is another town that is expanding its scope to attract visitors and vacationers to its wilderness attractions, golf courses and ski hills. As has become apparent, this is becoming a big business in the interior of B.C. and is creating competition between the various valleys and communities. Golden also places us on the Columbia River again; we are back in the valley that runs north of Invermere.

The Columbia continues north from here, swings in a large arc to the west, and then back to the south through the town of Revelstoke. Until a few decades ago the highway followed that long and tortuous route. Now the road goes along a more direct path, through the spectacular, but treacherous, Rogers Pass.

This is the pass that the CPR used right from the beginning as its only feasible route through the Selkirk Mountains. What is surprising is that the route was not located by the survey chief, Major Rogers, until after the construction of the railway across the southern prairies had already started. The Rogers Pass is not only narrow, but it also receives enormous amounts of snow in the winter. Frequently, huge avalanches come tearing down the steep mountain slopes. To counteract this danger, long stretches of the rail line were covered over with hefty wooden sheds, which deflected the falling tons of snow farther down the valley. Even then, many people were killed in avalanches and the route was often blocked for days by snow. Later, a tunnel was blasted into the mountainside to avoid the most difficult section.

The highway did not follow this same route until more than seventy-five years later, due to the difficulties and the dangers. The Trans-Canada Highway was officially completed here in the Rogers Pass in 1962. It has many snow sheds as well, and, in places, it is built over the railway track, due to the narrowness of the area.

We can spot concrete foundations beside the road at various intervals; these are mountings for cannons, which are fired during the winter to cause smaller, controlled avalanches to occur. The best advice is to just keep moving when you are driving this road in the winter.

At their centre at the top of the pass Parks Canada has an interpretive display about the construction of the railway and the highway through Rogers Pass, including an elaborate scale-model. I find that it is almost impossible to understand what is here without looking at that model.

We head down the western slope of the pass to reach Revelstoke. We are back on the Columbia River again, but now it does flow south. After all, it needs to get to Oregon somehow.

Not too far west of Revelstoke is Craigellachie, the site of the *Last Spike* on the CPR that was driven on November 7, 1885. With this connection, Canada's trans-continental railway was a reality, and the promise made to British Columbia that led it to join Canada in 1871 was fulfilled. It had been a long and difficult task, both physically and politically. John A. Macdonald had been forced to resign in 1873 over financial contributions linked to the railway. However, he came storming back in 1878 on a National Policy platform, which played on independence from the United States and committed to actually build the railway; its progress had stalled. Now, with the link firmly established, Canada could say it was "Sea to Sea," making true our national motto "A Mari Usque ad Mare." The commemorative plaque and small gift shop at the site certainly warrant a brief stop as you pass this way. The chance to heft one of the heavy, steel-driving hammers provides some sense of the hard work that was involved.

On this journey we are not going to continue west of Revelstoke however; instead, we are going south to investigate a couple more valleys and to trace the Columbia. We can follow the Upper Arrow Lake, which is part of the Columbia River system, crossing it on a local ferry and then working our way down to Nelson.

Nelson is an old mining town; it is now the regional centre for the lumber industry and for the tourist business linked to Kootenay Lake. Situated at the end of the West Arm of the lake, the town itself stretches along the lake shore, with parks, playgrounds and walking paths beside the water, as are the railway yards and wharves. The town centre works its way up the hillside, its neat streets lined with old-fashioned light poles, hanging flower pots, outdoor patio restaurants and colourful awnings on the store fronts. There are a number of brick and stone buildings, including the Court House. We cannot help but notice the mustard-yellow, four-story historic hotel on the main street. The town has over 400 heritage buildings, most of which we can tour.

Along the shores of the West Arm are a variety of homes, cottages, acreages and B&B's that have access to the narrow lake as it meanders through the mountain pass. We can see many boats moored along the shore. The main sections of Kootenay Lake, the North and South Arms, are longer and wider, being about 150 kilometers in total length and up to 8 kilometers wide, but they are generally less developed. This area is a longer drive from Calgary than the Invermere area, and even the Okanagan region that we will come to farther west, so there is a lot of undeveloped lakefront. At least for now, it is the destination for those who want a more remote location in the mountains, but with lake availability. The local villages are home to various painters, craft artisans and writers who find the quiet lifestyle very attractive and affordable.

Driving along the narrow roads that wind along the shore of Kootenay Lake, we frequently see signs that warn us about upcoming "Congested Areas." Then we come upon a spot that might have a small local store or perhaps a few cabins. It hardly seems congested and you wonder if they are serious, but even a few cars stopping at the same time on these narrow roads can plug things up and create a hazard.

Now, turning back southwest from Nelson, we follow the Kootenay River as it drops down more than a hundred meters to join the Columbia River at Castlegar. There is a series of power dams along the Kootenay, originally constructed in the 1890s to provide electricity to the developing mines. The region was rich in silver, copper, gold and lead. The surging waterfalls and bypasses at the dams are impressive, giving us a good sense of the energy of the river.

The towns along the southern border of British Columbia in this area all have a historic mining base: Trail, Rossland, Grand Forks and Greenwood. The lead/zinc smelter in Trail is touted as the world's largest.

Driving through this region, we are constantly going over high summits and dropping down into valleys The steep hills are covered with an evergreen forest, broken by periodic open meadows; lumber mills can be frequently spotted. Fast-flowing rivers carve deep gorges through the rocky passes.

We can get a sense of the history and heritage of the area from the signs and names. Grand Forks identifies itself with *Sunshine and Borsch*. Greenwood calls itself the *Smallest City in B.C.*, reflecting its past position as a significant mining centre; it has now become a small village. We can spot the Motherlode Store and the Gold Pan Café. Then there is a Saloon and Cappuccino Bar to bridge us back to the present

Rossland, the centre of a gold boom in the 1890s, shows signs of that era with its wide main street, stone buildings and the large churches on the hills around downtown. There is an attractive museum and a mine tour to help recall the town's history. At the peak of activity there were forty-two saloons, four breweries and two distilleries here. There were also seventeen law firms; some things haven't changed in the world, even after a hundred years.

Probably the best known town in the area, at least for Canadians of my generation, is Trail. And that has nothing to do with mining, forestry or tourism; it's all about hockey. The local junior team, the Trail Smoke Eaters, was the last Canadian amateur team to win the World Hockey Championship, in 1961. That also marked the end of an era. Canada had won 19 of the previous 28 Championships, going back to 1920, but we would not win another one until the pros did it in 1994, thirty-three years later. Trail calls itself the *Home of Champions*, being a little more modest than Edmonton.

Rock Creek is the start of the old Kettle River Railway right-of-way that has been converted to a popular hiking and biking trail; it wanders through the valleys from here to the Okanagan and Arrow Lake regions. It is used by tens of thousands of outdoor enthusiasts each year. One of its major attractions is the series of old wooden railway trestles that cross some of the deep canyons, but they suffered serious damage during the forest fires of 2003. There are commitments to repair and replace them; let's hope so.

Traveling along the southern border in central B.C., we climb over four high passes west of Rossland. The highest is the Nancy Green Summit, at 1535 meters above sea level. Canada's famous world champion skier was born in Rossland. There is a higher pass, the Kootenay Pass at 1774 meters elevation, back east between Creston and Trail, but we missed it on our route. That elevation is noticeably higher than the peaks we noted earlier on the Trans-Canada.

As we travel over the last of this series of passes we enter a new region of the province. We approach the town of Osoyoos by descending a steep, switch-backed section of the highway into a wide-open valley with a lake in the centre. Flat farmland stretches for long distances in every direction. On closer inspection, we find that the area is desert-like, and it will stay like that for the next fifty kilometers to the north. Irrigation has turned the area into a fertile agricultural region, with many orchards, vegetable fields and vineyards. Roadside stands advertise everything from apricots to peppers to perennial flowers.

The town of Oliver, just to the north, calls itself the *Wine Capital of Canada*. I wonder if they checked that out with the folks at Niagara-on-the-Lake. As we will see, there is a lot of wine created between here and the north end of the Okanagan Valley.

The scenes, as we drive by the miles of orchards, change with the season. In the spring, we can see the colourful expanse of the apple, cherry and peach blossoms. In mid-summer, the hanging clusters of the dark-red cherries are everywhere. In late summer, we find the oranges and yellows of the peaches and apricots. By fall, we see the reds and greens of the ripening apples. There is always a good excuse for stopping at the local markets.

The markets and local shops also have stone carvings for sale, made from the dark green B.C. jade or other colourful rocks, often pink and black blends. The most common carving seems to be of a bear, usually with a fish in its mouth. They must turn these out by the hundreds, if not the thousands, as they are everywhere.

At Penticton we get our first glimpse of Okanagan Lake. By the way, have you ever figured out when the word "Lake" should appear before the proper name and when it comes after? We have Lake Ontario, Lake Winnipeg and Lake Athabasca, but Bras d'Or Lake, Great Bear Lake and Kootenay Lake. I bring this up here since the maps all refer to Okanagan Lake but most people seem to call it Lake Okanagan. Actually, it's usually just shortened to "the Okanagan," although that does refer to the whole area, not just the lake itself. Another great Canadian mystery, like why do they only sell Red Rose Tea in Canada?

Penticton lies at the south end of the lake that stretches out for over 120 kilometers, although it is only a few kilometers wide. This city of 30,000 calls itself the *Peach City*, which is descriptive of the region. There is a wide, sandy beach across the southern lakeshore that attracts picnickers and water-sport enthusiasts. On the beach is a refreshment stand that is built in the shape and colours of a peach. This just cries out to be called the *Peach on the Beach*; the locals just call it "the big peach."

Continuing north along the west side of Okanagan Lake, we generally track through the hills that follow the shore, which is defined in many places by steep slopes and small, rocky cliffs. Periodically, we pass some small villages that have a beach and marina developed on the lakefront, but, for the most part, the southern half of the lake is undeveloped, especially the east side where access is limited. The western hillsides are populated with orchards and vineyards, notably around Summerland and Peachland, great names for towns.

At mid-lake, we find the major population centre of the Okanagan, Kelowna, on the east shore, and its neighbour, Westbank, predictably on the other side. They are joined by a 650-meter, floating bridge that creates a narrow causeway. It is a city of 100,000 people that seems even larger because of the many tourists and seasonal vacationers.

Halfway between Calgary and Vancouver, with moderate winters and hot sunny summers, this community is appealing to visitors and to retirees, as confirmed by its steadily growing population. The local economy seems strong, with the twin bases of agriculture and tourism, and its strong appeal as a place to live permanently.

New resorts, condos, homes and chalets are sprouting near the lake and in the surrounding hills that command a fantastic view of the valley. It is hard to find fault with living by a golf course, surrounded by an orchard or vineyard, near a ski hill, and looking over a large recreational lake in the mountains.

The forest fires of 2003 did impact this city, perhaps more than anywhere else in Canada. Homes were lost and thousands of people were evacuated. The newspaper photos and television pictures of those traveling walls of flames that swept through the treetops were mesmerizing and terrifying.

The year 2004 threatens to be a bad one for forest fires again. In early July there were over 400 fires burning in British Columbia.

The golf courses of the B.C. interior are some of the most spectacular in the country, with their natural setting of mountains, valleys, lakes and ravines. There are also some of the great names for courses, such as Predator Ridge, near Kelowna, and Bootleg Gap, back along the southern border. Most courses in the world have basic names such as the Local Town Golf and Country Club, or the overused phrases such as Happy Valley. Any combination of a bird, animal or tree with a geographic describer will do. You just join up one of Falcon, Quail, Deer, Fox, Pine or Spruce with Meadow, Valley, Hollow, Creek or Springs. The first really creative names that I recall hearing were for the courses north of Toronto called the Devil's Pulpit and the Devil's Cauldron. Now, those names can intimidate a golfer, even before you see the place, and more so when you actually play them.

The north end of Okanagan Lake has more cottage development than the south end, primarily because it is closer to Calgary, although we are still looking at a six or seven hour drive. It's more vacation country than a weekend retreat, except for the most determined. Vernon anchors the north end, as Penticton did the south.

Seventy-five kilometers farther north we rejoin the Trans-Canada Highway west of Revelstoke at Sicamous and start our visit to perhaps the best cottage country in all of British Columbia, the Shuswap.

Shuswap Lake is shaped somewhat like the letter "H," which gives it four "arms" of waterway and over 1000 kilometers of shoreline. Sicamous and Salmon Arm are the largest towns on the lake, with the full range of services, and there are a number of smaller villages scattered around the lake. There are also many homes, cottages, campgrounds, RV parks and lodges, but, with so much space, much of the lake is still undeveloped. Boating, fishing and water sports are big activities, along with all the usual suspects of golfing, hiking, skiing and river rafting.

Houseboating is a major attraction here. There are a number of companies that rent out these floating homes, which can be as large as 25 meters in length and can sleep up to 24 people. Families and groups will rent these by the week and have a fun-filled water-based vacation. They are fully equipped with modern appliances and conveniences, and they can have amenities such as hot tubs and water slides. You can travel along the more populated parts of the lake near lakeshore restaurants and attractions or you can search out the more remote, uninhabited sections. The shallow-draft, twin-hull design of the boats allows them to be easily beached along the shore on secluded beaches, where games or sand-castle building can fill the afternoons and campfires can be the centre of the evening entertainment. Supplementing them with jet skis or a water-ski boat adds to the enjoyment. Personally, I don't see anything wrong with a deck chair, a cold drink and a good book.

This is also one of the farthest-east areas where we can see a Pacific sockeye salmon spawning run. Here, the salmon have made their way from the salt water ocean by climbing rapids and fish ladders through the Fraser and Thompson Rivers. They arrive at the Adams River to lay and fertilize their eggs in these fresh water streams. Then they die. The individual fish live for four years; their cycle of river to ocean and back takes that long. Due to various natural and human-caused effects over time, the size of the spawning runs varies from year to year. The peak four-year cycle in this stream, i.e., 2002, 2006, etc., can bring as many as four million fish. The river is then literally churning with the bright-red, very tired, but determined, sockeye.

Going west again, we leave the Shuswap valley and enter a region of high hills and bluffs, with frequent steep cliff faces along the wide valleys. The region becomes noticeably drier, with fewer trees and short grasses covering the terrain. The agricultural fields along the valley bottoms are serviced with large, rolling irrigation systems.

An unusual sight is the fields that are draped in black plastic about two meters off the ground. These are ginseng crops. The covers keep the fields warm with the absorbed energy from the sun and keep the moisture in. There are huge expanses of these fields.

Kamloops is the largest city in this part of the B.C. interior, with a population of over 75,000 people. It is located at the junction of the North Thompson and South Thompson Rivers, with its residential and commercial developments spread through the surrounding dry hills. It is a pleasant city with parks and beach facilities along the river. Downtown we find a substantial convention centre and sports arena. The city seems to have a lot of hotels and motels for its size, which reflects its claim to be the *Tournament Capital of Canada*. They work hard to attract such events, and its not just sports such as hockey, soccer and baseball, but also secondary sports and other activities like bridge. The location is accessible, central to many attractions, and relatively affordable for most groups.

As we head west from Kamloops, we encounter a large B.C. Highways sign that points the way to two alternative routes to Vancouver: south via the Coquihalla Pass or west via the Fraser Canyon.

Going south, via the Coquihalla, is a modern four-lane highway that works its way along the high mountain ridges and passes and leads to the lower Fraser River at Hope. It is a very impressive drive, although it can have some treacherous driving conditions in the winter when storms occur at the high elevations, bringing snow, ice and avalanches. It is also a toll road, which is not mentioned on the signs until you have gone some 75 kilometers to Merritt, a logging and cattle ranching town in the heart of the region. The toll is a modest $10 per car and the route does reduce the trip from east of Sicamous to Vancouver by a couple of hours. Most of the traffic coming out of Kamloops takes this option, but we are going to go the other way and follow the historic route of the railways and the Trans-Canada to the Fraser River canyons.

Going west of Kamloops, we follow the Thompson River on a winding two-lane road, which works its way along the high, rolling hills. There are periodic farms, again with acres of plastic-covered ginseng fields, and cattle ranches, but most of the area is relatively rugged and uninhabited. The wide Thompson carves its path through the valleys.

We will see signs that advertise dude ranches from time to time. They could be fun, but I always think of the movie *City Slickers* and keep on going.

Beyond Cache Creek the river and highway swing south and the river valley becomes much narrower and steeper, making sharp turns that are bordered by high cliffs much of the time. The Thompson becomes a steady run of fast-flowing rapids, often filled with large boulder-fields that protrude well above the rushing water and which throw a steady spray high into the air.

There is now a railway line following along the base of the steep slopes on each side of the river, since we have been following both the CPR and the CNR since Kamloops. The CPR worked its way there via the Kicking Horse and Rogers Passes, as we saw earlier. The CNR arrived via Edmonton and the Yellowhead Pass. Now, they both follow this common route to Vancouver. The highway is perched above the railways, alternating sides via bridges from time to time when the opposite bank offers the best purchase.

At Lytton, where the Thompson River joins the Fraser River, the road and railways continue on in the same fashion, with the terrain becoming even more rugged. Lytton calls itself the *Rafting Capital*, which seems to be valid when we see the wild rivers here. They also advertise the local hot springs, which offers a great way to relax and warm up after rafting, although the weather can be quite hot here. This is the warmest part of Canada, with average temperatures over 10^0C (50^0F).

The most dramatic section of the river is just south of Boston Bar. It is called Hell's Gate. Here the river channel narrows to just 33 meters in width, making sharp turns and creating wildly churning whirlpools. The volume of water surging through this small gap is twice that of Niagara Falls! We can feel the energy here. There is a tramway that takes us across the gorge, high above the water, to a restaurant and gift shop on the far bank, an exciting experience. Again, down below, we can see the two railway lines clinging to the cliffs. Because of the railway construction and rock slides that were caused a century ago, there is a series of fish ladders through the canyon that allow the returning salmon to make their way upstream to their spawning grounds

The highway continues south, sometimes requiring tunnels to penetrate the protruding cliffs, and emerges from the canyon country into the wide Lower Fraser River Valley at Hope, a town that claims the title of *Chainsaw Carving Capital*. This small town has many impressive carved figures along its avenues, all three or four meters high: fish, birds, animals and humans (pioneers, natives, Mounties).

The local label for this region is the "lower mainland," a name that goes back in history as a reference to this area's location relative to Victoria and Vancouver Island, which were developed earlier in time. The mountains are set well back from the river; the flat valley has been developed as a prime agricultural area on both the north and south sides. We can spot orchards, berry fields, chicken coops, horse barns and dairy herds along the route, interspersed with small villages and isolated general stores.

It is about 100 kilometers west of Hope before we reach the outskirts of Greater Vancouver. The cities en route, especially on the south side of the Fraser, have been growing steadily. Chilliwack and Abbotsford are substantial cities with active town centres in their own right. They also have rapidly growing residential subdivisions that are becoming, more and more, home to Vancouver commuters.

Once we pass Langley, the site of the original 1840 Hudson's Bay Company fort for the area, we are into the big and busy reality of Vancouver. With two million people in its metropolitan area, it is Canada's third largest city, and it continues to grow at rates comparable to Toronto and Calgary.

Vancouver has the most spectacular natural setting of any major city in Canada. Combine the mountain views of Calgary, the river valley of Winnipeg, the downtown hills of Montreal, the harbour of Halifax, the beaches of PEI, the oceanside location of Saint John, and the general ruggedness of St. John's, and you have Vancouver. The only distractions are that it has all of the traffic issues of those cities, combined, and it does rain a lot.

Vancouver's city centre sits on a peninsula that protrudes into English Bay and which provides shelter for the inner harbour of the Burrard Inlet. The hilly profile of the peninsula accentuates the downtown skyline. It has a very different look from other cities' downtowns, in that the dominant image is one of green glass, created by the dozens of 20 to 30 story buildings with a glass façade. This image is also repeated in some of the suburbs, where tall condos line the hills.

Vancouver's inner harbour is always full of activity, from the ferries, float planes and pleasure boats that cluster around the downtown area wharves to the huge ocean-going freighters and container ships that ply their way to the industrial docks; these line the inlet for 25 kilometers or more inland to Port Moody and beyond. Those inner shores are filled with warehouses, industrial plants and piles of commodities such as lumber and bright yellow sulphur. Near the city centre, the shore is lined with marinas, restaurants and hotels that command great views. The focal point is the Pan Pacific Centre, with its white sail-like architectural design that can be seen from everywhere.

The original terminus of the CPR was at Port Moody, a tidewater port at the head of the inlet, but it was soon moved to the western shore, which stimulated the growth of Vancouver. In 1886, prior to the railway's completion, Vancouver had just 2,000 people. With the railway arriving in 1887 and regular shipping to the Far East beginning in 1891, the place boomed. By 1900 the population was 100,000.

Just north of downtown, at the end of the peninsula, is Stanley Park, without doubt the greatest city park in Canada. With over 1,000 acres of west coast forest, open meadows, waterfront walks and many facilities, it can be a vacation destination of its own.

It also anchors the Lions Gate Bridge, the long, high span that connects to the communities of North and West Vancouver and on to the villages up the coast. The residential views from North Van and West Van may be the best anywhere. Clinging to the steep hillsides, they look back over the downtown and inner harbour, and across the outer harbour to the bluffs of Point Grey, the spectacular location of the University of British Columbia.

We all recognize UBC as one of the leading universities in the country. You can always identify a grad of UBC by the way they say it, as a single fast-spoken syllable, sort of "youbesee," without any interior inflection. It takes as much practice as Antigonish or Miramichi; I must admit that I cannot quite get it right. In any case, its location on a huge tract of land, surrounded by forest and overlooking the water, is one of the finest anywhere.

The shore from UBC on Point Grey, back along English Bay, is lined with parks and beaches that have a full view of downtown, Stanley Park and the residential hills of the north shore. Huge driftwood logs are lined up along the beaches for hundreds of meters, four-rows deep, to serve as resting spots for the folks using the beaches.

Driving through some of the established residential communities in the heart of the city, we realize that we are in a very different growth zone for plants and trees. Everything is so green and lush, and so big! Things do grow here. Trees in the yards can be over thirty meters tall. Hedges around properties are composed of trimmed narrow cedar trees, which are often ten meters in height. Large flowering bushes, in a blaze of colour from the early spring, fill the boulevards. Looking up the gated, tree-lined driveways, we can glimpse elaborate flower gardens and manicured lawns. "What winter?" you ask.

Vancouver is served by a commuter train system that provides the daily transportation for many people in the outlying cities, using double-decker train cars. There is also a rapid-transit rail system, often set on pillars high above the ground, to service the closer-in suburbs. In the city itself, there are trolley buses that cruise through the traffic, tethered to two overhead wires. I wonder if there are trolley buses still running anywhere else? The Vancouver systems are very similar to Toronto with its Go-Trains, underground subway system and ground-level street cars.

Vancouver has some impressive galleries, especially those dealing in northwest native art. Galleries fill the upscale historic shopping zone called Gastown, not far from the downtown shopping corridor of Granville Mall. There is also the unique converted industrial area of Granville Island, across False Creek, south of the city centre. The Broadway and 4th Avenue area is becoming very trendy, what used to be called *yuppie,* I guess. Shops specialize in kitchen gadgets, modern furniture and household decorations. Sidewalk markets are filled with fresh fruit, vegetables and flowers. Restaurant signs emphasize curry, sushi and many other ethnic specialties, with the word *organic* always prominent. I do have to wonder about the shop that specializes in baked goods for dogs.

The south end of the city is divided by the channels of the Fraser River. Again, this is navigable far inland and is lined with wharves, warehouses and loading docks past New Westminster and on to Port Coquitlam. We can see many booms of logs tethered along the river, having been floated down the river to the local sawmills.

I recall staying in a hotel along the river in New Westminster one time and waking up in the morning to a very loud barking sound. It was the sound of sea lions. They had worked there way up the river to where they could lie in wait for the salmon to come swimming downstream to them, presenting a tasty breakfast opportunity.

The Fraser River delta is very fertile; huge tracts in the Richmond/Delta area are preserved as farmland. City developments are not allowed to encroach, an amazing feat given the potential commercial value of the land.

On an island in the middle of the delta is the Vancouver airport. Over the past decade or more we have all seen the significant transformations of airports into shopping havens, often with elaborate displays of art. The

Vancouver Airport is one of the leading examples, particularly due to the massive, but intricate, west coast carvings that are on display everywhere. I think the entrance to the Canadian Customs and Immigration area here is the most impressive entryway to any country in the world. I wonder if it, in itself, didn't influence a couple of votes on the International Olympic Committee that awarded the 2010 Winter Games to Vancouver/Whistler.

Just south of the airport, across the channels of the Fraser River, we can make a brief stop at the fishing village of Steveston. Its wharves and warehouses are rustic and weathered, but the seafood restaurants are some of the best anywhere. Freshness is a given, and the ambience is casual and friendly, with the fishing boats along the docks and the netting and rigging drying on the racks.

Vancouverites love their city. They just shrug off any inconveniences, such as the traffic or the rain, which outside visitors might notice. They can't imagine living anywhere else. It's not the "centre of the universe" phenomenon of Toronto; in fact, it's quite the opposite — it's the independence from the outside world that appeals to them. They know Toronto, Montreal, Ottawa and Calgary are back there, "over the mountains"; they just don't care. The west coast is a different place.

There seems to be a strangeness factor in British Columbia politics. I think the last five or so elected premiers have all had some sort of legal problem or controversy, and they have represented all of the leading political parties. There is equal opportunity craziness here. I wonder who their future equivalent to Arnold Schwarzenegger will be. It must be the west coast water, or the fog.

Whistler, the mountain village 100 kilometers north of Vancouver, is something else again. You get there by taking the Sea-to-Sky Highway, which starts out from the ferry terminal at Horseshoe Bay on the coast just north of the city. To say the road is narrow and winding is like saying the mountains are high or the ocean is wet, a gross understatement. Presumably this will be upgraded as part of the preparation for the Olympics, which means seven years of continuing construction delays for traffic.

The first half of the trip north from Vancouver follows the steep shoreline of Howe Sound, offering amazing views of the bright-blue waters, the deep-green, forest-covered islands, and the rugged mountain slopes with their brilliant-white snowy peaks. On a sunny day, this is one of the most scenic drives in the country. On a foggy or rainy day, this is one of the most harrowing drives anywhere.

Along Howe Sound there are a few small villages and some new vacation/residential developments at spots such as Lion's Bay and Furry Creek. Britannia Beach is the site of an old abandoned mine and the B.C. Museum of Mining, which has a collection of historic mining equipment and offers informative mine tours.

At the head of the sound is the small city of Squamish, the *Outdoor Recreation Capital of Canada*. Squamish comes from the Indian word for "mother of the wind," which has to tell us something about the weather here. To be sure, there are a lot of outdoor activities available here, ranging from hiking, biking and rock climbing on land, to rafting and fishing in the rivers, and boating, kayaking and wind surfing in the sound. Yes, there's golf.

This is the area Mother Nature struck with heavy rains and floods in the fall of 2003, a dramatic offset to the forest fires of the summer.

And for skiing, well, let's just carry on for the remaining half of our trip up here, head inland through the rugged mountain pass along the fast-running Cheakamus River, and experience Whistler itself.

This has to be the most upscale recreation and resort spot in Canada. Anchored by the ski hills of Whistler and Blackcomb Mountains, it is an all-season destination now, with a multitude of outdoor attractions. What is amazing is that it only started in 1966 with the first ski lift, and that the centrepiece "Village" was not built until 1980. Now the hills are filling with new hotels, condos, homes and chalets, plus all of the peripheral elements of restaurants, galleries and quality shops. It is a classy place. Construction is booming everywhere, and now there is the pending impact of the 2010 Olympics.

Okay, it's time to return back south and to locate transportation to Vancouver Island. From Vancouver we can fly, either by commercial jet or by the more entertaining float-planes that give a closer view of the water and the islands on the way. Also, we can take a ferry from Horseshoe Bay, north of Vancouver, or from Tsawwassen, south of the city. Let's take this latter option, as it will give us a close-up view of the Gulf Islands and lead us to Victoria.

The Tsawwassen ferry terminal sits on a long causeway that has been built out from the mainland to reach beyond the shallow waters and sand bars of the Fraser River Delta.

You can tell a local resident from a visitor by their pronunciation of this name, actually by the fact they can pronounce it at all without stumbling. Old-timers will start with a bit of an "S" sound; think of the analogy with the Russian word for king, Tsar, that's often written as Czar to help pronunciation. However the "T" sound of T'wassen is most dominant now.

The tip of the ferry jetty at Tsawwassen is exactly on the 49th parallel, the border between Canada and the United States. In fact, there is a little nipple of land jutting south from the mainland here that is part of the U.S.; it's called Point Roberts. This makes it the only heavily populated part of the U.S. lower-48 states that is attached to another country but not to the U.S. itself. Obviously, the inhabitants make a lot of border crossings.

(There is a similar isolated spit of U.S. land that juts into the Lake of the Woods from the eastern edge of Manitoba.)

As we cross the water on a B.C. Ferry, we get a good view of the Strait of Georgia and the approaching Gulf Islands. This is probably a good time to review the history of British Columbia, since so much of it was focused right here.

Conventional history has held that the northwest coast of North America was not explored by European nations until the mid- to late-1700s, almost 300 years after the voyages of Columbus encountered the continent. By then, South and Central America had been well defined, as had every other ocean coast in the world except for the Antarctic and Arctic regions. The general reason for that was that it took a lot of effort to get to the Pacific coast of North America, either by sailing around Africa or South America, or by traipsing across Panama and building a ship on the other side. Having reached there, the riches of South America, such as gold, silver and emeralds, overcame any curiosity about the forests and mountains to the north.

It is now quite well established that Francis Drake explored the coasts of British Columbia and southern Alaska, even sailing around Vancouver Island and seeing the mouth of the Fraser River in 1579. However, this was lost to history for centuries. The trip was designed to look for the possible opening to a passage across the top of North America that would provide a more direct access to England. It was treated as secret by the government of Queen Elizabeth I. As a result, reports of the voyage were suppressed; maps that were released to describe Drake's trip around the world were modified. On the west coast of North America they mapped everything 10^0 south of the true latitudes. There is an excellent account of all this in *The Secret Voyages of Sir Francis Drake* by Samuel Bawlf. This conspiracy is much more credible than the one about John Franklin.

In any case, the legacy of Drake's maps was twofold, and was wrong on both accounts. First of all, people have been searching the coast of California near San Francisco for the past couple of hundred years, looking for remnants of Drake's voyage. In fact, he never even touched the American coast much south of the Columbia River. Drake's winter harbour was closer to 48° N. (Strait of Juan de Fuca) than 38° N. (San Francisco Bay). I doubt that the proprietors of the Sir Francis Drake Hotel in San Francisco like to acknowledge this.

The second legacy was that piecemeal leakage of the details of Drake's voyage, combined with the falsified latitudes, resulted in California being depicted as an island on many world maps for 150 years. Without realizing it, they were superimposing Vancouver Island onto the California Baja. This was always a mystifying piece of history. The reality is that explorers were careful about their observations and certainly were able to determine latitude very accurately. How could California be depicted as an island? It was attributed to legend, but that was never credible in its explanation, even hundreds of years later. Now, we finally know the truth.

It was not until the 1700s that anything happened here again. In 1741 Bering, a Russian explorer, reached the Alaskan coast and discovered the rich harvest of seal and sea lion pelts that could be had. These became valuable commodities in trading for the riches of the Far East. As a result, Spanish traders also started to appear in the northern waters in the 1770s.

The most famous explorer to visit the shores of this region was James Cook in 1778. His maps became the definitive ones for the area, mostly because he was the first to accurately and credibly determine the longitude of the coast. The earlier Russian maps, based on Bering's voyages, were relatively accurate but they were not given credence in Western Europe. Determining longitude requires an accurate timepiece that will withstand the turbulent ride on a ship traveling around the world for a few years. This was not available until an Englishman, Harrison, invented one and provided a copy to Cook.

Cook sailed and mapped most of the Pacific Ocean, from the Arctic to the Antarctic and from America to Australia; he was truly the most successful explorer of that era. He was killed by the natives in Hawaii in a confusing conflict of cultures and legends, thus preventing him from completing his complete circuit of the Pacific; he missed the Japanese, Chinese and Indonesian areas.

Over the next decade, the 1780s, traders from England, Spain and the newly-independent United States, which was then still limited to the thirteen states on the Atlantic Ocean, scoured the west coast and hassled each other. In the early 1790s, the English and Spanish established a truce of sorts, and then jointly surveyed the area around the big island that they called Quadra's and Vancouver's Island, after the two sea captains that led the survey. In 1794, the two nations agreed to jointly occupy the area, but the Spanish slowly disappeared as other world events became more pressing. Thus, the island became simply Vancouver Island and the British now controlled the area. Recall that it was about this same time, 1793, that Mackenzie had reached the Pacific coast by an overland route.

As an aside, George Vancouver called the open waters between Vancouver Island and the mainland the Gulf of Georgia. The name was later changed to the Strait of Georgia, when more details of its geography were known. This is why we find Gulf Islands but no Gulf here.

Over the next decades the competition for control of the area shifted to the British versus the Americans. In 1803 the United States made the Louisiana Purchase from France. This gave them title to the Mississippi

River Valley and the northern plains as far as the Rocky Mountains, significantly expanding their borders from the Appalachians.

Within six months, the U.S. sent an expedition to explore for a route to the Pacific. This is the famous Lewis and Clark Expedition of 1804-06, which started out from the Mississippi, went through the Missouri River system to Montana, crossed over the mountain divide to the Snake River, and then carried on to the mouth of the Columbia River. (With the bi-centennial of that expedition now upon us, we will be seeing a lot of re-enactments, documentaries and celebrations in the U.S.)

The British were doing similar things farther north. David Thompson, perhaps the greatest inland explorer of them all, surveyed the Saskatchewan, Nelson, Athabasca and Columbia Rivers from 1790 to 1811. However, he arrived at the mouth of the Columbia after Lewis and Clark, which affected later land claims. Simon Fraser defined the river that flows out at Vancouver, and which bears his name, in 1808, having survived the Hell's Gate Rapids and all the other challenges.

In 1817 Britain and the U.S. defined the border through the Great Lakes; in 1818 they established the 49th parallel across the prairies to the Rockies (recall the Lake-of-the-Woods anomaly). Nothing had been settled west of the mountain front.

By the 1840s the Hudson's Bay Company controlled much of the area in today's British Columbia and Washington State. Their Fort of Victoria was established in 1843. The Americans were striving to extend to the west at the same time, having established a presence in Oregon, south of the Columbia River.

So, the situation in 1844 was: the Mexicans controlled California, having split from Spain; the Americans were in Oregon; the British were established north of the Columbia and on Vancouver Island; and the Russians controlled Alaska, including the coast down to 54^0 40' N. latitude.

In the presidential election of 1844, James Polk was victorious using the ridiculous slogan of "54.40 or Fight," meaning he planned to drive the British off the Pacific coast. Once he was elected, however, things settled down and they negotiated a border. Although the British tried to claim all lands north of the Columbia River, it was finally agreed to just extend the border along the 49th parallel over the Rockies to the mainland coast, but to leave all of Vancouver Island as British.

In 1849 Vancouver Island was established as a crown colony, similar to the colonies back east of Nova Scotia, Newfoundland, Prince Edward Island and Canada (with its two provinces, Upper and Lower Canada, today's Ontario and Quebec). Victoria was named the capital of the new colony.

1858 became a turning point for the region. First, gold was found on the Fraser River, then farther inland in the Cariboo area, and finally in the Kootenay valley. Within weeks tens of thousands of prospectors and adventurers arrived in Victoria and then moved on into the interior, the "lower mainland." To establish some sense of order and to maintain control of the area from the Americans, who were still looking to expand north, the crown colony of British Columbia was established with New Westminster as its capital. James Douglas, who had been the HBC leader in the area, and who was then Governor of Vancouver Island, was also made Governor of British Columbia.

Eight years later, in 1866, the two colonies joined into one. It was called British Columbia, with Victoria becoming the capital. Five years after that, they joined the new Canada on the promise of a transcontinental railway; the rest is history that we have already visited. Recall that the U.S. had purchased Alaska from the Russians in 1867.

I find it somewhat amazing that all of the physical definition of the west coast and its current political entities occurred over that relatively short period in the late 1700s and early 1800s. The rest of the continent took almost four centuries to sort itself out.

Anyway, let's get back to our trip, south down the Strait of Georgia towards Victoria. The ferries are large, carrying hundreds of cars, with comfortable lounge areas to relax in during the ninety-minute trip.

There is quite a saga about the ferries on these routes from Vancouver to Vancouver Island. A few years ago, the Government of British Columbia decided to invest in faster ferries. They commissioned a design involving catamaran-shaped aluminum hulls and turbine engines, which could reduce the trip to one hour. In constructing the assembly facilities, training the tradesmen in new skills such as welding aluminum, and actually building three ferries, they spent over 450 million dollars. Although the ferries were smaller than the existing "slow" ones, it was believed that they would be economic because they could make more runs in a day, and people would pay a premium for the added speed. Well, reality was something else.

The operating costs were very high because the fuel consumption per passenger was double the older ferries. They could not get up to speed, except for short stretches in the middle of the strait, because the wake they created played havoc with small power boats and sail boats in the area. The speed was also limited because of the many floating logs in the water, orphans from the coastal logging operations, which could damage the aluminum hulls and the turbine engines. So, they just ended up with smaller ferries that were more expensive to operate and that were no faster that the existing ones. They could not collect higher tolls either, since there was no time advantage. It was an economic and political disaster on the grandest scale. The next government sold them off for little more than scrap value, 25 million dollars.

The view of the Gulf Islands from the ferry is impressive, as we pass through the very narrow channels, sometimes not wide enough for two ferries to pass. The islands are tree-covered, rising above their solid rock shores, which are broken here and there by small beaches in local bays. Much of their shorelines are populated with impressive homes, as most of the islands are serviced by smaller, local ferries.

We can glimpse Salt Spring Island, the largest and most developed of the Gulf Islands, as we approach the ferry dock at Sidney on Vancouver Island itself. This is the town at the tip of the Saanich Peninsula, which juts into the water north of Victoria. The Victoria airport is nearby, for those who missed the boat.

Driving down the peninsula towards Victoria, we quickly develop a few impressions. First is that the area is very green and there are flowers everywhere. Next is that they really have kept the old-English look intact, with many stucco-and-batten buildings with dormer windows. Many of them are pubs. Third, and surprisingly, there are an amazing number of roadside billboards advertising hotels, tourist attractions and stores. It makes us feel that we have gone back fifty years, when these ugly things were common on highways everywhere.

Victoria is a surprising city for me. Its image as a quaint hidden corner of old England, having shops filled with woolens and porcelain, lounges where you can stop for afternoon tea, old bookstores and antique collections, double-decker buses and lots of Union Jacks, is all true, but there is so much more.

The inner harbour is the focus for a lot of the activity. On one side is the stately Empress Hotel, with its pink-and-brown stonework that is covered in creeping foliage, its many peaks and spires, and the expansive gardens out front.

On another side of the harbour is the British Columbia Legislature, perhaps the most impressive of all the provinces'. Set back from a deep lawn, the long white stone building, with the wide front steps and copper-domed roof, looks like an English castle. It is trimmed in lights that dramatically outline its massive size and shape at night, a concept that sounds a bit tacky but that actually works well.

Along the third side of the harbour are condos, hotels and restaurants. Let's stop and have a beer and some fresh mussels on one of the patios that look over the water. We can see the snow-capped mountains of Washington State in the background. On the water there are float planes landing, water taxis scurrying around to the various docks, and tour boats moving about that advertise fishing, whale watching and sightseeing. Along the wide walkways artists have set up their goods for visitors to peruse and street buskers are making music, acting out pantomimes, or juggling torches.

Sitting on the patio, we can understand why the weather here has been declared "the most comfortable in Canada" by Environment Canada when they combine the factors of sunshine, temperatures, precipitation and storms.

The downtown streets are busy. There are the usual stores, of course, including the Eaton Centre Mall that houses the Hudson's Bay store; how Canadian is that? There are also many galleries and specialty shops. We particularly notice the many Trading Companies that specialize in Canadiana, such as wool jackets, toques, maple syrup and native carvings. They have appropriately catchy names such as Moose Crossing, Bear River, James Bay and West Pacific Trading. One of my favourite book stores, Munro Books, with its stone front, old wooden floors and high stacks, is located here. It's always worth a visit. It was here that I bought the "conspiracy" books about Drake and Franklin, along with other Canadiana selections.

The University of Victoria has a special location in the north part of the city. It has a relatively protected campus that is circular in shape, with lots of open spaces and big trees. The buildings are relatively low with a finish of smooth stone and glass, which creates a very modern image. It is a quiet oasis in the middle of the busy city.

Victoria has a number of large parks, such as the Beacon Hill Park near downtown with its extensive lawns and walks, and the Mount Douglas Park north of the university with its deep, west-coast forest that forms a canopy over the road and its views of the open water between the offshore Gulf islands.

Because Victoria is on a point of land itself, it also has a long stretch of rugged coastline populated with upscale neighbourhoods, golf courses, marinas and restaurants. We need to travel away from the downtown to fully appreciate all the beauty of this city.

Leaving Victoria, we can take a trip along the south shore of the island toward the town of Sooke, one of the sites of the Spanish landings in 1790. Today it anchors the local tourist industry and a continuing lumbering business.

The road to Sooke goes west out of Victoria, past the harbour and naval training centre at Esquimalt, the *Home of Canada's Pacific Fleet*. Then we come to Royal Roads, once one of the major military universities in Canada. Now it's a private university, since the military has concentrated all of its senior education at the Royal Military College in Kingston, Ontario. We have seen many great campuses as we have crossed the country, but this one is amazing. Set behind high fences with stone pillars and iron railings, it is located deep in a thick forest of very high trees, all spread along the rocky shore. The many military-style buildings are anchored by the impressive, stone Hatley Castle, which serves as the administration centre. As you would expect from its history, there are extensive playing fields for sporting activities, but I can't help visualizing night-time maneuvers in that thick forest.

The highway to Sooke is marked by English-style pubs: Four Mile Pub, Six Mile Pub, Seventeen Mile Pub, etc. We can convince ourselves that we are on an olde-English highway, with the roadhouses being there to sustain our journey. We should definitely stop and check for Robin Hood and his band, or at least to get a pint and a beef-and-kidney pie.

The south shore is an attraction for visitors, with many campgrounds, lodges, guest houses and B&B's. I like to check the names they have chosen. As always, there are many such as Ocean View, Mountain View, Sea Breeze and Riverside, with creativity limited to substituting the word Vu for View. There are some local identities, such as Mrs. Smith's Farmhouse, and attempts at variety such as Peak-a-View. My favorite name here is Grouches Lair, which leaves you wondering if it applies to the owners or the guests. I'll bet it fills its space faster than the competition, just out of curiosity.

Backtracking a bit from Sooke and turning inland to the north, we can connect with the Trans-Canada Highway. It starts/ends in Victoria, as it does in St. John's. From here it goes up to Nanaimo and then crosses by ferry from there to Vancouver.

Just past the northern limits of Victoria is Goldstream Park, a relatively small natural area, but the site of a salmon stream that is easily accessible beside the highway. In the fall during the spawning season we can stand on the banks of this stream and watch the salmon that are just a few feet away. It is fascinating. The salmon are tired and appear generally lethargic due to the journey from the salt-water ocean up to this fresh-water gravel bed. They are also deformed due to the natural changes that occur at the end of their life cycle; their bodies seem to be rotting away before our eyes. They are here by the hundreds, packed close together in the shallow, fast-running water. The mating process involves the to-and-fro waltzing of a male and female, only distracted by the periodic need of the male to desperately lunge away and drive off a competing suitor. Eventually, the female creates a nest in the stream bed and deposits her eggs, followed by the fertilizing spray from the male. Then they drift off and die, having completed their role in the perpetual cycle. It's a fascinating, but melancholy, opportunity to see nature in action.

Continuing north, we climb over the relatively steep Malahat Pass, and then travel along the east shore of Vancouver Island, with its many towns and villages tucked along the local bays and beaches. Around Cowichan Bay there is a local micro-climate that is warm enough to grow grapes, which support a few local wineries. There is even a sign for an Estate Cidery, something new to me. Duncan is a historic mining centre; it has a couple of dozen carved totem poles along its main streets. Chemainus has a collection of some 30 murals on its buildings that depict the history of the area. We have seen such murals in many towns across Canada, but these are probably the most elaborate. Ladysmith is a colourful town with floral displays along the boulevards. It has won awards for its beauty.

There is one phenomenon we see along here that confuses me; in fact, it's present in Vancouver as well. The real estate advertising for homes that look out to the water calls the scenes "Ocean View." Yes, I know the strait is salt water and the tidal effects can be large, but to me it is not the ocean. I think the Pacific starts on the west side of Vancouver Island. I don't believe the folks on the Bay of Fundy or the Gulf of Mexico refer to their views as being of the ocean. Anyway, here it is called an ocean view, although no one talks about taking the ferries across the ocean when they cross the strait to the mainland.

Nanaimo is the second largest city on Vancouver Island, with almost 75,000 inhabitants. It was established over 150 years ago as a mining town and HBC trading fort. Its name comes from the Anglicization of the local Indian tribe's name, "Sneneymexw," although you have to wonder about the origins of that spelling. Today it is the regional centre for the central Island and is the gateway to the Island's ocean and forest vacationland. Called the *Harbour City*, it has a number of marinas and is the terminus for ferry connections to both Horseshoe Bay and Tsawwassen in Vancouver, which is directly east of here.

Diving is a popular activity here, with the waters full of fascinating sea life, centred on artificial reefs that have been created around two sunken ships. Being unable to swim and being prone to claustrophobia, I cannot give first-hand testimony to the details.

There is also a local golf course called Eagle Quest, which I think is a fine name, although, for me it would be more realistic to call it Birdie Hope, Par Hunt or Bogey Save.

The northern extent of the Gulf Islands chain occurs here at Gabriola Island, just offshore from Nanaimo. I have had the chance to visit there a number of times, since one of my sons and his wife live there. You can reach it via a short ferry ride from Nanaimo or by float plane from Vancouver. The latter mode is an effective way to get a bird's eye view of the activity in the strait and of the various small islands that are often stops on the way.

Gabriola is typical of the Gulf Islands; it rises out of the water into rolling, tree-filled hills. The shore is either sharp cliffs or wind-and-water-weathered rock, which is intriguing to explore. I am always amazed at the intricate patterns, smooth pock marks and gnarly holes that have been carved in the hard rock surface. In places it seems like we are walking on a moonscape. The shallow intratidal pools are teaming with small scurrying crabs, pulsating barnacles and waving anemone. The lower rock faces are covered in green kelp, which attracts the hungry but cautious seals to the shores.

The islands are generally populated with artists, artisans, writers and researchers, all of whom are attracted to the quiet spaces and relaxed pace of activities here. I think some of them have been here for decades, even since the times of the first hippies and flower children. Visitors quickly adapt to it all and enjoy visiting the seashore and searching out all the home-based galleries.

Back to Vancouver Island and heading north from Nanaimo, we will follow the original two-lane road that winds its way along the coast and passes through all of the local villages. There is a modern four-lane highway, inland a bit, but we are here to see things, not just get somewhere.

The towns of Parksville and Qualicum Beach start the beach vacation country. They are attractive towns with seaside parks and a wide selection of hotels, motels, lodges, cottages and townhouses to accommodate the many summertime visitors. One of the main attractions is their sandy beaches, being both long and, more importantly, very wide at low tide. The sea floor is very shallow here and the tides can be as much as three meters in height, which creates hard packed beaches that can extend out from the shore for a kilometer or more when the water is low. This is the time for walking and beachcombing for pretty shells or artistic driftwood pieces, especially when its sunrise or sunset and the skies are filled with colourful hues. One of the activities that spring up on the beaches on hot summer days is the building of elaborate sand castles — fun for everyone, at least until we experience the unavoidable angst of watching them slump away as the tide rises.

The next sixty kilometers along the shore is populated with small villages tucked into local bays, all with their beaches, campgrounds and roadhouses. The tourist facilities have generally been here for awhile and include our old favourites such as Sea Breeze, Shady Shores and Sea View.

Mud Bay and Fanny Bay are the source of huge quantities of oysters. In Union Bay, we spot a restaurant called *Critters Café* that somehow doesn't lure me in. Probably we are missing something good; I recall that in Australia they use the term "bugs" for small crayfish or lobsters.

By the way, I am sure you knew without me pointing it out that every town we have passed since leaving Victoria has a golf course.

The cities of Courtney and Comox line a large harbour and a peninsula that protrudes into the strait. This coast and the valley that follows back up the local river is again an active vacation region with both wilderness and seaside attractions. The spine of Vancouver Island is a range of mountains, some of which rise to sharp snow-topped peaks that contain extensive glaciers. Thus, inland from here there are ski hills to attract winter vacationers as well.

I expect there will be a sharp increase in the number of visitors who wander through the area around Comox Harbour looking for artifacts from four hundred years ago, now that we know this was the famous landing point for Sir Francis Drake, rather than somewhere in Oregon or California.

The shore of Vancouver Island continues on north in a similar fashion to that south of Courtney/Comox. Oyster Bay is a very wide area, with a rocky edge and sandy flats, and bordered by a shoreline park and picnic grounds.

Campbell River, a city of 30,000, declares itself the *Salmon Capital of the World*. It certainly has developed a reputation as "the place to go" for sports fishing and general wilderness enjoyment, with many lodges and resorts. The upper end of Georgia Strait and all of the many fast-flowing tidal channels in the area provide many opportunities for catching halibut, red snapper and cod, but salmon is king. The waterfront is lined with kiosks that offer fishing charters, boat rentals and expert guides. We learn that there are many varieties of salmon: Coho, Chinook, Sockeye and Pink, but that a Tyee is not a type. It's any salmon larger than 30 pounds, and catching one is considered to be a big achievement. Apparently it is common, even expected, that everyone shouts out "Tyee-e-e" whenever someone in a group catches such a big one, or even suspects they may have one on the line.

I was surprised the first time I saw this part of Vancouver Island. Having heard so much about the salmon fishing and the rustic lodges, I wasn't quite prepared to see such an established city. It's the composite of all those things we have observed across B.C. There are the sea-based activities of kayaking, diving, surfing, waterskiing, beachcombing and whale watching. Inland there is fresh-water fishing for char and trout, hiking, climbing, river rafting and caving. There are also tours to observe grizzly bears that live and forage along the more remote shores.

The harbour is active with boats and ferries. It is also busy with commercial activities, as this is the base of a large fishing fleet and the hub of the local forestry industry. We can see that the nearby offshore islands have also been developed with cottages and lodges. As in so many places along the coasts, it's great entertainment to sit on a patio deck having a seafood lunch and watching all of the activity. Pass the oysters, please.

Now, let's find that inland highway I mentioned and go back south for an hour or so. Then, we can travel west from Qualicum Beach to the interior of Vancouver Island.

Almost immediately after we leave Qualicum, we are climbing through forested hills along a narrow, sharply-curved road. We pass Cameron Lake, a long and narrow, modest-sized lake set in the woods with some cottages along its shore. We might almost imagine ourselves in the woods of any province across Canada, at least until we get a glimpse of a rocky, snow-capped mountain peeking (peaking?) through the trees.

Our next stop, however, could not be anywhere but on the west coast — Cathedral Grove. Even on a bright sunny day everything darkens here, as the high canopy of the towering trees blocks out much of the light. The "old growth" firs, cedars and hemlocks can be over 70 meters high and have trunks that are more than three meters in diameter. Their substantial roots protrude through the fern-filled undergrowth. Moss covers everything: the tree trunks and limbs, old stumps and logs and the soft forest floor. There is a distinctive smell in the air from all of the foliage and pervasive dampness; we are in a rain forest and can easily imagine ourselves in an African or South American jungle.

The Cathedral Grove Provincial Park has preserved this stand of old forest. The term "old growth" refers to trees that are more than 150 years old — in other words, trees that existed before the forestry industry arrived. Most of the forests of British Columbia have been cut at least once. This is not always obvious when you can see "new" trees that are over 30 meters high. In Cathedral Grove the trees are up to 500 years old, although many are "only" 300 years in age, the result of a forest fire that has been dated to around 1700.

From here we continue west and climb over a divide that's more than 300 meters (1000 feet) above sea level, and then immediately slalom back down to sea level on the winding road. We next come to Port Alberni, with its highway sign that says "Welcome to the West Coast." This is a bit of a surprise, in that we are less than a third of the way across the Island and here we are at a sea port. As we saw around Prince Rupert, the long narrow fjords penetrate far inland from the Pacific coast.

Port Alberni, a pleasant city of about 20,000, is the centre of the local fishing and forestry industry, as well as a destination for outdoor enthusiasts. With proximity to various inland fresh water lakes and access to the ocean shore, it is a fisherman's dream. The main harbour and the marinas on the local river are full of pleasure craft and commercial fishing boats.

They advertise a daily trip through the fjord on board a small freighter that delivers mail and supplies to the isolated villages and camps along the way. I plan to go back and try that; it sounds like it would be a nice adventure.

One thing we notice as we leave the various places out here, such as Port Alberni, is a road sign that informs us that there is no gasoline service available for the next "X" kilometers. At Port Alberni the distance is 85 kilometers. Of course, since this sign is located outside the city, if we need gas sooner than the stated distance we need to turn around and go back. Somehow there must be a better place for the signs, say as a warning as you enter the town.

Back on the road west, we continue to pass lakes and fast-running rivers that cut gorges through the rocky terrain. Cottages and visitor lodges appear from time to time. At one point, we can spot a narrow waterfall that drops down from a very high, rugged hill, reminiscent of western Newfoundland.

When we reach the west shore of Vancouver Island, we find the Pacific Rim National Park, which runs for 30 kilometers along the coast. It is bracketed by two historic villages, which are now active and booming vacation destinations, Ucluelet and Tofino.

Ucluelet ("you-clue-let") sits on a spit of land that separates the open ocean from a sheltered bay. Naturally, the marinas and tourist facilities are centred on the bay, although some newer lodging and residential developments are now rising along the hillsides and cliffs that front the ocean. They always have impressive views, but sometimes tough weather conditions.

Tofino is located at the end of a peninsula that separates the ocean from a series of inland channels and smaller islands. There are extensive developments of impressive resorts and vacation homes with views of the ocean or the bays.

In both places there are numerous attractions for the visitor on land and water, just as there have been at so many spots on the Island. Everything is here. The scenery in the bays, with the mountain backdrop, is spectacular. There are amazing opportunities for nature watching: whales, seals, eagles, bears and so much more.

We can also find a wide range of sights along the Pacific coast in the national park. There are miles of beaches that slope gently into the ocean surf. These are broken by knobby rock protrusions and jutting headlands. Behind the sandy beaches are dunes covered with blowing sea grasses. Driftwood and sea shells provide our entertainment as we walk along the hard sand and listen to the waves and the ocean birds.

In one section of the park there is another micro-area of rain forest, similar to Cathedral Grove, with tall trees, ferns, mosses and a dark moist atmosphere. There are hiking paths a kilometer or two in length which allow us to become immersed in the environment and feel we are a long way from the outside world.

There are also sections of rocky cliffs with a panoramic view of the open ocean, a fitting place to end our trip. When we started this adventure, we were on Signal Hill above St. John's, looking out at the grey North Atlantic and imagining the early arrival of John Cabot and all of the events that would follow. Here, we can stare out at the blue Pacific and visualize Francis Drake and James Cook, who first defined this other side of the continent and stimulated its exploration and settlement. We have truly traveled *A Mari Usque ad Mare*.

The end of a journey is always met with mixed feelings. There is the pleasure and satisfaction of actually having done it and having experienced so many things. There is also the inevitable melancholy and slight regret that it is over. However, it always leaves many memories, and starts the anticipation of the next trip. Let's finish by sharing some thoughts about what we have seen across this great land of Canada.

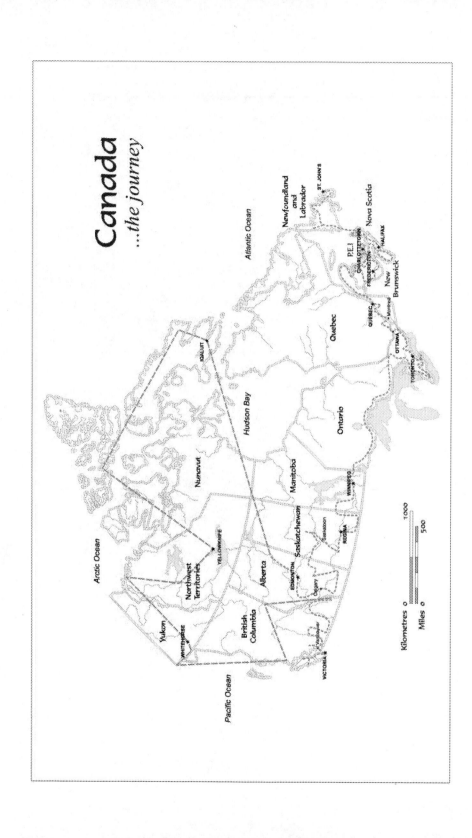

Afterthoughts

It has been quite a trip. I find it somewhat surprising, but very satisfying, that we have been able to cross the country and visit all of the provinces and territories in a manageable way. Our country is large and diverse, but many common threads do tie it together. For me the overriding result of this journey has been the development of a broad, but integrated, perspective of Canada:

- The sights were awe-inspiring, from the icebergs of Newfoundland to the rain forests of British Columbia.

- The vastness of our geography was overwhelming, from the open prairies of Manitoba to the towering Rocky Mountains of Alberta.

- The historical crossroads were fascinating, from the old sections of Quebec City to the hamlet of Batoche, Saskatchewan.

- The remoteness of our frontiers, from Nunavut to the Yukon, reminded me of the bravery and resourcefulness of the early explorers.

- The cultural heritage centres recalled our roots, from Pier 21 in Nova Scotia to the trading posts of the west.

- The early settlements in each region increased my admiration for our forefathers, from the Acadians of New Brunswick to the prospectors in the North.

- The richness of our land was evident from the ever-present forests to the prairie grain fields.

- The events were wonderfully entertaining, from the elaborate festival stages of Ontario to the small town fall fairs everywhere.

- The sounds were memorable, from the roar of nature at Niagara Falls and the din of human activity in the big cities to the melancholy call of a loon on a quiet northern lake.

- People everywhere reinforced my awareness of the energy and goodwill that is so evident in the country.

As I said in the Foreword, my hope in writing this book has been to inspire Canadians to see more of our country first-hand and to learn more about our rich history and heritage. It is very encouraging to see that there are more and more books, documentaries and entertaining interpretive sites being created about every part of Canada. The Canadiana sections of bookstores are bursting with new items.

I find that the first question that I am invariably asked by people when they hear that I have written a book about Canada is, "What is your favourite place?" This is an impossible question to answer since there are so many dimensions to our country. I invariably answer with the somewhat glib response that my favourite place is the one that I am going to next; I love to explore this nation and there are many places that I have not yet seen.

Nevertheless, in response to that inevitable question, and in the modern tradition of David Letterman, I have created some *Top Ten Lists* for Canada in the Appendices. Compare them to your own and share them with family and friends as you plan your next trip.

For amusement, I have also created a little trivia quiz that can test your knowledge of some of our geography and history. The answers can be found in the book. (They are given in the Appendices as well.)

Thank you for your company on our trip. I wish you many happy times and interesting adventures in your future travels.

Barry Stewart

Appendices

I) "Top Ten" Favourites

My lists of favourite sights and experiences in Canada are obviously just that, my opinion. How many of these have you actually seen or done yourself? After you have finished reading mine, make up your own list of missed highlights and start packing.

There are five lists of ten items each: Natural Sights, Places Created by People, Images and Sounds, Events and Experiences, and Out-of-the-way Places. Score yourself on those you have seen, two points each. Partial scores are allowed if you have seen or done part of the item. It's a tough scale since the lists cover many remote spots and local events across the country.

If:	Status:
0 – 20 points	Canadian, eh? You stay close to home.
21 – 40 points	Canadian, eh. You venture out some.
41 – 60 points	Canadian, eh! You have hit the highways.
61 – 80 points	Canadian, yay! You have hit the byways.
80 – 100 points	Canadian expert. Write a book.

A) Natural Sights (East to West)

Icebergs. The gleaming-white towers of ice floating majestically along the Newfoundland coast create a sense of awe and of hesitation, as we remember the Titanic and all the other ships they have sunk.

Bay of Fundy Tides. The surging power of the world-class tides are amazing, whether at the cliffs along the Hopewell Rocks, the river flats of Truro, the power plant at Annapolis Royal, or the Reversing Falls of Saint John.

Gaspé Peninsula. The St. Lawrence River and its Gulf shape the rugged shores of this rural landscape, with its ravines, forests and the rock at Percé, all enhanced by the quiet, shoreline villages.

Ontario Cottage Country. The lakes and woods that stretch from the Ottawa Valley across the Kawarthas and Muskoka to Georgian Bay contain a fabulous selection of vacation retreats.

Niagara Falls. An absolute "must see" for everyone. Ignore the tourists and the shops; just admire the raw energy of the sight, probe its inner nooks and crannies, and cruise through its churning lower rapids.

The Canadian Shield. Recall TRRLPAM? The trees, rocks, rivers, lakes, ponds and marshes of the northern forests define Canada's main geography. The rushing rivers, calm beaver ponds and elusive animals are captivating.

Open Prairies. The flat landscape that runs to the farthest horizon, filled with the waves of the grain fields blowing in the western winds, all beneath the sunny "big sky," is a wonder to experience.

Banff–Jasper Trail. The Rocky Mountains are an awesome presence; along this route they are the most spectacular, with snow-capped peaks, emerald-green lakes, tumbling rivers, deep ravines and ancient ice fields.

Pacific Fjords. The long, narrow, steep-sided inlets that penetrate far inland through the high, rugged Coastal Mountains are spectacular, from Vancouver Island to Alaska; the ones leading to the Chilkoot Pass and the Klondike are especially historic.

Rain Forest. Huge fir and cedar trees forming a canopy over the moss and fern-covered undergrowth, preserving a damp and fragrant environment, make us feel like we are in the tropical jungles, a unique Canadian experience.

B) Places Created by People (Alphabetical) (Almost always with great settings)

Charlottetown. This stately old colonial city has its roots embedded in the creation of Canada as a nation — all well-presented in the Founders Hall. The whole province of PEI is a gem, from its bridge, beaches and golf courses to the attractions of Anne of Green Gables.

Forts. All of the old forts from colonial times, with their summertime re-enactments, give us a sense of the French-English-American conflicts in our country's history, e.g., Louisbourg, Halifax, Quebec, Henry, York and George.

Historical Villages. These re-creations give us a sense of our heritage and culture as it evolved in the new nation, e.g., Grand Pré, Caraquet, Upper Canada Village, Sainte-Marie-Among-the-Hurons, Ft. William, Ft. Garry and Batoche.

Niagara-on-the-Lake. This is a fascinating town, with its colonial facades and chintz hotels, the artistic and entertaining Shaw Festival, and its setting among orchards and vineyards with their Cellars, Estates and Boutiques.

Nova Scotia's South Shore. Atlantic Canada's entire coastline is ruggedly attractive, with its coves and villages full of colourful homes, docks, boats and traps. This area is the most beautiful, from Peggy's Cove to Shelburne.

Okanagan/Shuswap. The B.C. interior qualifies for its natural beauty alone, but it is all enhanced with great vacation facilities and its orchards and vineyards – a combination of Ontario's cottage country and Niagara On-the-Lake.

Quebec City. Did I say I didn't have one favourite place to visit? Maybe I lied. The old-world charm of the walled city, the quaint hotels, the fine restaurants, the amazing shops and boutiques, and the historic battlefield and citadel: they are all here to enjoy.

Railway Hotels. These grand old edifices anchor our cities and reflect our history: Chateau Frontenac, Royal York, Bessborough, Banff Springs, Lake Louise, The Empress, the log structures of Montebello and Jasper Park Lodge...

Tyrrell Museum. The Alberta Badlands have their own appeal, with the high cliffs and stone pillars that rise above the river valley, but the attraction is this amazing centre that explains our natural history from the time of the dinosaurs.

Vancouver. The city with it all: mountains, ocean, rivers, parks, universities, nightlife, galleries, the arts and the west-coast lifestyle. Then they have the fabulous Sea-to-Sky drive to Whistler and the ferries to wonderful Victoria.

C) Images and Sounds (Alphabetical)

Animals. The wild animals in Canada are exciting to see: beaver, bison, coyote, fox, wolf, bears (black, grizzly, polar), bighorn sheep, mountain goat, deer, elk, caribou and the elusive moose. The search for them enhances any trip.

Fall Colours. The blaze of colours across the land in the fall alone is worth a trip: the eastern forests with their many hues of reds, yellows and golds; fields alight in orange pumpkins; golden wheat fields billowing in the wind, mountain ash dripping in red berries; larches turning gold.

Canada Geese. The high, "V-shaped" formations of these large, impressive birds, loudly honking their way through the skies, is always a memorable sight, as are the flocks of white snow geese covering the prairie fields by the millions.

Great Lakes. These large bodies of water generate more feelings than great visual sights. Their scope and might is impressive, conjuring up the images of the early explorers and traders on their arduous journeys, or large ships floundering in a violent storm.

Loon. This beautiful bird, with its plaintive call that can be heard for miles across a quiet northern lake at sunset, is one of the most enthralling sounds anywhere. (Its affiliation with our currency, the "loonie," is a national bonus.)

Midnight Sun and Noontime Dark. The land above the Arctic Circle, with its extremes of seasons and daylight, is so remote and forlorn, yet awesome and intriguing. Be sure to take a book of Robert Service's poems.

Northern Lights. These amazing displays of colourful sheets of light (white, red, green, purple) surging across the northern skies take our breath away, especially if we are holding it in anticipation of the sound that never comes.

Puffins and Whales. Along every coast of Canada we can search for whales and be amazed by their size and grace, and we can see the millions of sea birds that nest along the shores. Most special are the puffins At Witless Bay.

Ste. Catherine Street. Downtown Montreal, our most cosmopolitan centre, in the evening, is a major happening. The animated energy and laughter of the many people walking the streets and filling the restaurants and clubs is unique.

Yonge, Bay, King, Queen. Downtown Toronto, our commercial centre, during the daytime, is a beehive of activity. From high in the towers to the underground tunnels, everyone stoically rushes to their appointed destinations.

D) Events and Experiences (Alphabetical)

Blue Jay Baseball. The skills and strategies of major league baseball in the fabulous Skydome; a Blue Jays game is just plain fun. Who can forget the World Series years? "How about those Blue Jays?"

The Brier. First class curling is very addictive, at least for those who have played the game, in spite of that uniquely irritating screaming by the skips, "Hurry, Haaaard." The Worlds and International Skins events are a bonus.

The Calgary Stampede. The exhibition and rodeo is the centrepiece event for this vibrant city. Everyone is a cowboy for the ten days. Free pancake breakfasts on the street seem normal after a night of partying. Then, it's on to Banff.

The Grey Cup. As a single event, it's perhaps the most Canadian of sports experiences. The historical rivalries are well established. Attending a game only gets full points if it is held outside, in freezing weather, with the wind blowing; domes, #!&#@$.

Live Theatre. The full-blown production of famous plays in the big-city theatres is always entertaining, but so are the small town troupes and the special theme groups (mystery, comedy, musical, train trips, dinner theatre). I enjoy the enthusiasm.

Lobster Dinners. This most special of all meals has to be experienced in a community hall in Atlantic Canada. To help determine which is best, you need to try it in each of the four provinces; just don't tell anyone your conclusion.

Maple Syrup. This great Canadian treat only counts if you watch them gather the sap from the trees and then boil it down into syrup and sugar in the big outdoor kettles. Even without a sweet tooth, this is good.

Olympics. These games, which are the crowning achievement for so many young athletes, are pure spectacle, from opening ceremony to closing awards. We have had Montreal and Calgary; Vancouver/Whistler, here we come.

RCMP Musical Ride. The riders, in their scarlet tunics and mounted on their prancing black horses, create a vivid scene as they maneuver in formation and through their drills in time with the lively music. It sure beats roaring jet planes.

The Stanley Cup. Hockey is Canada; attending any game, be it NHL, Junior or in your community, is fun. The pinnacle is the Stanley Cup playoffs, of course. I can still vividly remember Calgary's victory in 1989. Just wait 'til next year.

E) Out-of-the-way Places (West to East)

Queen Charlotte Islands. I have been close by, but have never visited these special Pacific Coast islands. Then I can see more of the spectacular fjords and coastal mountains and can go salmon fishing, another new experience.

Dawson City. Having made it to the Chilkoot Pass and Whitehorse, I need to finish the experience and visit the actual site of the Klondike gold rush. Perhaps a West Coast cruise is the answer.

Waterton Lakes. Should I admit that I haven't visited this great national park, with its famous Prince of Wales Hotel on the lake shore, when it is only a few hours away from where I live?

Churchill. It is off the beaten track, but where else can I see polar bears up close and in the wild. This also can provide a chance to see some of the original Hudson's Bay Company sites and envision the history of the area.

Iqaluit. While I am in the North again, I must visit Iqaluit, the capital of our newest territory. On Frobisher Bay, this is the site of the first Arctic expeditions from Europe following on the discoveries by Columbus and Cabot.

The Laurentians. My travels in the hills and lake country of Quebec have been limited to the areas just north of Montreal and east of Ottawa. There is so much more to see.

Quebec City Winter Carnival. Although I now avoid winter as much as I can, this extraordinary event beckons. It will just add another dimension to my favourite city to visit.

Southwest New Brunswick. I have probably visited New Brunswick less than the other provinces and have totally missed the coastal region southwest of Saint John. The villages of St. George and St. Andrew and the islands await.

Atlantic Deep-Sea Fishing. Again, I have been to all of the cities and villages where this is available but I have not done it. It's time.

L'Anse-Aux-Meadows. The Viking Trail up the northwest arm of Newfoundland leads to the sites of the earliest Viking landings in North America. From there, a visit to the shores of Labrador and the Inuit settlements can follow.

II) Canadiana Quiz

There are fifty questions covering the range of subjects we discussed: "people, places, history and idiosyncrasies." The answers can be found in the book, of course, and also on the last page for easier checking – just don't peek too soon. This test is tough as well; it is trivia detail, after all. Give yourself two points for each right answer.

The answers to the quiz appear on the bottom of page 266, or can be found in the book if you read it carefully.

If:	You:
0 – 20 points	Just read the cover and guessed.
21 – 40 points	Only scanned through quickly.
41 – 60 points	Did read the book or travel a lot.
61 – 80 points	Paid attention to my stories, thanks.
81 - 100 points	Took notes or have a photographic memory.

The Canadiana Quiz

1. What percentage of Canada's total population lives north of the 49th parallel?
    a) 33%   b) 50%   c) 67%   d) 75%

2. The final battle between the French and British for control of Canada was at?
    a) Louisbourg   b) Montreal   c) Quebec City   d) St. John's

3. The "yellow" in Yellowknife comes from the colour of?
    a) Bone   b) Copper   c) Gold   d) The sun

4. Which of these cities is farthest west?
    a) Prince Rupert   b) Vancouver   c) Victoria   d) Whitehorse

5. Louis Riel was captured, later to be hanged, after a battle at what location?
    a) Batoche   b) Frog Lake   c) Regina   d) Winnipeg

6. The hiking trail across Newfoundland is called?
    a) B'y the B'y   b) Joey's Jaunt   c) Smallway   d) T'Railway

7. Which province has not had a referendum election on separation from Canada?
    a) B.C.   b) Newfoundland   c) Nova Scotia   d) Quebec

8. The first European explorer to navigate and map the British Columbia coast was?
    a) Cook   b) Drake   c) Juan de Fuca   d) Vancouver

9. The highest mountain in Canada is located in?
    a) Alberta   b) British Columbia   c) Nunavut   d) Yukon

10. The Acadians established their "capital" in which province?
    a) New Brunswick   b) Newfoundland   c) Nova Scotia   d) Quebec

11. The first oil well in the world was located where?
    a) Alberta   b) New Brunswick   c) Ontario   d) Pennsylvania

12. Which one of these colonies joined the Canadian confederation most recently?
    a) British Columbia   b) New Brunswick   c) Nova Scotia   d) PEI

13. What percentage of new immigrants goes immediately to the Toronto area?
    a) 25%   b) 33%   c) 50%   d) 67%

14. The highest elevation on the Trans-Canada Highway is near which city?
a) Golden b) Kamloops c) Revelstoke d) Vancouver

15. The largest fresh-water island in the world is?
a) Akimiski b) Anticosti c) Manitoulin d) Pelee

16. The city of St. John's, Newfoundland, is at similar latitude to?
a) Calgary b) Edmonton c) Seattle d) Vancouver

17. The capital of New Brunswick is?
a) Bathurst b) Fredericton c) Moncton d) Saint John

18. Alexander Graham Bell invented the first operating telephone in which city?
a) Baddeck b) Brampton c) Brantford d) Boston

19. How many rivers flow into the St. Lawrence River at Trois-Rivières?
a) One b) Two c) Three d) Four

20. The flood diversion canal around Winnipeg is colloquially called?
a) Bison Bypass b) Duff's Ditch c) Gumbo Gulch d) Peg's Path

21. A pingo is?
a) Arctic ice mound b) Atlantic bird c) PEI party d) Quebec treat

22. The first capital of the Northwest Territories was where?
a) Battleford b) Edmonton c) Regina d) Yellowknife

23. The last Canadian amateur team to be World Hockey Champions was from?
a) Brandon b) Flin Flon c) Kenora d) Trail

24. The rainiest city in Canada is?
a) Halifax b) Prince Rupert c) St. John's d) Vancouver

25. The "Iceberg Capital of the World" is?
a) Gambo b) Iqaluit c) Twillingate d) Witless Bay

26. The highest point between Calgary and Labrador is in?
a) Manitoba b) Ontario c) Quebec d) Saskatchewan

27. The cafe in Oungre, Saskatchewan specializes in chicken...?
a) Drumsticks b) Gizzards c) Hearts d) Necks

28. Klondike Days is the summer festival in which city?
a) Dawson City b) Edmonton c) Skagway d) Whitehorse

29. The warmest over-all weather in Canada is in?
     a) Fraser River valley b) Niagara Falls c) Ottawa d) Windsor

30. Which of these lakes is the smallest?
     a) Great Bear b) Great Slave c) Ontario d) Winnipeg

31. The city with the most hours of sunshine per year is?
     a) Calgary b) Inuvik c) Medicine Hat d) Swift Current

32. The highway from Vancouver to Whistler is called?
     a) Cliffside b) Oceanview c) Sea-to-Sky d) Sea-to-Ski

33. The NWT is predicted to produce up to what share of the world's
     diamonds?
     a) 20% b) 30% c) 40% d) 50%

34. The "Reversing Falls" are located in?
     a) Churchill b) Saint John c) St. John's d) Whiteshell

35. National Park officials complained that the Field, B.C., ice rink
     was too?
     a) Big b) Close to Highway c) Noisy d) White

36. Pile-O-Bones was the original name of?
     a) Brandon b) Moose Jaw c) Regina d) Toronto

37. Which Prime Minister was not born in Ontario?
     a) Diefenbaker b) Martin c) Pearson d) Turner

38. Longfellow wrote his poem *Evangeline* about the?
     a) Acadians b) Iroquois c) Loyalists d) Métis

39. The colour of potash mined in Saskatchewan is?
     a) Blue b) Green c) Pink d) White

40. The tunnels in Banff's Tunnel Mountain are?
     a) Highway b) Imaginary c) Railway d) River channels

41. Which city has never been the capital of Canada?
     a) Charlottetown b) Kingston c) Ottawa d) Montreal

42. Niagara-on-the-lake hosts which festival?
     a) Brock b) Leacock c) Shaw d) Shakespeare

43. The only province that does not use Daylight Saving Time is?
     a) Alberta b) B.C. c) New Brunswick d) Saskatchewan

44. The easternmost point in North America is?
     a) Cape Cod   b) Cape Spear   c) Iqaluit   d) Louisbourg

45. Fiddleheads are a?
     a) Cod delicacy   b) Green vegetable   c) N.B. beer   d) Shellfish

46. Lake Shuswap in B.C. is famous for its?
     a) Canoes   b) House boats   c) Power boats   d) Sail boats

47. The historic immigration terminal in Halifax is?
     a) Founders' Hall   b) Pier 21   c) The Wharf   d) Welcome Island

48. Which city has roadside taverns called 17-Mile Pub, 6-Mile Pub,
     4-Mile Pub?
     a) Charlottetown   b) London   c) Stratford   d) Victoria

49. The southernmost point in Canada is in?
     a) Lake Erie   b) Lake Ontario   c) Nova Scotia   d) Vancouver Island

50. The "Midnight Madness" in Yellowknife involves?
     a) Fishing   b) Golf   c) Hunting polar bears   d) Northern Lights

50.b	49.a	48.d	47.b	46.b	45.b	44.b	43.d	42.c	41.a
40.b	39.c	38.a	37.d	36.c	35.d	34.b	33.d	32.c	31.c
30.c	29.a	28.b	27.b	26.d	25.c	24.b	23.d	22.a	21.a
20.b	19.a	18.d	17.b	16.c	15.c	14.a	13.c	12.d	11.c
10.a	9.d	8.b	7.b	6.d	5.a	4.b	3.b	2.d	1.a

Reviews for
"Across the Land
...a Canadian journey of discovery"

"(The book is) an uncritical upbeat trip from sea to sea to sea."

"(It's) contagious. Not far into the book, the reader is tempted to pack a bag, get in the car and go find the Canada that Stewart sees."

"He mixes well-known and oft-visited places with unnoticed corners."
Calgary Herald, Canada Day Special

"(a book) to fuel the imagination... (with) compelling stories to inspire a visit."

"(The author) includes a historical and cultural perspective for each region (with) the people and history of a city or town as a backdrop"
Airlines Magazine

"(The) book is a nationwide adventure..."

"(It) puts to rest some of the preconceived notions Canadians have of their fellow Canadians...providing readers with a sense of history and culture that often gets lost"
Rocky Mountain Outlook

If you wish to purchase another copy of this book, please contact your local bookstore. If they do not have it in stock, they can order it from the publisher, Trafford Publishing.

If you prefer to buy books online, this can be done from the publisher via their bookstore, at www.trafford.com, with the reference number #04-0104, or by phone at (866) 752-6820. It is also available through the major commercial websites such as Amazon, Chapters, Barnes and Noble or Baker & Taylor Book Distributors.

The author would appreciate hearing any comments or to know of any errors that have occurred. The beauty of on-demand printing is that corrections and modifications can easily be made for future production runs.

If you wish to discuss sales promotions, special events, author's participation or volume purchases, please contact the author at bstewart@barizco.com

ISBN 141202276-2

9 781412 022767